# George Lokert
## LATE-SCHOLASTIC LOGICIAN

*Patri optimo*

# GEORGE LOKERT

*Late-Scholastic Logician*

by
ALEXANDER
BROADIE

EDINBURGH UNIVERSITY PRESS

© A. Broadie 1983

Edinburgh University Press
22 George Square, Edinburgh

Set in Linoterm Plantin by
Speedspools, Edinburgh, and
printed in Great Britain by
Redwood Burn Limited, Trowbridge.

British Library Cataloguing
   in Publication Data
Broadie, Alexander
George Lokert
1. Lokert, George—Logic
I. Title
160'.92'4     B785·L/
ISBN 0 85224 469 X

# CONTENTS

*Acknowledgements* vii

*A note on spelling* viii

ONE. Historical Background 1

TWO. Terms 32

THREE. Exponibilia 81

FOUR. Consequences 125

FIVE. Opposed Propositions 165

SIX. Lokert's Place in Medieval Logic 184

APPENDIX. Latin Texts 192

*Notes* 234

*Lokert's Published Works* 242

*Bibliography* 243

*Index* 246

# ACKNOWLEDGEMENTS

I am pleased to be able to record, especially here, my gratitude to two colleagues at the University of Glasgow, Dr Ian B. Cowan and Dr John Durkan, for invaluable discussion of Pre-Reformation Scottish history, and to two logicians, Professor E. J. Ashworth and Professor G. Nuchelmans, from whose writings on late-scholastic logica I have learned so much.

A debt of a different kind is owed to the late Arthur Prior. It is a matter of the deepest regret to me that he could not see this book.

My thanks are due also to members of staff of Glasgow University Library for their help in securing copies of rare texts.

The staff of Edinburgh University Press guided the book, with tact and understanding, through its various stages, and I am grateful to them.

A. Broadie
*Glasgow* 1983

# A Note on Spelling

Lokert spelt his name 'Lokert' on the title page of the various editions of his works. Elsewhere in sixteenth-century sources it occurs as 'Locard', 'Lockart', 'Lokart' and 'Loquart'. While some modern writers, for example, Ashworth and Élie, spell the name as Lokert did, others, for example, Durkan and Watt, prefer the modern variant 'Lockhart'. I have followed the practice of the bearer of the name, but readers searching for Lokert's name in indexes should keep in mind the modern variant.

# CHAPTER ONE

# Historical Background

## I

George Lokert, active in Scottish affairs during the period of development that culminated in the convulsions of the Scottish Reformation, did not operate in a cultural vacuum; on the contrary the cultural scene was rich, and is represented by works of lasting value. More especially the period is now regarded, culturally, as the age of the makars, the lowland poets amongst whom the best known are Robert Henryson, William Dunbar and Gavin Douglas, though that there were many more is clear from Dunbar's *Lament for the Makaris*, which lists the names of many poets whose works are now lost. Yet it is not hard to defend the claim that this great period is no less well represented by its philosophers than its poets. Though it is true that Scotland has never lost sight of its major poets of that period while at the same time hardly giving a thought to the philosophers, the failure to keep alive the latter aspect of the Scottish tradition is due less to considerations of intrinsic merit than to contingent political and religious factors.

But the philosophical spirit of Lokert and of other members of the distinguished academic circle to which he belonged did not die with them; nor indeed was it born with them, for Scotland has a long tradition, stretching back at least as far as Duns Scotus, of producing men of great philosophical stature. Hence the intense philosophical activity in the Scottish universities in the century and a half before the Reformation was not, in Scottish terms, unusual. As elsewhere, the chief bone of contention was the question of whether, as the realists held, universals were real individuals, or whether, as the nominalists held, they were not. The first rector of St Andrews University (founded 1411–12), Laurence of Lindores, who had gained a considerable reputation on the continent as a proponent of the nominalism of John Buridan, even succeeded in persuading the Arts Faculty[1] to ban the teaching of the realism of Albertus Magnus – though the ban was revoked twenty years later.[2]

Laurence of Lindores' conduct in spending years abroad at conti-

nental universities before returning to make a contribution to the
Scottish academic scene was the norm among Scottish academics.
Languages, at any rate, were no barrier, for Latin was the lingua
franca of academic discourse – to be used even on the playing fields as
well as in the classroom.[3] It is an important feature of the Scottish
educational scene that those grammar school pupils who, having mas-
tered Latin, wished to have a university education but preferred not to
attend a Scottish university for their first degree generally went abroad
rather than to England. Balliol College was the only college in either
Oxford or Cambridge which attracted substantial numbers of Scottish
students during this period. Very many of those who did go abroad
went to France. But they did not go in any way as exiles, for there was
a considerable movement of Scots scholars in both directions. Certainly a high proportion of the Scottish universities' teaching staff had
a degree from a foreign university.

It would be easy to misinterpret the significance of this last point.
Nothing could be either further from the historical facts or more
unjust to Scotland's intellectual achievements than to see the Scots
scholars abroad as merely recipients of what foreign universities had
to offer. In reality the Scots played a much more active role, and as
regards the University of Paris, the continental university with which
we shall be chiefly concerned, the contribution of the Scottish contingent was immense. In illustration of this fact we need only note that in
the period before the Reformation that contingent provided the University with more than a dozen of its rectors. Without doubt the
University would have been immeasurably the poorer had the Scottish contribution not been made. Certain aspects of that contribution
will shortly be described since otherwise an essential aspect of Lokert's achievement will have been left out of account.

To consider for the moment the other side of this coin, we shall have
to bear in mind that Scotland benefited from this international traffic
in scholars not only by gaining from it men who could teach, in
Scotland, to the highest standards found anywhere, but also by gaining men who brought home as part of their intellectual baggage ideas
about university organisation. This aspect of the movement of scholars between universities, to which as we shall see George Lokert made
a contribution, is of crucial importance for understanding the Scottish
university scene, for the period with which we are concerned, and
especially the century into which Lokert was born, saw the founding
of the first three Scottish universities, St Andrews (1411–12), Glasgow
(1451) and Aberdeen (1495). Most especially, for our purposes, the
men who were primarily responsible for organising Scotland's first

university, St Andrews, upon the experiences of which the other two medieval foundations and also Edinburgh University, drew heavily, had close acquaintance with the University of Paris. In many ways, indeed, St Andrews University constituted a re-establishment of the University of Paris in Scotland. Of course, many modifications had to be made to accommodate the new institution to the changed environment, but this does not serve to conceal the extent to which Scotland, in this respect, was repaid for the contribution Scots had made to Paris.

We may mention, as one small example of the adoption of a continental principle of organisation, the fact that Laurence of Lindores, during his rectorship of St Andrews, persuaded the University to accept, in imitation of Paris, an arrangement whereby the academic body was divided into four 'nations' of which each was to appoint, annually, a representative (an 'intrant') whose job was to elect a rector who could act as spokesman for the entire University. This arrangement, we shall observe, had an important effect on Lokert's career.

However, our chief concern is not with organisational and administrative matters. While it is important to note the large contribution that Scots made in an administrative role in Paris, whether as rectors or as members of important committees, the fact remains that those immensely talented men were there in the first place in virtue of their scholarship and were there primarily to pass on their knowledge and to contribute new ideas. In particular, during the first half of the sixteenth century Scotland provided Paris with some of its most distinguished philosophers and theologians. Of that galaxy of scholars none was then more exalted than John Major (also spelt 'Mair', of which 'Major' is merely the Latinised version) who, during the first three decades of the sixteenth century, was regarded as pre-eminent in Paris in both philosophy and theology, a role which carried heavy moral responsibilities, since the period during which he was acclaimed as 'prince of philosophers and theologians'[4] was the period which saw the rise of Luther and Protestantism, a movement with many of whose chief protagonists, especially in Scotland, Major was in close contact.

John Major, having arrived in Paris, did not so immerse himself in indigenous French matters as to lose sight of his origins. He can in fact fairly be judged the leader of Scottish intellectual life in Paris during his residence there. More specifically he was the leader of a group of philosopher-theologians, the circle of John Major, which included men of great stature. Among the Scots in the circle were David Cranston (Major's favourite pupil, who died tragically young some twelve weeks after receiving his doctorate of theology) and William Mander-

ston. The neglect of their writings, especially in Scotland and by
Scots, can in no way be attributed to those writings not meriting close
scrutiny.

George Lokert was a leading figure in this remarkable circle, a close
friend and collaborator of Major, substantially influenced by him but
an independent thinker. And whatever the explanation for his neglect
it cannot be that he did not leave behind him sufficient writings for us
to be able to form a well grounded judgment about his thinking.

Of course, one thinks of the eighteenth century as the *saeculum
mirabile* of Scottish philosophy, and no doubt even after a thorough
investigation of Major's circle no justification will be discovered for
suggesting that the sixteenth century challenges the eighteenth in this
respect. But nevertheless it should be said that, in the first place, such
a judgment cannot be passed without prior investigation, and secondly the sixteenth need not vie with the eighteenth for the earlier period
to have been a time of great philosophical achievement. Clearly consideration of Lokert's contribution is a small part of a much larger
examination that needs to be carried out.

In approaching Lokert's own contribution to Scotland's philosophical inheritance I shall begin with the fact that his intellectual
context was, most importantly, the circle of John Major in the University of Paris during the earlier part of the sixteenth century. We
shall therefore start with Major himself, and fit Lokert into the framework thus provided.

## II

Major was born in the village of Gleghornie near Haddington in East
Lothian. The date of his birth has been a matter of dispute, but there
are strong reasons for placing it in 1467 or 1468,[5] some seventeen or
eighteen years before that of Lokert. Like his pupil John Knox, who
was also an East Lothian man, he received his early education in
Haddington, which he refers to as 'the town which fostered the begin-
nings of my own studies, and in whose kindly embraces I was nour-
ished as a novice with the sweetest milk of the art of grammar . . . So
that many persons call me not wrongly a Haddington man'.[6]

Major's movements after leaving grammar school are unclear. It is
possible but only conjectural that he was a student at St Andrews
before leaving Scotland. So far as is known his first university, ex-
ceptionally for a Scot, was Cambridge, where he spent a year c.1491 at
the college of Godshouse (to become known in 1505 as Christ's College). His next movement, a more natural one as we have seen, was to
Paris, to the College of Sainte Barbe. He received his master's degree

in 1494, and the following year incepted as a regent in arts, that is, became a full time lecturer. At the same time he began the study of theology under Jan Standonck at the College of Montaigu, then one of the poorest and also one of the leading colleges in Paris. Coincidentally a fellow regent in Montaigu was another Haddington man Robert Walterston (who did not forget his birth place – he was granted a charter of lands in Haddington to support a chaplain at the local Church of the Holy Trinity), though another member of the College, indeed its principal for many years, Noel Beda, was to have a far greater influence on Major, as indeed also on Lokert who was closely associated with him. When Standonck was banished from Paris in 1499 Major and Beda took charge of the College, though about this time Major also became attached to the College of Navarre, a wealthy and prestigious college which boasted amongst its earlier masters Nicole d'Oresme and John Gerson (Doctor Christianissimus). Major nevertheless continued to teach logic and philosophy at Montaigu. Evidently he did not resent the extremely ascetic conditions at that College for he afterwards called Montaigu 'the nurse of my studies and never to be named without reverence', though Major's colleague at the College, Erasmus, with whom Major enjoyed a long association, and whose lives touched at many points, disliked the regimen intensely. The Scot had perhaps been more accustomed at home to rigorous living conditions. Neither were others deterred by the harsh living conditions imposed by Standonck on all members. George Lokert, who taught at Montaigu for a number of years, appears to have said nothing in criticism of those conditions. Another member, Ignatius Loyola, also appears to have been better able to cope than Erasmus.

In 1506, while still at the College of Navarre, Major took his doctorate of theology, and began to teach theology (the *Sentences* of Peter Lombard) in the Sorbonne, a college pre-eminent in Paris for theology, and one of the great centres in Europe in that field. The Sorbonne was the headquarters of the faculty of theology in the University of Paris, consisting of the doctors of theology of the University who were working either in the University or in clerical posts in the Paris area. The membership varied between seventy and eighty, and though far from being unanimous even on matters of fundamental doctrine (in the thirty years from 1503 fifteen of its members were investigated for heresy – a high proportion of its total membership) it was all the same in its general tone a highly conservative body, as witness the fact that as late as August 1523, after discussing the translations of sacred texts, it passed judgment that such translations from Greek into Latin, or from Latin into French, should be entirely suppressed and not tolerated.[7] When, against a background of criticism, the scholar Jerome Aleandro introduced the teaching of Greek to Paris one of his pupils was Major. Aleandro wrote 'There are many Scottish scholars to be found in France who are earnest students in various of the sciences and some were my most faithful hearers – John Major, the Scot, doctor of theology and David Cranston, my illustrious friends'.[8] But despite this association with a man especially identified with, and indeed held partly responsible for, the new humanistic trend in Paris, Major's own stance on a wide range of Church matters was hardly, if at all, less conservative than that of the Sorbonne as a whole. However, as we shall see, for all his unswerving loyalty on doctrinal matters, Major's writings reveal him to have been as sharply critical as anyone of many Church practices. His numerous writings bear wide testimony to his intense hostility to many aspects of ecclesiastical morality.

Major was indeed an immensely prolific writer. He began in 1499 with a work on a subject which claimed the close attention of many medieval logicians, namely, exponibilia, terms such as 'only', 'except', 'in so far as' and 'different from', expressions which contribute in interesting logical ways to the validity, or otherwise, of syllogisms. This field largely disappeared from view after the middle ages, though there are signs of a renascent interest in its. Major's substantial contribution to the topic, and indeed its relation to Lokert's own later book on the subject, have never received their due attention. Major then went on to cover the whole range of Aristotelian logic and philosophy, finishing in 1530 with a critical edition of Aristotle's *Nicomachean Ethics*. His great intellectual energy is evidenced by the fact that, despite recurrent bouts of illness, he had within twenty years of the start of the series already completed at least forty-six books.

The range of Major's writings is in fact wider than so far suggested, for in 1521 he published a *History of Greater Britain* (i.e. England and Scotland). It is possible that Major was motivated to write this very large book at least partly by the wish to enhance the idea of a union of the two countries,[9] and certainly the dedicatee of the book, James V, who was the son of a Scottish king (James IV) and grandson of an English king (Henry VII), was a particularly appropriate symbol of the closeness of the relation between the two countries. But the reason Major himself gave for writing the book, a reason which also goes some way towards explaining why a theologian, at any rate a moral theologian, should have engaged in such a task was that 'you may learn not only the thing that was done but also how it ought to have been done'. Major tells us that the first law of the historian is to tell the truth and that it is 'of more moment to understand aright, and clearly to lay down the truth on any matter, than to use elegant and highly coloured language'.[10] But having told 'the truth' he had a good deal to say about whether what was done ought to have been done or ought not. Thus for example he criticised David I of Scotland for endowing religious foundations with great wealth, arguing that such endowments eventually did the cause of religion immense damage.

Major's *History*, which has been termed the first critical history of Scotland, was distinguished among its rivals by the scepticism with which the country's myths and legends were treated. Ranald Nicholson has argued that 'had his *History* become more widely known, European historiography might have jumped forward two hundred years. In that humanistic age Major was damned for his unfashionable Latin style'.[11]

By the time Major came to write the *History* he had returned to Scotland for his first lengthy stay since his original departure for France some twenty-six years earlier. He had left at the height of his reputation. That reputation was based on two things.

The first was the quality of his teaching. There are many testimonies of the deep respect which his teaching inspired in his pupils. Juan Gomez, writing to Jerome de Cabanyelle, the Spanish king's envoy in France, said: 'I am following the theology course of John Major with great interest, as he is a deeply knowledgeable man whose virtue is as great as his faith . . . May the eternal King deign to grant him long life that he may for long years be useful to our Alma Mater, the University of Paris'.[12] Major did indeed attract a substantial number of Spanish philosophers to his lectures, some of whom went on to become leading figures in the University. It was one of their number, the logician and theologian Antonio Coronel, a pupil of Major's at Montaigu, who described his teacher as 'the prince of theologians and philosophers at Paris'. The dry 'Sorbonnic' style of his books, which was ill received by his humanistic successors in the University, who preferred their Ciceronian way of putting things, was either not employed by him in his lectures or, which is more likely, was enhanced by the personality of the speaker.

The second reason for Major's pre-eminent position was his leadership of a team of scholars who were both pupils of his and also important figures in their own right. The members of this team not only produced their own works on logic and philosophy but also edited in a scientific, critical spirit works of Aristotle and also of a number of their great medieval predecessors. Thus for example in 1512 Antonio Coronel published an edition of the *Prima Secundae* of St Thomas Aquinas' *Summa Theologiae*, and in the same year Pieter Crockaert, a

Dominican and regent in arts at Montaigu, published an edition of the *Secunda Secundae*. Major himself, amongst his other works, edited in 1504 John Dorp's commentary on the *Summulae Logicales* of John Buridan. And an edition of Buridan's writings on physics was produced in 1516 by George Lokert. We shall discuss that edition later.

In 1505 Major published his collected writings on logic. In the Preface he tells us that it was at the insistence of his favourite pupils that he decided, despite bouts of fever and an overwhelming workload, to prepare his logic lectures for publication. The pupils he names include the Scots David Cranston, Robert Caubraith ( = Galbraith) and George Lokert).

Of these three, Robert Caubraith, though an authority on Roman law, of which he went on to become professor at the College of Coqueret, published, so far as is known, just one book, and that on logic. It was a four-part work, his *Quadrupertitum* (1510), on propositional opposites, propositional conversions, hypotheticals and modal propositions. He claimed that in this work he had resolved all problems of dialectic!

David Cranston, who came from Glasgow to study at Montaigu, began teaching at that College in 1499, and numbered among his pupils George Lokert, who was thus a pupil, and also a pupil of a pupil, of Major. In 1512 there appeared two editions of his treatise on insoluble problems and obligations (the logical rules under which a disputation is conducted). The second contained an appended poem 'On the death of our master David Cranston, the Scot', for he died too soon to see that edition through the presses. The edition was read and corrected by two of Cranston's pupils, one of whom was Antoine Silvestre, regent in arts at Montaigu. The other was William Manderston.

In view of his close links with Lokert some salient features of Manderston's career should be mentioned. He was born in the diocese of St Andrews probably in the mid-1480s and was thus a close contemporary of Lokert. He did not attend his local university but matriculated at Glasgow University in 1503, taking his bachelor's degree in 1506. He then went to study at Paris, rising to become professor at the College of Sainte Barbe and then, in 1525, rector of the University.

His name first appears in connection with a publication when in 1516 he was one of the two editors of the index of Lokert's edition of the writings on physics of Albert of Saxony, Thimon and Buridan. In the following years he published three books. The first to appear, in 1517, was in effect his course of logic lectures, a three-part work (a *Tripartitum*) on the principles of dialectic. The following year came a two-part work (the *Bipartitum*) on moral philosophy, and in 1522 appeared a short treatise on future contingent propositions.

Manderston's *Tripartitum* led to his departure, in unhappy circumstances, from Paris shortly after taking up the rectorship. The cause of the trouble was Jerome de Hangest, a philosopher, logician and anti-Lutheran theologian. In the period between 1504 and 1518 Hangest published a number of works on logic and philosophy. These include his *Logical Problems* (1504), *Problems about Exponibles* (1507) and *On Causes* (1515). In 1525 or 1526 Hangest accused Manderston of plagiarism in the *Tripartitum*. Whatever the merits of the accusation, and there is good reason for scepticism about it, Manderston left France and never returned. It seems probable that there are other, presently unknown reasons for Hangest's animosity towards Manderston, and that the accusation of plagiarism served merely as a pretext for an attack that was intended to damage Manderston's career. One possible explanation lies in Manderston's teaching on the Lutheran doctrine of justification by faith alone, a doctrine which Manderston discusses in his 1518 moral philosophy work while expounding Aristotle's theory of the will.[13] Certainly his discussion approaches the Lutheran position more closely than the implacably anti-Lutheran Hangest could have approved. That Manderston's position is at any rate not nearly as extreme as that of his pupil in Paris, Patrick Hamilton, proto-martyr of the Scottish Reformation, does not diminish what may well have seemed to Hangest to be the University rector's drift towards heresy. In the absence of documentary evidence on this matter the foregoing can only be speculation. The outcome, however, is not in dispute. Paris's loss of a distinguished philosopher was to the advantage of Scotland. For Manderston took up his career in the University of St Andrews, becoming for a period that University's rector. By coincidence, about the time Manderston was leaving Paris for Scotland, his colleague George Lokert was returning to Paris after a three year stay in Scotland which he spent as rector of St Andrews.

At the same time that Lokert was returning to Paris so also was Major, though in his case after a rather longer stay in Scotland. When he left Paris in 1518, to become in effect principal of the University of Glasgow, the shadow of Manderston's difficulty with Hangest was some way in the future. In 1518 Major, a Scottish patriot, must have derived great pleasure from the performance of his Scottish pupils and colleagues, most especially perhaps from Lokert himself. Major's patriotism, despite his voluntary long stay in Paris, is undeniable in view of the many expressions of it in his writings. Thus, for example, in his dedication of the *Commentary of the Fourth Book of the Sentences of Peter Lombard*, a dedication to Alexander Stewart, son of James IV and pupil of Major's colleague Erasmus, he writes 'Our native soil attracts us with a secret and inexpressible sweetness and does not permit us to forget it'.

Nevertheless Major was faced with at least one tempting offer of a post in Scotland for which, despite what must have been formidable pleading, he refused to leave Paris. The offer was made through Gavin Douglas who, along with Henryson and Dunbar, was one of the great triumvirate of makars and had since 1503 been provost of the Collegiate Church of St Giles in Edinburgh. The post for which Major was sought was that of treasurership of the Chapel Royal at Stirling. His reasons for not returning are not now known, though one may speculate that he did not wish to terminate that immensely productive stage of his career, productive with respect to his own books, the books of his pupils, and also with respect to teaching. In addition he could certainly have claimed that he was serving the interests of Scotland hardly less effectively where he was, in Paris, than he would have been doing had he been in Scotland, especially as he was first and foremost an academic whereas the post on offer was one in ecclesiastical administration (though no doubt he would have been free to give just as much, or as little, of his attention to the treasurership as he chose).

Perhaps it was as a result of the powers of argument Gavin Douglas revealed while trying to persuade Major to take the treasurership that in the following year Major composed a dialogue (published in the 1510 edition of the *Commentary on the First Book of the Sentences of Peter Lombard*) between Gavin Douglas and David Cranston on the relation between the methods of philosophy and theology and the extent of the usefulness of either for the other. Douglas comes over as a formidable arguer.

The intellectual and diplomatic qualities of Gavin Douglas, son of Archibald, fifth earl of Angus and head of the Red Douglases, were appreciated by the Scottish authorities. For in 1517, by which time he had been elevated to the bishopric of Dunkeld, he was back in France, this time to participate in the negotiations preceding the reaffirmation, in the Treaty of Rouen, of the Auld Alliance. It is possible that on this trip also Douglas attempted to persuade Major to return to Scotland. Whatever be the truth of the case Major did in fact return the following year, for an eight year stay.

With pupils and colleagues, such as Lokert, Manderston, Peter Houston, Gilbert Crab and Robert Caubraith still maintaining the

Scottish contribution to Paris, Major became principal of the University of Glasgow. As well as the administrative role associated with that office, he also taught in both arts and theology at the University.

His writings meantime continued apace. The massive *History of Greater Britain* must have been written during the first two or three years of his principalship of Glasgow; for in 1521 he was back in Paris supervising its printing, and he wrote the dedication to James V at the College of Montaigu (from which College Lokert had two years earlier moved to the College of La Marche).

Major's trip to Paris to oversee the printing of his latest book highlights an important feature of Scottish cultural life that has to be borne in mind, namely, that for all the pioneering work of Chapman and Millar, and despite the presence of three univerities, there was no press in Scotland that would have been able to cope with a book of the size of Major's *History*; and hence Major had no option but to export the task. In any case, for three reasons the obvious place for him to send his manuscript to was Paris. First, he was one of the great figures of the Parisian academic scene. Paris had for about twenty-six years been his University, and he for much of that time one of its most distinguished members. Secondly, Paris had a huge and thriving printing industry which had no peer anywhere, even in Venice. And thirdly, Paris had one of the greatest and largest universities in Europe, and hence an enormous book-buying population was on the doorstep of the printing houses. Major could not have been assured of greater sales anywhere else. Moreover, granted the highly cosmopolitan nature of the University of Paris, Major's ideas would be exported much more readily from Paris than they could possibly have been from any of the Scottish universities, including that of Glasgow which was far smaller than the great universities on the continent and certainly did not have a cosmopolitan character. Like St Andrews and Aberdeen, it was a university where Scots taught Scots. In the light of all this it comes as no surprise to discover that all of George Lokert's books were printed on French presses – and indeed of the known twenty-three editions of his works published in his lifetime, twenty-two were printed in Paris.

After the publication of the *History* Major produced no more books for a further five years. But he did not meantime stop writing. Still in 1521, immediately upon his return to Glasgow from Paris he wrote a set of questions on metaphysics, which he dedicated to two Glasgow philosophers (one of whom, William Gibson, had matriculated at the University of Glasgow with Manderston). The questions were eventually published as an appendix to Major's 1526 edition of the *Physics* of Aristotle. Other works also were in preparation. We know that about this time he began work on his edition of Aristotle's *Nicomachean Ethics*, which was not to come out for a further nine years. And his great commentary on the Four Gospels must then have been in incubation. However, by Major's own extraordinary standards these were quiet years as far as concerns his writing. On the other hand his administrative work-load must have been appreciably greater than he would have been accustomed to in Paris.

During the period of his principalship he was on close terms with James Beaton, second archbishop of Glasgow. In October 1522 Beaton was translated to the See of St Andrews, the primatial See in Scotland, receiving the pallium in December of that year. While there is no clear evidence for this, it is plausible to suppose a connection between Beaton's translation and Major's move to St Andrews in the following year, rather less than five years after his arrival in Glasgow.

Major was incorporated into the University of St Andrews on 9 June 1523. On the same day Patrick Hamilton, who as we have seen certainly studied under Manderston in Paris, and may also have attended Major's lectures there, was incorporated into St Andrews. The coincidence was ironic. Hamilton was to be put to death for that against which Major stood out as a bastion of orthodoxy.

James Beaton was not the only person whose presence at St Andrews might have drawn Major to that university, for the previous year Lokert had been installed as rector. In other respects also Paris was well represented at St Andrews, and indeed that representation was more than merely symbolic. It was to be expected that changes that had to be made would be made in the direction of, or at least in the light of, the Paris system. In 1523–5 Major served as assessor to the dean in the Arts Faculty, and in this capacity served on a committee, on which Lokert also sat, which made extensive recommendations, along Paris lines, regarding the forms of examining in St Andrews. The recommendations were duly adopted.

Unlike Lokert, who so far as is known did not teach during his period of rectorship, Major taught in both arts and theology while at St Andrews.[14] Nominalism, which in the early years of St Andrews University had been so vigorously defended by its internationally known rector, Laurence of Lindores, was a century later being taught there by a man of even greater international reputation. And once again a top ranking terminist logician was rector.

In 1526 both Major and Lokert were back in Paris. Lokert took up a post at the Scots College in Paris and, as fellow of the College of Sorbonne, took an active part in the business of that college and of the faculty of theology. In particular he sat on an important committee set up to investigate certain writings of Erasmus for evidence of heresy. We shall examine this aspect of Lokert's career in some detail in the next section. Major, whose non-membership of the aforementioned committee set up to examine Erasmus suggests that he returned to Paris after Lokert, for he was an obvious candidate for such an appointment, probably went to the College of Sainte Barbe, the college at which he had started as an undergraduate at Paris, and there lectured on theology. Among the students then at Paris who may well have heard him lecturing were Calvin, Loyola, Rabelais and George Buchanan.

Another of the great scholars under whom those students of Paris would otherwise have been able to study was Erasmus himself. But Erasmus refused to make himself available. He had meantime been invited to become head of the newly founded Royal College in Paris, but had decided in the face of developments that acceptance would be imprudent. His caution appears to have been justified by events, for the faculty of theology condemned certain of his writings, but in his absence he could not be touched by the civil authorities. His translator Berquin, despite enjoying royal patronage, was less fortunate. In 1523 he had been arrested and was released only because François I intervened. Three years later he was again arrested and this time it was the king's sister who intervened on his behalf. In 1529 he was again arrested, despite repeated warnings from Erasmus not to be over-provocative, and this time was burned at the stake before his appeal could reach his royal patrons.

Among the martyrs to the Protestant cause at this period one, whose burning must have deeply affected Major, Lokert, Manderston, and others of the Major circle, was Patrick Hamilton. By being in Paris and not in St Andrews Major and Lokert were at least spared the pain of being present at, and perhaps even active participants in the legal processes that culminated in the burning on 29 February (the statutory day for the election of the St Andrews rector) 1528 before the college of St Salvator.

However, Major makes it clear that he was utterly opposed to Hamilton's heretical views. For all his compassionate nature Major does not let us forget that on matters of fundamental doctrine his orthodoxy is unshakable. The personal tragedy of Hamilton, a highly courageous man and fine theologian, had to be set against the fact that he was after all a heretic. Major's attitude emerges in the dedicatory epistle of his *Commentary* on the Gospel of St Matthew published in 1528, shortly after Hamilton's death. The dedication was to Major's friend of many years standing Archbishop James Beaton of St Andrews. There he congratulated Beaton for 'removing, not without the ill-will of many, a noble but unhappy follower of the Lutheran heresy'.

As regards Manderston, whatever his personal views of the burning of his former pupil, and on this matter he seems nowhere to have been as explicit as Major, there can at any rate be no doubt that on crucial moral theological issues his position was orthodox and far removed from Hamilton's. For Manderston, in line with Thomist teaching, held that the human will is dispositionally free, and that our freedom is in no way diminished by the grace conferred by baptism – there is no hint of a 'determinism by grace' doctrine in his writings. Hence our acting in a state of grace is not to be understood as grace acting through us, and consequently if, in a state of grace, we act virtuously we thereby act meritoriously.[15] Hamilton, on the contrary, taught that men do not have a free will nor can any action we perform be meritorious. We are sinners, and the cause of our sin is God's removal of grace from us, and we can cleanse ourselves of sin only by repentance and faith in the blood of Christ.

However, conformity with the Church's teaching on matters of fundamental doctrine is not to be interpreted as uncritical support – least of all in interpreting the positions of the inveterate logicians who formed the Major circle. But in any case it has to be remembered that on many matters of great religious importance the Church did not speak with one voice. As regards the criticisms levelled at the Church, we find, for example, in a discussion of the excommunication of the Scottish king Alexander II, Major writing: 'If it [an excommunication] is unjust to the degree of being null, it is in no way to be dreaded . . . unjust excommunication is no more excommunication than a corpse is a man . . . Whence it comes that we reckon a vast number of excommunicated persons who are in a state of grace. A sophistical excommunication can harm no man in things spiritual, whether his body lie in holy ground or in a place unconsecrated'.[16] Major was indeed prepared to speak out against a wide range of malpractices in the Church, and not only against the widespread misuse of the machinery of excommunication. He attacks plural holdings, commendations, absenteeism, the extensive neglect of ordinary pastoral duties, and the personal moral laxness of many clergymen. In reference to such features of ecclesiastical corruption he says: 'Those deceive themselves who think that the approval of even the Supreme Pontiff can reconcile such things to the dictates of conscience'.[17] It should perhaps be added, however, that with regard to absenteeism neither Major (who was for many years vicar of Dunlop) nor Lokert (whose full-time job in Paris did not prevent him holding a Church post in Scotland) could have been entirely guiltless.

One must nevertheless not lose sight of the fact that a willingness to criticise ecclesiastical malpractices and to call for reform to stamp out those malpractices committed one merely to a reformist programme within the Church and in no way constituted a heretical attack involving a commitment to wreck the existing Church and replace it by another one. There is no evidence that as regards essentials Major and Lokert ever wavered an inch. Major's attack on 'the grasping abbots who make things hard for the husbandmen' [*Commentary on Matthew* fol.74v] cannot, without great injustice to Major's position, be taken as evidence of such wavering.

One area where there might seem to be such wavering concerns Major's attitude to the authority of the Pope. While allowing that the Pope has sovereign authority in all routine matters, Major held that in certain circumstances the Pope's authority can be legitimately questioned and even resisted. But here Major was simply taking sides in a centuries-old debate on each side of which were to be found unquestionably orthodox churchmen. The debate concerned whether a legitimately convened general council of the Church could overrule the Pope. Major's position was conciliarist. He held indeed that for certain offences a Pope could be deposed by such a council. It is not now possible to estimate what influence Major's acceptance of this position might have had on his pupil John Knox.

After his commentary on the four Gospels Major produced just one further work, an edition of Aristotle's *Nicomachean Ethics*. The book, which was published in 1530, had been started, as we noted earlier, while Major was still principal of Glasgow University. The dedication was to his friend Cardinal Wolsey. Three reasons are given for that choice of dedicatee. The first was their shared love of 'our common country', for Scotland and England are 'enclosed in one Britain'. So even in this dedication Major expresses the view, which emerges so clearly in the *History*, that though it was with France that Scotland was in alliance, England the traditional enemy was nevertheless the natural ally of the Scots. Major nowhere suggests that Scotland should unite as a single country with France.

The second reason given was their common religion and study, and the third was that he wished to express his gratitude for the frequent hospitality he enjoyed in England. He mentions here the year spent, forty years previously, at Godshouse in Cambridge before his first stay in Paris. We also learn in this dedication that Wolsey had offered Major a teaching post at Christ Church College in Oxford which

Wolsey was just founding. The reason given for rejecting that offer is interesting since it may shed light on the reason for Gavin Douglas's failure to persuade Major to return to Scotland. Major wrote: 'So great a love possessed me for the University of Paris, my mother, and for my fellows in study, besides the desire to complete the books which I had already begun, that I could not accept the post . . .'.

One further interesting passage in this dedication must be noted since nothing else Major wrote so fully reveals him as a schoolman of the middle ages rather than as a renaissance humanist. The passage in question expresses Major's attitude to Aristotle, an attitude he must have sought to inculcate in his pupils: 'In almost all [Aristotle's] opinions he agrees with the Catholic and truest Christian faith in all its integrity . . . in so great and manifold a work, if it be read as we explain it, you meet scarcely a single opinion unworthy of a Christian gentleman'.

A further interesting fact, which the dedication does not reveal, is that it was written after Wolsey, having been stripped systematically of his honours, had fallen far from grace. Major's introductory epistle could have been written only out of real affection for the dedicatee.

One year after the publication of his text of the *Nicomachean Ethics* Major returned to St Andrews, and remained there till his death in 1550. A chief source of information about Major and especially about his motives, namely, the dedications and prefaces of his books, dries up after the publication of the aforementioned *Ethics*. Hence one matter about which we can now only speculate are his reasons for his departure from France. Perhaps he felt less and less at home in Paris as the spirit of renaissance humanism took an ever greater hold there, making Major's contribution to the life of the university seem increasingly dated, out of touch with the times. Yet in that case it has to be said that St Andrews was, though marginally more slowly, also moving with the times.

Or perhaps we should look to the increasingly troubled and agitated atmosphere in the University of Paris, arising from the steady encroachment of reformist tendencies, fuelled by the writings of, for example, Erasmus, a friend of Major's. Heresy huntings and burnings, under the enthusiastic guidance of Major's friend since his earliest Montaigu days, Noel Beda, led to a turbulent atmosphere, which could not have been conducive to academic labours. But, again, it should be said that St Andrews, where two years earlier Patrick Hamilton had been burned, did not provide an atmosphere notably calmer than that of Paris. It was not to be many years before St Andrews University, which had been founded to resist heresies and 'errors', was to become a centre of Protestant resistance against the forces of the Counter-reformation. And while it is true that that role was yet some years in the future, there was already a good deal of unrest in the academic community. The Feast of St John the Evangelist before the Latin Gate, a university feast of friendship and love, symbolising the brotherhood and unity of the Faculty of Arts, was discontinued just four years after Major's arrival, probably because the extent of religious disagreements within the academic body would have made a mockery of the symbolism of the Feast. It has indeed been argued that 'its discontinuance in 1534 denotes the break-up of the medieval conception of the Faculty – and indeed of the University as a branch of the Roman Church'.[18] Perhaps, after all, a simpler explanation for Major's return was that he was homesick. And perhaps underlying all this was the fact that he was by then sixty-two, a considerable age in the sixteenth century, and preferred to die in his native country which he had always regarded, as we know, with the deepest affection. The thought of death far from home must have been vivid enough for him. Among those of his distinguished pupils who had died while yet young, he could not have forgotten his favourite pupil David Cranston, from Glasgow, buried beside Jan Standonck in the chapel of the College of Montaigu.

Major held two appointments after his return to St Andrews. He was from 1534 provost of one of its colleges, the Collegiate Church of St Salvator, and was also dean of the Faculty of Theology. Among friends with whom he was reunited upon his return was William Manderston, who the previous year had been elected rector of St Andrews, just four years after his abrupt departure from Paris. Clearly the University of St Andrews did not take Hangest's accusation seriously.

Despite his administrative work Major continued to teach. His most distinguished pupil was John Knox. For it is now generally accepted that Theodore Beza's assertion that Knox was taught by Major at St Andrews was correct. The probability is that Knox went up to St Andrews in 1529 and after studying arts for about two years spent three to four years in the study of theology under Major at St Salvator's. Indeed Beza claimed that it was at one time thought that Knox would eventually be a more subtle sophist than even Major, but that Knox changed direction after study of the writings of St Jerome and St Augustine revealed to him the mistakes in traditional learning.

During this critical period Major was in contact with many of the most important actors in the Scottish Reformation. But much as he would have liked to there was, of course, nothing whatever he could do to stop the Reformation. At the very most he did nothing to help it maintain momentum, and there may even have been some who were dissuaded by either the arguments, or even the living example, of Major from following that road.

There is no doubt that had anyone then been able to obstruct reform at all effectively it would have been Major. His immense reputation, which had enhanced even the University of Paris, could do no less for St Andrews. As in the days of Laurence of Lindores, it was possible in St Andrews for Scots to be taught by Scots at the highest levels available anywhere. There could not at that period have been in any university in Europe a tutorial between two more formidable men than Major and Knox. Evidently, and even on Knox's evidence, Major was regarded with awe at this stage of his career. In a famous phrase Knox refers to his theology teacher as a man 'whose word was then held as an oracle on matters of religion'.[19] And no doubt that formidable reputation was only enhanced by the presence in Scotland of certain of his distinguished pupils from his Paris days, such as George Lokert, now holding high office in the Church.

However, Major, for all his reputation for, and commitment to, orthodoxy, was not one to see a heretic under every bed. For example, in 1541 a St Andrews student, David Guild, was charged with heresy on account of assertions he had made during a quodlibetal exercise in an examination, and Major signed a letter rejecting the charge. The letter appears to have been effective. And Guild evidently came through the ordeal with an untarnished reputation, for twelve years later he became dean of the Arts Faculty, a post he held for three years.

But during that bitter period other accusations of heresy were made to stick. In 1546 George Wishart, who had furthered the cause of radical Protestantism in Scotland with his Scots translation of the *First Helvetic Confession,* was burned before the residence of David Beaton, Cardinal Archbishop of St Andrews. Knox, a supporter of Wishart, was caught up in the aftermath of that execution, an aftermath that included the assassination of the Archbishop. The following year Major was present at the first public sermon preached by Knox. Knox preached the Protestant doctrine of justification by faith alone, attacking, with numerous Biblical references, justification by pilgrimages, pardons, 'and other sic baggage'. He then issued a challenge to the congregation to reveal, if they could, wherein lay his errors about the Bible or history. Major, at least, offered no criticism then or, so far as is recorded, later. But by then he was in his eightieth year, and he cannot be supposed to have assented either to the theological doctrines or to the spirit in which they were propounded. Major's criticism of the Church had always dealt with incompetent or corrupt administration and with individual immorality, never, as we noted earlier, with basic doctrine. Thus for example, we learn from Knox that in 1534 a friar, William Arth, who had been accused of heresy by John Hepburn, Bishop of Brechin, went to Major with his offending sermon to seek judgment on the matter, and was given an assurance that what he had said, which had provoked the Bishop's accusation, was indeed defensible, and that he, Major, was willing to defend it. Thus encouraged, William Arth delivered the sermon again, in the presence of a number of notables, including, Knox tells us, Major himself and also George Lokert.[20]

The sermon was on the text 'Truth is the strongest of all things'. Its contents are extensively reported by Knox, and it is clear that the sermon was chiefly on ecclesiastical malpractices. In particular Arth condemned the frivolous use of excommunication: 'If it was rightly used, it was the most fearful thing upon the face of the earth; for it was the very separation of man from God . . . But now the avarice of priests, and the ignorance of their office, has caused it altogether to be vilipended'. And he attacked the frivolous way claims about the occurrence of miracles were made and the disreputable way those claims were then used: 'But now, the greediness of priests not only receives false miracles, but also they cherish and fee knaves for that purpose, that their chapels may be better renowned, and their offerand [receipts from offerings] may be augmented'. The only part of the sermon, as reported by Knox, which was not on the malpractices of the clergy, concerned the claim 'That the Civil Magistrate might correct the Churchmen, and deprive them of their benefices, for open vice',[21] a claim running entirely counter to the Church's position that a secular court has no jurisdiction over a priest. But it has to be noted that despite the strength of the criticisms made by Arth and despite his hostile modes of expression, the sermon did not raise questions about the validity of fundamental doctrine. And indeed, as regards the criticism of the misuse of the instrument of excommunication, Arth's criticism was not couched in stronger language than that employed by Major in making the same basic point.

Knox's sermon of 1547 was however a very different matter. Basic doctrinal issues were involved then. And it is therefore not possible to extrapolate from Major's sympathy for Arth's sermon to Major's attitude to his former pupil Knox, even though Arth helped to create the climate of opinion which allowed Knox, who helped to formulate the ideological underpinning of Arth's moral criticism, to flourish.

By the time Major died, on 1 May 1550, he must have seen as clearly as anyone could that the kind of world, essentially medieval, to which he had dedicated his life, was gone forever.

## III

We shall turn now from a consideration of Lokert's academic background to a closer examination of certain important aspects of the foreground. Points merely mentioned in the previous section will here be expanded.

Lokert's date of birth is unknown, but it is possible to extrapolate from the fact that his doctorate, which he received in 1520, could be bestowed, by university statute, only upon a person aged at least thirty-five. We also know that Lokert appears to have attended no university before going to Paris, and also that even if he was not a high-flier his rate of progress up the academic ladder was quite brisk. The probability is, therefore, that he was born in 1485. He was born in Ayr, on the south-west coast of Scotland, to John Lokkert and Marion Multray. His mother died in 1500 when he must have been about fifteen and can be presumed to have still been at grammar school.

The first reference to him in the University of Paris occurs when he is mentioned, along with his half-brother John, in 1504 in the *Book of Receipts* of the German Nation in the University of Paris (one of the four nations to which members of the university were assigned roughly according to nationality – Scots, along with English, Flemish and Dutch students were placed in the German nation).

George Lokert studied arts under David Cranston at Montaigu and, along with his brother John, took his master's degree in 1505. In that year he gave his inaugural lecture as a regent in arts. With his theology studies under way he taught arts in the College of Reims where he gave a full (i.e. three and a half years) course before returning to teach arts at Montaigu, as a colleague of Noel Beda, Major and Cranston. Beda was then principal of the college, an office he held till resigning it to Pierre Tempete in 1514.

Lokert had found time to serve the German Nation in several administrative roles, being successively proctor, reformer and receiver between 1511 and 1513. But this activity had not hindered his advancing sufficiently to be accepted by the College of Sorbonne as a *hospes* in 1512, that is, as a kind of guest of the college awaiting election to a fellowship. Two years later, having completed a course on the *Sentences* of Peter Lombard, he became a bachelor of theology, and in the same year published his first book, a work on the philosophy of mind entitled *On Notions*. A notion is a quality which represents something, or in some way, immediately to the cognitive faculty. This concept will be examined in chapter two. At this stage it may merely be noted that Lokert's book was sufficiently well received in Paris to go through at least five further editions within ten years of its first appearance.

In 1516 Lokert published his edition of the writings on physics of Buridan, Thimon and Albert of Saxony. This large volume includes Albert's commentary on Aristotle's *Physics* and Buridan's comment-aries on several Aristotelian or pseudo-Aristotelian writings including the *De Sensu et Sensato* and the *De Memoria et Reminiscentia*. It has been argued[22] that this edition links Lokert with Laurence of Lin-dores, two rectors of St Andrews whose terms of office were separated by a century, for just as it was through the writings of Laurence that Copernicus in Cracow came to learn of Buridan's theory of impetus, a theory propounded to explain how a projectile can remain in motion after it has left the projector, so, as it has been held, it was through Lokert's edition that Buridan's theory reached Galileo.

In the same year as the publication of the edition just discussed Lokert was elected a fellow of the College of Sorbonne.

Three years later, as evidence of the good relations between master and former pupil, Lokert edited the alphabetic table of contents of the fourth edition of Major's *Commentary on the Fourth Book of Sentences*. And during that year he became *prior*, that is, head of the College of Sorbonne. About this time he moved from Montaigu to the College of La Marche, where he continued lecturing on logic, bringing out with-in a year a commentary on Aristotle's *Posterior Analytics*.

But though he was by now a distinguished professor of theology in Paris he had been in permanent residence in Paris for about twenty years, and the thought of a post in his home country was attractive to him. He may also have been influenced by Major's departure for Glasgow late in 1518. It has to be added that he was returning to Scotland to take up positions commensurate with his status in Paris, and it is therefore at least possible that an emissary, one more success-ful than Gavin Douglas had been in the case of Major, had been sent to Paris to attract Lokert back to Scotland. Major himself may have played a part. But whatever the means, the outcome was that by late 1521 Lokert had returned to his native country.

He is known to have been provost of the Collegiate Church of Crichton, in the village of Crichton some miles south of Edinburgh, by 14 December 1521.[23] The last known reference to his predecessor, Halkerston, is on 13 March 1519.[24] But since the pension arrange-ments with Halkerston would take place at about the time of his resignation, and since those arrangements were made on 22 May

1522,[25] the presumption is that it was on or shortly before 14 December 1521 that Lokert took up this post.

Some words should be said here about the kind of church of which Lokert was now provost, and of which about forty had been founded in Scotland in the three centuries prior to the Scottish Reformation. First, a collegiate church,[26] an *ecclesia collegiata*, was a college, a body of secular clergy 'associated for a specific purpose in furtherance of which it was in corporate possession of property or endowments'.[27] Its size was not fixed, though it could not have fewer than three members. Nor was its function fixed. It involved the performance of religious services, but might also be concerned with education, or even legal administration.

One type of college was the collegiate church. Easson lists its typical features as a staff of clergy, one of whom was head (the 'provost' or 'dean'); a common table, emphasising the collegiate life of its members; a common purse for common purposes; a common chest for custody of records, funds and seal; and a common seal. Patronage of the provostship was not determined in a uniform way. But in Crichton, as in many other collegiate churches, it lay with the founder and his heirs. The role of provost was to preside in chapter and choir, to install the prebendaries and receive their profession of obedience, to exercise jurisdiction over the inmates of the college, and to secure, if necessary by pecuniary penalties, the observance of its statutes and the proper performance of its services.

There were two kinds of collegiate church. Some churches had never been other than collegiate. One example of this to which we have already referred is the College of St Salvator's in St Andrews of which Major was provost from 1534 till his death. Other churches had a college grafted onto them. Thus, for example, Crichton Church had been an ordinary parish church till 26 December 1449 when Sir William Crichton, Chancellor of Scotland, had it transformed into a collegiate church for a provost, eight prebendaries and two singing boys. It subsequently acquired a song school and a grammar school, though Sir William had not specified these in the foundation document.[28]

Although parish churches which were raised to the status of collegiate church did not thereby cease to be parish churches, the general story is that they less and less fulfilled their pastoral role of caring for the spiritual needs of the parishioners. For the chief function of collegiate churches, the function which their founders had in mind first and foremost, was the celebration of votive masses for themselves and their families. Hence, as Easson tells us, 'ministration to the laity, far from being a primary concern, was at best an unavoidable necessity; and the extent to which these churches catered for their parishioners is shown at Crichton, where the surviving building has a choir and transepts, but the nave was never built'.[29] There can be little doubt that this failure of the collegiate churches contributed to the growing dissatisfaction with the Church which eventually led to the Reformation. In view of Major's strictures against the Church for failing to fulfil its duty to its flock, there is a certain irony in the fact that both he and Lokert (as indeed also Robert Walterston, their Montaigu colleague from Haddington), were provosts of collegiate churches – though admittedly Major's church (St Salvator's) was never specifically a *parish* church.

On 14 December 1521 George Lokert, described as doctor of theology of Paris and provost of Crichton, and his brother John, canon of Moray and rector of Inverkeithny, were incorporated in the University of St Andrews. Ten weeks later, on the last day of February 1522 George Lokert was elected rector. Lokert's election involved a considerable departure from the normal procedure at St Andrews.[30] Till 1471 records of the rectorship are very sparse, but it seems that the practice was in general to elect former students of the university who were also distinguished churchmen. Between 1472 and 1579 the great majority of the rectors had been former students of the university. George Lokert appears to have been the first person to have been incorporated specifically as a preliminary to electing him rector. Coincidentally the second person was William Manderston, who was incorporated on 27 February 1530 and elected (three and a half months after the statutory date for the election of rector) on 14 June 1530. Manderston is described in his incorporation as doctor of medicine (a title he had gained at Paris in 1525) and rector of the parish church of Gogar. *Dominus* Thomas Manderston, brother of William, was incorporated on the same day.

In the absence of the appropriate records it is now impossible to say to what extent Lokert carried out his duties as provost of Crichton, though it is at least clear that he was not in permanent residence in Crichton during his provostship. For throughout that period he also held other important posts elsewhere in Scotland, and even in France, that must have made substantial demands on his time. Certainly he took very seriously the office of rector of St Andrews and was in no sense merely a figurehead rector. His post, which was in theory a major one, had always been so treated in practice. From the foundation of the University the rector was the head of the academic body, and possessed, by the original charter of privileges, the right to sit in judgment upon, and also to punish, other members of the academic community. The rectorship benefited by the strength of character of Laurence of Lindores who had worked to ensure that the powers theoretically granted to the rector were his in practice as well as in theory. And it is to be expected that Lokert, who came to the post armed with the experience of headship of the Sorbonne as well as of fifteen years of distinguished service at one of the greatest universities in Europe, and the university moreover which more than any other served as a model for St Andrews, would act with competence and confidence in his new post.

The chief area in which he left his mark was in the field of examination procedures. In 1520, while he was still in Paris, that University had extensively reformed its examination regulations. The changes made were studied in St Andrews by a committee which included Lokert, John Major, who had arrived in St Andrews the previous year, and Peter Chaplain (who had studied in Paris and was eventually to take over from Major as provost of St Salvator's). The outcome of the committee's deliberations was a new set of examination statutes in 1524. The thrust of the changes, which closely followed the Paris revisions, was towards a simplification of procedures, in particular by providing, at the Lenten examinations, for open disputation between the examiner and each examinee individually, and by providing for a single means of electing examiners both for the determination (the first faculty test, usually conducted in the third year of undergraduate studies) and for the fourth year examinations which formed part of the requirement for the licence to lecture and dispute.

There is no evidence that Lokert taught during the period of his rectorship, in contrast with Major who, as we know, taught arts and theology both in Glasgow (despite holding the principalship) and in St Andrews (where his official position appears to have been that of principal of the body called the Pedagogium, and shortly after to be re-established as St Mary's College). Whether, even if not teaching, Lokert continued his logic studies, is uncertain. In 1523 he published a long work, the *De Oppositionibus*, running to some forty-five folios, which may well have been completed after his return to Scotland, though the book is almost certainly based on lectures he gave while yet in Paris. And it is also possible that the *De Terminis* was published in 1523. Certainly a letter dated October 1523, written by Robert Caubraith to James Henryson, a councillor of James V, was included as a preface to an otherwise undated edition of the *De Terminis*. It is not, of course, sound procedure to fix the date of an edition of a book solely by reference to the date of an accompanying letter. But it is at least most unlikely that the edition would have appeared earlier than the letter's date. It seems in any event probable that that edition was published during the period of the rectorship, and Lokert may well have been working on it during that time.

It is, however, certain that several editions of his works were published while he was still rector, in particular, two editions of his *De Noticiis* and one edition of the *De Sillogismis*, all of which came out in Paris in 1524. It is possible that Lokert spent some time in Paris during this period in order to see one or more of these editions through the presses. But this does not, of course, provide evidence that he was working on logic at this time. Indeed, all the evidence suggests that by the time he came to take up the rectorship of St Andrews the great bulk of his contribution to terminist logic had already been made.

On the last day of February 1525 John Weddall replaced Lokert as rector of St Andrews. Sometime after that, but before 15 January of the following year, Lokert returned to Paris. He resumed his fellowship of the College of Sorbonne and membership of the Faculty of Theology. He also took up an appointment with the Scots College in Paris. The latter is a shadowy body. It was founded in 1325 by David, bishop of Moray, in the year before his death, and was paid for from funds from some houses and land in the village of Grisy, several kilometres south-east of Paris. The purpose of the funds was to provide bursaries for scholars from the bishop's diocese to study in Paris; and up till the Reformation it was the bishops themselves who elected and funded the bursars. The probability is that the bursars were theology students, though at least one arts student is recorded among the bursars, when in 1384 during Alexander Bur's occupancy of the Moray bishopric William de Camera was in receipt of the Grisy benefaction. A distant successor of Alexander Bur, James Hepburn, bishop of Moray 1516–24, founded a 'bursarie for the trayning up a certane number of Scottes youthes specallie of the diocie of Moray in the knowledge of the Greek towng'.[31] Hepburn's immediate successor, Robert Shaw, bishop of Moray 1525–7 and educated in Paris, 'provydit Mr. George Lokart, professor of theologie . . . then resident at Paris, ourseer of the studentis' of the Scots College.[32] The appointment, made on 15 January 1526, gave Lokert the right to exercise jurisdiction over recipients of the Grisy bursary and to punish miscreants.

It is evident that the Scots College was a college in the strict sense in which, say, a collegiate church was a college. It was, to repeat Easson's words, 'a body of persons associated for a specific purpose in furtherance of which it was in corporate possession of property or endowment'. And as with collegiate churches the patronage of the headship lay with the founder and his successors. However, there is no evidence that the Scots College had a college building,[33] though the recipients of the bursary seem to have preferred the upper part of Mont Ste. Geneviève in the area of the street now called 'rue d'Ecosse'. But the corporate possession of property is not necessary for a college, so long as the body is in possession of endowments. However, it may be the absence of a college building that explains why almost all the papers associated with the routine running of the College have disappeared. In particular, if a Register was kept, and surely it was, it seems not to have survived, and we are therefore in no position to know how Lokert exercised his office as overseer.

But other aspects of his stay in Paris after his rectorship of St Andrews are better documented. In particular he was involved in the attempt, largely inspired and masterminded by Noel Beda, to have certain of Erasmus's works condemned as heretical. The attempt reveals a great deal about the religious and political tensions in the University of Paris while Lokert was there, and a consideration of the drama in which he played a part will afford insight into his character also, as well as into that of the University.

The *Index librorum prohibitorum,* the list of books banned by the Church of Rome, was established in 1557. Before that date there was no single centralised censorship authority. At most, individual countries had their own such authorities. And an obvious move was to employ in such a body a pre-eminent faculty of theology in a university of the country. France in the early sixteenth century had fifteen universities. But the Faculty of Theology of the University of Paris was not only unrivalled in France, it was also one of the most distinguished in Europe. Hence it was bound to play a major role in the decision procedures concerning the censorship of books in France.

It has already been noted that the Faculty was a conservative body. It is true that from time to time questions were raised about the orthodoxy of certain of its members; on one occasion it was claimed that many members either were Lutherans or at least favoured 'that most damned sect' and were disclosing Faculty secrets to it, and all Faculty members were required to swear an oath denying the claim.[34] But the general tenor of the Faculty was undeniably conservative. One cause of this was the authority of Noel Beda who, in 1520, became the first occupant of the newly created post of syndic of the Faculty – a post he occupied for thirteen years. As syndic he was required to ensure that deliberations were conducted in a satisfactory manner, that adequate minutes of those deliberations were kept, and that the decisions of Faculty were implemented.[35] He used the considerable authority of the post to lead, highly effectively, the right wing of the Faculty and to swing the other members behind him.

However, the powers of the Faculty of Theology were closely circumscribed. It could pass judgment on matters concerning faith, particularly on matters regarding the definition of doctrine and the point at which an opinion slides into heresy, but it was not an ecclesiastical court, and hence it could not pass sentence on anyone it judged guilty of heresy.[36] In this respect the syndic of the Faculty of Theology had less power than the bishops who controlled the ecclesiastical courts. And in view of the religious authority of the bishops their word could be expected to carry weight with the civil authorities who were liable to be involved in cases of alleged heresy. For in sixteenth-century France heresy came very close to treachery against his very Christian majesty François I.

The chief civil authority in question here is the Parlement de Paris, which was chiefly concerned with legislation and legal administration. And in particular it was from time to time faced with the question of whether to act on the civil implications of a theological judgment passed by the Faculty of Theology operating under Noel Beda. At such times the Parlement could not ignore the wishes of François I even if it could not always be fully compliant.

The triangle of authority consisting of the king, the Parlement and the Faculty of Theology is seen in operation in 1521 when the Parlement forbade printers 'to print books in French or Latin concerning the Christian faith or the interpretation of Holy Scripture unless those books have first been seen by the Faculty of Theology or its deputies'.[37] The prohibition was requested by François I who was himself acting on a request from the University rector.

But relations between king and Faculty did not always run so smoothly. A conspicuous case concerns Louis Berquin, the Flemish translator of Erasmus. Berquin faced the Faculty for the first time on 15 June 1523, and 'presented to the Faculty a certain letter from our most Christian king'. The king wished the speediest possible examination of certain writings which were causing a scandal in Paris. The letter was at least evidence that Berquin had friends in high places. The Faculty refused to be impressed by this. The following day it condemned Berquin's book *On the Use and Efficacy of the Mass*, and in a series of judgments on subsequent days it condemned several others of his books. On 24 June 1523 Berquin reappeared before the Faculty with a letter from François I demanding that they cease their examination and judgment of his books. Yet two days later the Faculty

completed their dossier on Berquin's condemned books and passed it
on to the Parlement with a note saying that Berquin's work spoke
rashly and ignorantly of the Mass and dealt impiously with the ritual
of the Church. Notwithstanding the king's support for Berquin, the
books were burned, by the authority of the court of the Parlement,
before Notre Dame Cathedral.

Yet Berquin was principally a translator, especially of the writings
of Erasmus. If he was censured for publicising books by Erasmus then
Erasmus was bound to be under threat of censure for writing the
books. Such a move by the Faculty was however certain to bring it
into conflict with the king, who was trying to attract Erasmus to a
major appointment in Paris. The Faculty was undeterred. In May
1525 it investigated three French translations of Erasmus's writings,
and its judgment was that 'they contain many things which are im-
pious or absurd or pernicious or heretical; the printing of the translations should in no way be permitted, but they should be entirely
suppressed as they offend pious ears in many matters'.[38] And the
following month a further French translation of a book by Erasmus
was condemned, and even judged worthy of burning. In May 1526
Erasmus's *Colloquia* was brought under scrutiny and it was judged
that the reading of the work should be forbidden, especially to the
youth since they would be corrupted by it, and that by all possible
means an attempt should be made to have the book suppressed.[39]
Things were clearly reaching a climax.

On 9 July 1526 the Faculty received a request from the Parlement of
Paris to investigate Erasmus's work *A Refutation of the Erroneous
Censures of Noel Beda*. The work contained a strong attack on the
syndic of the Faculty. Thirteen members of the Faculty were nominated to sit on a commission to investigate the work. Lokert was one
of those nominated. He was in fact the sole Scotsman on the commission, but he was by no means isolated; whether by accident or not,
of the thirteen men chosen to investigate the attack on the former
principal of the College of Montaigu, at least six were Montaigu men.[40]

The commission could not have been more openly in conflict with
the king; and this makes Lokert's position particularly interesting. It
was earlier that year that Manderston, faced with an opponent with
friends in high places, had returned to Scotland. It is to be imagined
that Lokert's motives for sitting on the commission, which may have
included personal loyalty to Noel Beda as well, of course, as a desire to
help extirpate heresy, were tinged with a degree of apprehensiveness
in the face of his comparative vulnerability as a foreign national standing out in opposition to the king.

The king used the Parlement as his mouthpiece for calling the Faculty to order. The immediate excuse was a short work by Noel Beda, attacking Erasmus. On 16 May, seven weeks before the commission was set up, Beda presented to the Faculty a paper highly critical of Erasmus's recent works paraphrasing the Gospels and the Pauline Epistles. Faculty 'consented to and permitted'[41] the publication of Beda's paper. But on 17 August Beda was called before the Parlement. He was then informed that the king had just sanctioned the seizure of Beda's writings against Erasmus, and had ordered that the sale of those works be forbidden until the king himself revoked the prohibition; and furthermore the Faculty of Theology was to publish nothing attacking anybody without the agreement of the Parlement, though this was to be understood as a prohibition on personal attacks, not attacks on doctrines as such.[42]

The commission set up to investigate Erasmus's criticisms of Beda had clearly had its teeth drawn. The Faculty, which was a self-perpetuating body, unlike the Parlement, and relied far less heavily on royal patronage, could, and indeed did, continue to pass judgments hostile to Erasmus. But in the absence of support from the secular arm of the law (or indeed from the ecclesiastical courts – which were under the control of bishops appointed by the king) the Faculty was unable to push successfully for the prosecution of those of whom it disapproved. One of the rare occasions thereafter when the Faculty did secure the co-operation of the Parlement is briefly mentioned in a Faculty minute: 'On this Sabbath day 17th April 1529 Louis Berquin was condemned to the flames'.[43]

This must have been a stressful and anxious time for George Lokert, and it may be that we need not look beyond the tensions generated by his membership of the Faculty of Theology to discover why he published no more works. We do get occasional glimpses of him in happier circumstances during his second stay in Paris, as when in 1526 and the following year he was, with John Major, a guest at banquets given by the German nation in the University of Paris.[44] However, the Reformation was casting long shadows and could have brought no pleasure at all to a man who was clearly as dedicated as anyone could be to the old order. He may indeed have been regretting his departure from Scotland after his successful period as rector of St Andrews. Whether from desire for a quieter life, or from homesickness, or for some other reason, he returned to Scotland, and even, after a short period, to the west coast of Scotland from where he had originally come.

He had returned by 1533. He was still provost of the Collegiate Church of Crichton, but was interested in securing the archdeaconry of Teviotdale, in the Scottish borders, which became vacant on the death of Thomas Ker in July or August of 1533.[45] But a complex struggle developed for the post. At least two other men, James Lamb and John Lauder, were also candidates. James Lamb petitioned the Pope for the benefice on 9 October 1533,[46] but just one week later John Lauder, in petitioning for the benefice, claimed that Lamb had died at Marseilles.[47] Lamb had possessed some rights to the deanery of Glasgow, and on 17 October Lauder also petitioned for the deanery.[48] However, on 4 February of the following year Lokert himself petitioned the Pope for the deanery of Glasgow, and in that petition he referred to himself as the provost of the Collegiate Church of Crichton, professor of sacred theology 'who also holds the canonry of Morebattle [i.e. the archdeaconry of Teviotdale], prebend of Glasgow'.[49] In a similar petition dated 5 February 1534 Lokert obtained a dispensation to retain the provostship of Crichton and the archdeaconry with the deanery.[50] However he seems not to have retained all three posts. He appears instead to have come to an agreement with John Lauder by which Lauder obtained the archdeaconry[51] and Lokert obtained the deanery of Glasgow.[52] Thus Lokert's possession of the archdeaconry was shortlived. He secured the post some time between July 1533 and 4 February 1534 but exchanged his rights for those in the deanery on 4 March 1534.

Thereafter until his death in 1547 Lokert's chief role was as dean of Glasgow, though he also appears to have held the provostship of Crichton until his death. As dean he was required to be present in Glasgow for six months in the year. He was head of the Chapter and presided over Chapter meetings, which entailed his dealing with such concerns as lands, endowments and disciplining of the clergy, as well as with details relating to the Cathedral services. One task that might have faced Lokert, but did not, was the election of the archbishop of Glasgow. Gavin Dunbar was the archbishop for all but the last six weeks of Lokert's period as dean (Dunbar died in April 1547) but complications arose over the election of his successor, and the post was not filled till some time after Lokert's death.

It is probable that Lokert devoted the greater part of his time to the deanship. The post brought considerable influence and prestige, more indeed than did his provostship of Crichton, though in the face of Lokert's record of diligence and application it is unlikely that he ignored the demands of the provostship. It would also not be at all surprising if he made periodic trips to St Andrews where friends of his of many years standing were in high places putting at the disposal of their students the priceless gift of many years' experience at the University of Paris.

He died on 22 June 1547. In 1542 he had arranged that an anniversary mass for the souls of his parents should be said in the Church of St John the Baptist in Ayr, and had further arranged that such a mass was to be said on his death for himself and his brother John. And the Register of Decisions of the Sorbonne Community for 8 June 1549 records that 'with the consent of all' it was agreed that on the day after Quasimodo Sunday an obit was to be said for 'our master Loquart'.

Like John Major, his friend for over forty years, Lokert had dedicated his life to the service of ideas and ideals which were under fierce attack. He was a devout man on the conservative wing of the Church[53] and was also a scholastic logician and philosopher. To such a man the Reformation and the encroachment of renaissance humanism must have appeared as threatening almost everything he stood for. However he could hardly have done more than he did to help preserve what mattered most to him. He lived a very full life, with his actions sharply focused on what he identified as essentials, namely, academic values and the Church.

But it has to be added that it would be grossly unfair to Lokert to omit reference to the fact that much of his work was a contribution to specifically Scottish academic and religious life. The many years spent in Paris are in no way evidence against this. In Paris he worked first under, and then with Scots; he brought his expertise back to Scotland and placed it at the services of St Andrews University; and on his return to Paris he took the post of overseer of the Scots College. He returned home to a major Church appointment in the west of Scotland, where he had his roots. And he died in his native country.

This distinguished Scot published, as we have seen, a series of treatises on logic and philosophy. It is to an assessment of those treatises that the remaining chapters are devoted.

## CHAPTER TWO
## Terms

### I

In most of his writings Lokert devotes at least some space to discussion of the properties of terms and principles of classifications of
terms. But just one of his works, the *De Terminis*, is concerned
exclusively with those topics, and it is therefore on that book that our
attention will be primarily focused in this chapter, though we shall
often find it helpful, and sometimes necessary, to take into account
what he has to say elsewhere.

The *De Terminis* is in two large sections. The first [3v–21v] presents a number of definitions of technical terms in logic and discusses
possible objections to those definitions and possible replies to the
objections. The second section [21v–36r] presents an exposition of
six fundamental principles of division for terms, and makes extensive
use of the terminology explained in the earlier section. Exhaustiveness
is not claimed for the six principles, nor could it reasonably be; but
few divisions of terms, if any, could be more important than those six.
Several are still in common currency, and none should be lost sight of.
I shall discuss some of the many definitions of the first section of the
*De Terminis* and shall then go on to consider certain points raised by
Lokert regarding the six divisions, where what he has to say either has
relevance to contemporary discussions, or at least merits discussion in
contemporary terms.

### II

The word *terminus* (which I shall hereinafter translate as 'term') has a
wide range of meanings. John Major asserts that: 'in the physical
sense it refers to things outside; in this sense we speak of the term *from
which* and the term *to which*'.[1] This corresponds closely to the English
word 'terminus' as in 'railway terminus'. And, more generally, we can
speak of the terms, that is, the end points, of a relation. Thus Major
points out that, for example, a word in a sentence can be a term in the
physical sense, as is 'men' in 'Men are mortal' because 'men' is
physically at one end of the written sentence.

But in the quoted sentence 'men' is a term also in the logical sense. In this sense of 'term' every term is sayable. Medieval logicians distinguished many kinds of term in the logical sense of the word. Major himself presented five. He writes: 'Terms belong to the sayable in five ways. In the first way it [sc. 'term'] is taken broadly for every sign placeable in a proposition. In the second it is taken, less broadly, for every sign taken significatively which is placeable in a proposition, whether the sign be complex or not. In the third way it is taken strictly for every incomplex sign taken significatively, and placeable in a proposition. In the fourth way, most strictly it is taken for everything which, taken significatively, could be an extreme of a proposition in relation to a personal verb in the finite mood. In the fifth way, it is taken most narrowly for an incomplex which can be an extreme taken significatively'.[2]

Lokert nowhere gives a single list containing all these items, though each of these ways of taking the word 'term' is mentioned by him and we shall be discussing them in the course of the chapter. However, in general where he employs the word 'term' he can be taken to be using it in the first of the five logical ways listed above, namely, as signifying any sign, complex or otherwise, placeable in a proposition.

The notion of a sign placeable in a proposition is basic to the remaining four items in Major's list. And indeed it was a standard way of defining the word 'term' so far as that was understood in its logical sense. Lokert, however, unlike Major, did not begin his treatise on terms by defining the word 'term'. Instead he began by examining the notion of 'definition' itself. For since the first half of Lokert's *De Terminis* is taken up with the presentation and discussion of a series of definitions, he recognised that a prior examination of the notion of a definition and of a 'definitum' or the term to be defined was therefore logically called for.

Three requirements are laid down for a good definition (see appendix, no.2). First, the definitum and its definition must be mutually convertible. Lokert gives as an example the mutual convertibility of the definitum 'term' and its definition 'sign placeable in a proposition', for, he says [3v]: 'given anything of which the word "term" is true with the verb "to be" in any of its forms mediating, the phrase "sign placeable in a proposition" is also true with the verb "to be" in the same form mediating'. Hence, given something X such that it is, was or will be a term, then X also is, was or will be a sign placeable in a proposition. The second requirement laid down is that the definition should explain or clarify the nature of what is expressed or referred to by the definitum. The notion of 'nature' here invoked is very wide: 'it is not just taken for the intrinsic cause, but for any cause, condition or property of the thing'. And thirdly, it is laid down that a definition should contain nothing superfluous, nothing, that is, whose removal would leave a definition which no less well expresses what is expressed by the definitum than did the expression containing the superfluous part. This third requirement is evidently not a requirement of a definition in the way the first two are, as Lokert seems to acknowledge in saying that he adds it because it is customary to do so.

The kind of definition just described is classified as a 'near definition', and is contrasted with what is termed a 'remote definition'. Similarly a distinction is drawn between a 'near' and a 'remote definitum' (see appendix, no.3). Briefly, whatever is signified by the definitum of a near definition is a remote definitum of that definition. Thus, for example, given that 'sign placeable in a proposition' is the near definition of 'term' then that definition is also the remote definition of anything signified by the word 'term', that is to say, of anything of which the word 'term' is truly predicated. Correspondingly the word 'term' is the near definitum of its near definition and anything which is a term is a remote definitum of the near definition of 'term'.

It should be noted that it is possible for some terms, in relation to a given definition, to be a near definitum and remote definitum. Lokert[3] instances the term 'term' itself, for since the word 'term' signifies, amongst other things, the word 'term' itself, 'term' is a near and also a remote definitum of the one definition [7r]. Clearly not all terms can be both near and remote definita of the same definition; the definitum 'man', to take Lokert's example, is not both near and remote in relation to its definition 'rational animal' [7r].

Evidently the notion of a remote definition does not coincide with what we should ordinarily call a 'definition', for while 'dog' and 'house' do not share what we would regard as a definition they do have the same remote definition in so far as they are both terms and therefore are both remotely defined as 'sign placeable in a proposition'. On the other hand while we would have no qualms about accepting the near definition 'sign placeable in a proposition' as a definition (even if not perhaps a good one) of 'term', there are certain aspects of the notion of a near definition which would make us hesitate to accept the notion of a near definition as corresponding closely to our concept of a definition. In particular the first requirement laid down, namely, that definitum and definition should be mutually convertible, implies that no term can be a definitum unless it can be true of something, and from this it follows that only terms which signify something, that is, so called 'categorematic terms', can be defined. And hence logical terms, such as 'all', 'some', 'or', 'and', 'if' and 'not', so called 'syncategore-matic terms', cannot be defined. This is Lokert's position on the matter. He asks whether every term can be defined and replies: 'The negative answer is obvious from the foregoing. Syncategorematic terms cannot be defined, only categorematic terms can' [5r].

That is not to say, of course, that no exposition can be given of the role such logical terms play in a proposition, for, as we shall see, they do signify *in some way*, that is, while not signifying some thing they signify in such a way as to have certain characteristic effects on the truth value of propositions in which they occur. Lokert agrees [5v] that the term 'syncategorematic' can itself be defined, for a syncate-gorematic term is, by definition, one which signifies *in some way* (see appendix, no.4), but, as he immediately adds, the term 'syncategore-matic' is not itself syncategorematic for it can be predicated truly of things of a certain kind, namely, logical terms, as in the proposition '"If" is syncategorematic'. But it is essential to note that in the fore-going proposition in quotes the word 'if' does not function as a syn-categorematic term; that is, it does not signify syncategorematically, for it signifies something, namely, the term 'if' itself. Hence what is being described as syncategorematic cannot actually be signifying syncategorematically in the proposition in which it is being so de-scribed.

The term 'if' was taken to be indefinable on account of its incon-vertibility with any other term, and it was deemed inconvertible be-cause it could not occur as either the subject or the predicate of a proposition. As we noted, the underlying consideration here is that there is nothing that 'if' signifies, and what signifies nothing cannot be subject or predicate in a proposition. The basic form of a proposition consists of two terms which do signify something (that is, two cate-gorematic terms) plus a coupling device, a 'copula', which holds the two categorematic terms together. In the basic proposition the coupl-ing device is a present tense indicative form of the verb 'to be'. Thus the basic proposition is of the form 'A is B', where 'A' and 'B' are signs of things. The terms preceding and following the copula, which are respectively the subject and predicate, are the 'extremes' of the basic proposition. A proposition of the kind just described is termed 'cate-gorical'; and it would have been categorical even had the copula had a different tense, or the proposition had been negated, or both.

However, a proposition does not require the overt form of subject plus copula plus predicate to count as categorical. In the *De Sillogismis* Lokert points out that in 'Socrates runs' no term is predicated of a subject [1r²]. The reason is that subject and predicate terms are

extremes coupled by a copula, and in 'Socrates runs' there is no copula. Nevertheless, this surface feature of the proposition's structure is
not sufficient ground for denying that the proposition is categorical;
it was Lokert's view that the copula was present, not 'formally' but
only 'virtually'. That is, though 'Socrates runs' lacks an overt copula,
were it rewritten in such a way that the logical *form* of the proposition
was perspicuously displayed the copula would be formally present, as
also would be the predicate which in 'Socrates runs' is also present
only virtually. Rewritten to display its logical form the proposition is
'Socrates is running'. Thus, in 'Socrates runs' 'runs', though grammatically unitary, is not to be treated as a logical unit for it is a
confused combination of copula and predicate. In a similar way
Lokert warns against treating 'sees', in 'Socrates sees Plato', as the
copula uniting the two extremes 'Socrates' and 'Plato' [*De Sill.* 2r[1]].
The proposition is indeed categorical, but the copula, once again, is
present only virtually, not formally. Rewritten to display its logical
form the sentence is 'Socrates is seeing Plato' or, perhaps better,
'Socrates is a-seer-of-Plato'.

The perspicuous version just printed corresponds term for term
with the mental proposition correlative with it, the mental proposition
being the proposition we think when we think what we say when we
say 'Socrates sees Plato'. The distinction between mental, spoken and
written terms and propositions is one of the six divisions discussed in
the second half of *De Terminis*, and we shall be considering this vital
distinction later in this chapter.

Categorical propositions are not the only kind; there is also the
hypothetical proposition, which is 'one in which formally or equivalently several propositions are combined . . . through some connective'
[*De Term.* 4r] (see appendix, no. 5). Such propositions are classifiable
on the basis of the nature of the connective term, and indeed take their
names from those terms. If the connective is 'or' or an equivalent the
hypothetical proposition is a disjunction; if the connective is 'and' or
an equivalent it is a conjunction. Evidently the terminology here
could mislead, for the 'hypothetical proposition' in medieval logic is
not necessarily hypothetical in the modern sense.

But two kinds of hypothetical proposition discussed by Lokert [*De
Term.* 4r] are closely related to the modern notion. One is the consequence, a compound proposition consisting of an antecedent (which
may be composed of a single premiss or a conjunction of several
premisses), a connective term ('therefore') and a consequent (the
conclusion). The second type is called a conditional; it contains the
mark of consequence ('if'), an antecedent immediately following the

'if', and a consequent which may either precede the 'if' or follow the antecedent. That is, it can be of the form 'q, if p' or 'If p, q'.

The connective terms will be discussed later when we consider Lokert's discussion of the contribution they make to the truth value of the propositions in which they operate. However, we cannot enter upon an exposition of his discussion of truth conditions without prior detailed consideration of his account of two crucial properties of terms, namely, signification and supposition.

Signification is treated as a property possessed by a thing in virtue of its place in a three-way relationship. Lokert defines 'signify' as 'to represent something, or in some way, to a cognitive faculty' [*De Term.* 4r]. There is thus that which does the representing, namely, the sign; the cognitive faculty to which the sign is presented; and thirdly, the 'something' or 'in some way' which the sign represents. Clearly the 'something' is introduced into this definition in order to indicate the kind of representative function of categorematic terms, and the 'in some way' is introduced in order to leave room for saying that syn-categorematic terms also signify, even if there is no *thing* signified by them.

The cognitive faculty to which the sign is represented is modified by the sign being presented to it, the modification produced by the pre-sentation to the mind of the term being itself a term, a 'mental term',[4] while the modification produced by reading or listening to a proposi-tion is a 'mental proposition'. As regards the notion of a mental term, we need at this stage in our exposition merely note that it is no part of Lokert's doctrine that spoken terms directly signify mental terms, and that it is mental terms alone that signify things. The spoken term 'man' directly signifies any thing A such that 'A is a man' is true. The point that should be made, however, is that even though a spoken or written term can signify a thing directly, as can a mental term, they could not signify at all unless there were a corresponding mental term, corresponding in the sense that it is the modification produced in the cognitive faculty by the presentation to it of the spoken or written term. A mental term, on the other hand, can signify without the existence of a correlative spoken or written term. Spoken words re-quire to be understandable if they are indeed to be signs, but the cognitive grasp we have of something is itself an act of understanding and does not require a further act of understanding. In this sense spoken and written words are mediated by mental terms and mental terms are not, at least in the normal case, mediated by further mental terms. And in that sense it can be said that mental terms 'came first'; we require a cognitive grasp of things before we can talk about them.

One of the ways in which medieval logicians couched their discussions of this matter was in terms of the distinction between the 'natural' and the 'conventional' (see appendix, no.6). Spoken and written terms signify conventionally by imposition. A term, we are told, signifies by formal imposition when it is introduced 'through a formal act of will of someone with authority or through several such acts of several people' [*De Term.* 4v], and where the imposition is not formal it is said to be 'virtual'. Lokert refers to two kinds of case of virtual imposition, though the two kinds are not mutually exclusive. In the first kind of case a term comes to have a given signification through custom alone; and secondly, after the formal imposition of a term, that term can come by virtual imposition to have a further signification by virtue of its association with the original signification, as when a portrait of a man is called a 'man' (as in 'There is a man in the painting'). However, the main point to note here is that by whatever means a set of sounds or visible marks comes to have signification as terms, their mode of signification is essentially conventional, whereas the modification of the cognitive faculty which occurs whenever we think of something is not itself conventional, however conventional may be the manner of our expression of that thought.

Nevertheless, Lokert recognised that his exposition of the division into natural and conventional signification of terms was not entirely plain sailing, and consequently he follows up that exposition by raising a question as to whether the division was in fact satisfactory. Since he cannot answer that question without first explaining what constitutes a satisfactory division he first furnishes that explanation.

Two conditions for a satisfactory division are laid down [*De Term.* 12r] (see appendix, no.7). Suppose we try to divide A's into those which are B's and those which are C's. If this division is to be satisfactory the first condition to be satisfied is that all the members of the class of A's should be A's which are B or A's which are C. Lokert puts this by saying that the divisum (A), that is, what is being divided, ought not to exceed the disjunction of heads of division, namely B and C; and the disjunction of heads of division ought not to exceed the divisum. The second condition is that 'the heads of division in a good division ought not to be true of the same thing on the same basis' [*De Term.* 12r], that is, the heads of division should be so related that nothing falling under the divisum ought on formal grounds to fall under both heads of division. The first condition ensures that the heads of division are jointly exhaustive, and the second that they are mutually exclusive.

A further requirement that Lokert discusses, though he does not lay it down as a third condition, is that the divisum must be taken univocally [*De Term.* 13r-v]. The difficulty he has in mind here is that a term can be taken analogically as well as literally, and failure to notice the equivocation may lead to the formulation of two heads of division, of which one has relevance only for the term literally understood and the other for the term analogically understood. The example Lokert provides is the division 'Of men, some are real men and others are painted men', and he argues as follows: 'Either in the foregoing proposition the phrase "of men" is taken according to that signification by which it signifies real men, and so the second part of the foregoing conjunction is impossible; or the "of men" is taken according to the signification by which it signifies painted men, and then the first part of the aforesaid conjunction is impossible. But for the impossibility of an affirmative conjunction it is sufficient that one part be impossible. Therefore [the division is unsatisfactory]'. No doubt Lokert does not present a condition explicitly designed to rule out this type of division because the fault, namely, trading on an equivocation, would be on a different logical level from the two conditions that he does present. For in all circumstances, whether dealing with divisions or not, trading on an equivocation is a logical malpractice.

In the light of this it must now be asked whether the division of 'signify' into 'signify naturally' and 'signify conventionally' is satisfactory. The immediate cause for doubt arises from Lokert's definition of 'signify', namely 'to represent something or in some way to a cognitive faculty', for it follows from this definition that anything whatever is a sign of itself, since whatever else anything might represent to a cognitive faculty it always at least represents itself if it is grasped cognitively. And in representing itself it signifies naturally, for no formal or virtual imposition is required for anything to signify itself. But if everything signifies naturally it follows that whatever signifies conventionally also signifies naturally, and hence the two heads of division appear to overlap. Lokert states this argument briefly as follows: 'The same term signifies naturally and conventionally. Therefore the division is insufficient. The antecedent is obvious as regards the word "man" which naturally signifies itself and conventionally signifies all men. Therefore [the conclusion is true]' [*De Term.* 12v].

As a first move in defence of the division Lokert makes a distinction: 'It might be said that it is not unsatisfactory for one and the same term to signify one thing naturally and another thing conventionally, but that it would be unsatisfactory for a term to signify the same thing naturally and conventionally' [*De Term.* 12v]. This move deals adequately with the problem of the term 'man', which certainly does not signify the same thing naturally and conventionally; but some other terms, in particular the so-called 'transcendental terms', which are employed in speaking about very general features of reality, are not so easily dealt with. Lokert gives one example: 'This spoken or written term "entity" signifies itself naturally and also itself conventionally, since it signifies all entities conventionally and is itself one entity' [*De Term.* 12v].

However, this does not prove that the two heads of division 'naturally' and 'conventionally' divide the divisum 'signify' unsatisfactorily, for the reason why 'entity' falls under the one head of division is quite different from the reason why it falls under the other. In the one case it falls under the head of division because it has been imposed, whether formally or virtually, to signify everything whatever, from which it follows that it signifies itself conventionally; and in the other case it signifies itself, just as everything whatever, in so far as it represents itself to a cognitive faculty, signifies itself, and thus signifies naturally. Hence the reason why a term signifies a given thing conventionally is quite different from the reason why that same term might signify that same thing naturally; and granted that the first condition also is satisfied, the proposed division of 'signify' is satisfactory [*De Term.* 13r].

Lokert has a good deal to say about the distinction between the natural and the conventional signification of a sign in terms of whether it signifies for everyone or not. Where the signification of a term derives from an act of imposition, whether formal or virtual, then of course only those will know the signification of the term who know what it was imposed to signify – in general that will mean those who speak the relevant language. But the manner in which things are experienced is taken to be common for all; it is only on the basis of that assumption that people think they understand each other when speaking the same language to each other, and it is only on that same basis that it is thought possible to translate from one language into another. Thus the different conventional languages are considered as underpinned by shared experiences which, considered as modifications of the cognitive power, are regarded as constituting a natural language which all language users understand.[5]

It might, then, be argued that there are after all no mental terms, for no terms can signify for all people [*De Term.* 14r]. A term in the mind of Socrates signifies only for Socrates; it is unique to him. But for Lokert this comment simply misses the point. It is of course true that a modification in the cognitive faculty of Socrates must be unique to Socrates. But any modification has properties which are intrinsic to it by virtue of which it is the particular kind of modification that it is, as well as having the relational property of being a modification in one cognitive faculty rather than in another, and the cognitive faculties of many people can be modified in the same way, that is, can undergo a modification that has the same intrinsic properties. It is in this sense that we are all said to share a natural language. Of course, members of different species may have different kinds of cognitive faculty, in the sense that the cognitive faculty of a member of one species may not be modifiable in a way in which the cognitive faculty of a member of another species is; there are certain kinds of thought that men can have that animals cannot. Lokert affirms: 'I say that the cognitive power of a man and the cognitive power of an ass or of another beast are not of the same kind, just as the intellectual and the sensitive powers are not of the same kind' [*De Term.* 14v], and his conclusion is that 'It is sufficient for a term signifying naturally that it signify for all *men*' [*De Term.* 14r]. However, not quite all men. Lokert lays down the requirement that a person must have a 'well disposed' cognitive faculty, for there may be a man with a malfunctioning cognitive faculty, and the inability of a term to represent to such a faculty should not be seen as conflicting with the claim that mental terms signify for all men. He writes: 'Any naturally signifying term, so far as regards its own way of signifying, is fitted to represent to every cognitive faculty, and if it is not able to represent to everyone there will be a defect and hindrance on the part of the cognitive faculty and not on the part of the signification of the term' [*De Term.* 14v] (see appendix, no.8).

We have so far considered the distinction between natural and conventional signs in terms of how the signs come to have their signification, whether by imposition or by nature. A further distinction between natural and conventional signs can be drawn on what is in effect the opposite basis, namely, how, if at all, a sign can lose its signification. Let us begin by asking whether it is in fact possible for a term to lose its signification. Lokert replies with two propositions as follows: 'First proposition: A term signifying naturally cannot lose that signification. Hence it is not possible to be such a term in fact and not to signify naturally. This proposition can be proved, since a term does not have natural signification from an extrinsic source but from its own nature. Second proposition: A term signifying conventionally can lose the signification by which it signifies conventionally. I mean that something now signifying conventionally can remain in the nature of things and not signify conventionally. This also can be proved, since it is by virtue of something extrinsic, viz. by a voluntary institution of some one person or of many people that a term signifies conventionally. But . . . the signification of such a term can be volun-

tarily renounced by the same person or by another having authority'
[*De Term.* 14v] (see appendix, no.9).

Lokert thinks the second proposition comparatively plain sailing,
but considers that the first requires defence against certain apparent
counter examples. In particular he is concerned about double negation (see appendix, no.10). He writes: 'Take the [mental] proposition "A man is not an animal". The negation in that proposition
naturally signifies negatively, viz. by negating the copula of the proposition. And yet it can lose that signification'. The argument which
Lokert sets up in defence of this claim is that the copula which is
negated by the negation in 'A man is not an animal' would cease to be
negated by it if the proposition just quoted were itself negated by
placing 'It is not the case that' immediately before it, for the outcome
of the double negativing is a proposition which is equivalent to a
proposition having no negation operator at all [*De Term.* 15r]. But
Lokert rejects the foregoing argument: 'It is denied that the negation
in this mental proposition "A man is not an animal" could lose its
signification; and granted that it signifies negatively it does not follow
that on account of the introduction of the second negation it loses its
earlier signification or negation'. Lokert's view is that it is by virtue of
the fact that the negation in the original proposition continues to
signify negatively that the later proposition containing two negations
is equivalent to one containing none. Had the later negation merely
cancelled the signification of the earlier one, the resultant sentence
would be a sentence with a single negation, namely, the 'It is not the
case that' at the start of the sentence, and the law of double negation
would not apply.

Since conventional signification arises by imposition Lokert discusses kinds of imposition, though he includes under the general
heading of 'imposition' acts which do not thereupon result in something having a conventional signification. Indeed, some very strange
animals are caught in his net. First he distinguishes between those
impositions which are sufficient and those which are not. A sufficient
imposition, which is the kind of primary concern, is an imposition by
which a term can be significative. Lokert refers to two kinds of sufficient imposition.

> Sometimes a term is imposed by a sufficient imposition simply
> and absolutely on some thing or in some way determinately for
> signifying, as when someone with authority imposes something
> for signifying Socrates, whatever be the kind of thing assigned
> and no matter what the time or place. Sometimes a term is im-
> posed with a dependent or conditional sufficient imposition,

when viz. it is imposed by someone having authority, but not imposed simply and absolutely . . . but on a certain condition . . . This also can be clarified by an example; if someone with authority imposed the letter A for signifying something if Socrates touched a pillar and not otherwise, the A would not signify by such an imposition unless the condition included in the imposition were fulfilled. [*De Term.* 16r] (see appendix, no. 11)

Insufficient imposition, which includes such cases as those where a term is imposed to signify something in particular (for example, a particular man) but where the significate is insufficiently determined (so that, for example, we do not know which man is the intended significate) need not for the present detain us. Our chief concern is with sufficient imposition. It is evident from Lokert's exposition that more than a bare act of imposition is required if a given term is in fact to signify something. He writes:

This is obvious first as regards an imposition made by someone lacking the authority. Also, granted that the imposition had been made by someone with the authority, that signification could have been set aside by the same man or by another man with authority. Furthermore, even without such a setting aside the signification could have been imposed by an insufficient imposition. And even when the term had been imposed by a sufficient imposition, if the imposition was dependent or conditioned it is not necessarily the case that the term will signify by such an imposition unless (a) the condition is fulfilled, or (b) that upon which the signification deriving from such an imposition depends occurs. [*De Term.* 16v]

The question of how words are imposed for signifying is answered only obscurely in *De Terminis*. It seems that for certain impositions a speech act deeming a word to have a given signification is the machinery by which imposition is effected. But obviously not all impositions could be effected in this way. As Lokert states the matter: 'Some terms were imposed through other terms; but not every term was imposed through others and hence it is not necessary to proceed to infinity in impositions, but one must come back to a first imposed term which was not imposed through previously imposed terms. But such a term was imposed through exterior signs' [*De Term.* 17r] (see appendix, no. 12), The 'exterior signs' in question are, in all probability, the gesture of pointing to what is being referred to, as a means of establishing, in the cognitive faculty of others, a relation between the sound being made while the speaker is pointing to something, and the something to which the speaker is pointing while making that sound.[6] If this account of how a word can come to have a signification has any plausibility it can have it only for words which stand for things such that the word can truly be predicated of a demonstrative pronoun which refers to the thing which the word signifies. It can have no plausibility whatever for syncategorematic terms. Hence Lokert affirms: 'It is necessary to concede that at first syncategorematic terms were not imposed, but categorematic terms came first and syncategorematic terms later' [De Term. 17r]. But it is left entirely unexplained how by using categorematic terms alone syncategorematic terms could be imposed. That Lokert recognised the problem is suggested by what he subsequently says on the difficulty of explaining the signification of syncategorematic terms: 'Perhaps it is impossible to explain in simple terms the manner of signifying of syncategorematic terms; but the signification of such terms could be explained partly through categorematic terms and partly through syncategorematic terms' [De Term. 20r] (see appendix, no.13). Lokert illustrates the point by explaining the signification of 'non-strictly'. That term signifies in, say, the proposition '"Flower" signifies non-strictly when it is said that he died in the flower of his years' by signalling that the term 'flower' in the sentence 'He died in the flower of his years' is not to be taken to signify what it was imposed to signify. Such a mode of explanation could be given when imposing some syncategorematic terms for signifying in some way, but clearly such explanation could not be given with the imposition of all syncategorematic terms because of the presence of such terms in the explanation. The question, then, remains unanswered as to how syncategorematic terms were imposed for signifying.

In fact, though Lokert does say that the first categorematic terms were imposed by 'exterior signs', that is, pointing, he nowhere gives a clear indication of his explanation of how the first syncategorematic terms were imposed. The focus of his interest in syncategorematic terms was not on how they came to be imposed but, rather, on the manner of their signification.

## III

We shall for the present take Lokert's discussion of signification no further, but shall turn to a closely related concept which cannot be understood without a prior grasp of what is meant by signification. The concept to which we now turn is that of supposition (see appendix, no.14). Once that concept has been expounded we shall be in a position to deal with Lokert's discussion of the truth conditions of the various kinds of categorical and hypothetical proposition.

Consider the sentence 'Socrates is a man'. In the context of that sentence 'man' signifies what it was imposed to signify, namely, men. That it signifies as it normally does is made clear by the subject of the sentence, for it is the name of a man. But in 'Man is a species' 'man' does not signify what it normally does, for Socrates, say, is a man but he is not a species and neither is any other man; and even if there were just one member of the species 'man' left, that remaining man would still not *be* the species. Finally in this sequence, in '"Man" is triliteral' 'man' stands for the actual word 'man', not for any individual man, as in the first sentence, nor even for the species man, as in the second. Thus although the term 'man' by itself, that is, outside of the context of a sentence, signifies individual men, within the context of a sentence it can play a quite different role, and the role it plays can be identified by a consideration of the other extreme. The different roles are different ways that the term supposits in the sentence. In the first sentence 'man' has *personal* supposition; it stands for, or 'personates', individual men. In the second sentence 'man' has *simple* supposition; in the context of that sentence the term stands not for men but for a mental term – for following the standard nominalist position Lokert regarded a species as a certain kind of modification of the cognitive faculty. And in the third sentence 'man' has *material* supposition; it stands for the word itself. In modern writing this kind of supposition is commonly signalled by placing the term in question within inverted commas.

It is evident from this why supposition is classified as a property which a term has within the context of a sentence, for in each of the foregoing three examples it is the other extreme in the sentence that signals the way 'man' is being used. For example, since neither individual men nor any species can be triliteral, the term 'man' in 'Man is triliteral' cannot have either personal or simple supposition.

In view of the fact that a term has a given supposition in virtue of its relation with the other extreme of the proposition supposition is to be seen as essentially a syntactic relation. In this respect it is entirely different from signification, since the latter is a property possessed by a term in virtue of its relation to a thing which it signifies and which gives us the interpretation of the term. That is to say the relation between sign and thing signified is a semantic relation, and signification is therefore a semantic property of a term.

A further distinction between signification and supposition follows from what has already been said. Signification is possessed no less by syncategorematic than by categorematic terms, but in view of the fact that what supposits must be able to serve as subject or predicate within a proposition it follows that supposition can be a property only of a categorematic term. It is, of course, possible to say meaningfully ' "And" is triliteral', even though the word 'and' is syncategorematic, but evidently in the proposition just mentioned 'and' in inverted commas signifies something, namely, the word itself, and thus that occurrence of 'and' does not signify as a syncategorematic term, and the proposition thus fails as a counter-example to the claim that only categorematic terms have supposition.

A further classification of supposition must now be introduced, this time involving personal supposition only. Consider the proposition 'Some dog is black'. If it is true then so also is the disjunctive proposition 'This is black or this is black or this . . .', where 'this' refers successively to all the dogs there are; and also any one of the disjuncts in the foregoing disjunction implies the original proposition. That is to say, to use the technical terminology usually employed, a *descent* can be made to a disjunction of singulars under the term 'dog' and an *ascent* can be made to the original proposition from any one of the disjoined singulars. If a term satisfies these two conditions of descent and ascent then it is said to have 'determinate supposition'. It is evident in that case that in 'Some dog is black' the term 'black' also has determinate supposition, for a descent can be made to a disjunction of singulars under 'black'; and from any one of the disjoined singulars an ascent can be made to the original proposition. In this context the metaphorical term 'descent' has to be understood as the replacement of a quantified term by singular terms; to ascend is to write the quantified term back into the sentence in place of the singulars.

Let us consider now 'All dogs are black'. A descent to singulars can be made under 'black' in the following way: 'All dogs are this or this or . . .' where 'this' refers successively to all things which are black. Hence a descent to singulars can be made under 'black' where the singulars form a disjunctive predicate. And further, an ascent can be made from any one of the disjuncts in the predicate to the original proposition. That is, if it were true that all dogs were this (black thing), as would be the case if there were just one dog and it was that black thing being indicated by the demonstrative pronoun, then it would be true that all dogs were black. In this case 'black' is said to have 'merely confused supposition'.

Thirdly, staying with 'All dogs are black', if that proposition is true then it is also true that 'This is black, and this is black, and this . . .', where the 'this' refers successively to all dogs, but it is not possible to infer the original proposition from any one of the conjuncts. Thus a descent can be made to singulars under the subject term where the descent is to a conjunction of singular propositions, but no ascent is possible from any one of the conjuncts. In this case 'dogs' is said to have 'confused and distributive supposition'.

Numerous syntactic rules for the identification of the kind of supposition possessed by a given term in a proposition were formulated. The most important, stated here without their hedge of provisos, were, first, that a term governed directly by a sign of universality ('all' and 'every') has confused and distributive supposition, as also does a term governed by 'not'; secondly, a term governed by a sign of particularity ('some') has determinate supposition; and thirdly, a term governed indirectly by a sign of universality has merely confused supposition. For example, in 'Every A is B' 'A' has distributive supposition since it is directly governed by 'every' and 'B' has merely confused supposition since it is indirectly governed by that same 'every'. In 'Some A is not B' 'A' has determinate supposition, and 'B' has distributive supposition.

Though such rules provide guidance in the identification of the kind of supposition that a term has, they give no help on the crucial question of how a sentence as a whole is to be analysed, for to analyse a sentence it is necessary to know the *order* in which a descent is to be made to singulars. For example, in the case of 'Some dog is not black' descent to singulars can be made under 'dog' and under 'black', and the order in which the descent is made affects the truth value of the sentence. Let us for the sake of simplicity suppose there to be just two dogs, whom we shall name '$A^1$' and '$A^2$', and just two black things, named '$B^1$' and '$B^2$'. If we descend under 'black' first in analysing

(1) 'Some dog is not black'

we derive

(1a) Some dog is not $B^1$ & Some dog is not $B^2$,

from which is derived next, by descent under 'dog':

(1b) ($A^1$ is not $B^1$ ∨ $A^2$ is not $B^1$) & ($A^1$ is not $B^2$ ∨ $A^2$ is not $B^2$).

What this says is that one or other of the two dogs is not the first of the two black things and one or other of the two dogs is not the other of the two black things. But this could be the case even if both dogs are black, and hence our sentence analysis totally fails to capture the sense of 'Some dog is not black'. What our unsuccessful analysis says is that there is a black thing that some dog is not. If however we descend first under 'dog' the outcome is quite different. We derive first:

(1c) $A^1$ is not black ∨ $A^2$ is not black

from which we derive next, by descent under 'black':

(1d) ($A^1$ is not $B^1$ & $A^1$ is not $B^2$) ∨ ($A^2$ is not $B^1$ & $A^2$ is not $B^2$).

This says that either the first dog is neither of the black things or the second dog is neither of the black things, that is, some dog is not black.

The lesson to be drawn from this example is that where one term has determinate supposition and the other has distributive supposition, descent should be made first under the term with determinate supposition. It can readily be shown that a term with merely confused supposition should be replaced by singulars after descent has been made under a term with either of the other two kinds of supposition. Thus the order of descent is first, determinate supposition, secondly, distributive supposition, and thirdly, merely confused supposition.

It is however possible to have a sentence in which both terms have determinate supposition, e.g. 'Some dog is black', or in which both have distributive supposition, e.g. 'All dogs are not black'. It was held that in this kind of case it did not matter in which order descent was made. The explanation can readily be seen from an example.

(2) Some dog is black

whose subject and predicate terms both have determinate supposition, is equivalent, after descent under 'dog' and then under 'black', to:

(2a) $(A^1 \text{ is } B^1 \vee A^1 \text{ is } B^2) \vee (A^2 \text{ is } B^1 \vee A^2 \text{ is } B^2)$.

If descent is made first under 'black' and then under 'dog' the result is:

(2b) $(A^1 \text{ is } B^1 \vee A^2 \text{ is } B^1) \vee (A^1 \text{ is } B^2 \vee A^2 \text{ is } B^2)$.

Clearly (2a) and (2b) are equivalent.

So far we have considered the standard form of sentence, namely, that consisting of two terms and a copula. However, a great many of Lokert's examples were not of the standard form, and we have to attend to the non-standard forms he used as examples, for most of his theorising concerned the non-standard forms. Perhaps the commonest was a sentence consisting of three terms and a copula, where one term stood in genitival, or possessive relation to another. His numerous examples, many of which (and their negations) occur as major premisses in the syllogisms of his *De Sillogismis,* conform to one or other of the following patterns:

(1) Some A of some B is C
(2) Some A of every B is C
(3) Every A of some B is C
(4) Every A of every B is C
(5) Of some B some A is C
(6) Of some B every A is C
(7) Of every B some A is C
(8) Of every B every A is C

In dealing with sentences of the sort just schematised Lokert generally took, as many logicians did during this period, the terms 'man',
'ass' and 'running'. Thus, for example, (6) becomes 'Of some man
every ass is running". Here 'man' has determinate supposition since it
is directly governed by the sign of particularity; 'ass' has distributive
supposition since it is governed by the sign of universality; and 'running' has merely confused supposition since it is governed indirectly
by the sign of universality. It follows from this that we should descend
to singulars first under 'man', then under 'ass' and finally under 'running'. There is in fact a further law of precedence which could be
invoked here to justify descending under 'man' before descending
under 'ass', namely, that, in the case of an expression consisting of
determinator plus determinable, descent is made under the determining term before it is made under the determinable term. Thus, in 'Of
some man every ass is running' the 'every ass' is made more determinate by the modifying or determining phrase 'Of some man'.

We can now start our analysis of (6). Assuming, for the sake of
keeping the formulae to a manageable length, that there are two A's,
two B's and two C's, we descend first to singulars under B, and reach:

(6a) $(Of B^1$ every A is C$) \vee (Of B^2$ every A is C$)$

Descent is made next under A:

(6b) $(Of B^1 A^1 is C \& Of B^1 A^2 is C) \vee (Of B^2 A^1 is C \& Of B^2 A^2 is C)$.

We next descend under 'C', which has merely confused supposition:

(6c) $[(Of B^1 A^1 is C^1 \vee C^2) \& (Of B^1 A^2 is C^1 \vee C^2)] \vee$
$[(Of B^2 A^1 is C^1 \vee C^2) \& (Of B^2 A^2 is C^1 \vee C^2)]$.

A further pattern of which Lokert makes use [e.g. *De Sill.* 19r[1],
19v[2]] is (8). This case, however, unlike the previous one, is not
entirely plain sailing. In (8) 'A' and 'B' both have distributive supposition since they are governed by a sign of universality, and 'C' has
merely confused supposition since it is governed indirectly by a sign of
universality. Hence in the order of descent 'C' must be dealt with last.
Furthermore, while in general it does not matter which of two terms
with distributive supposition is dealt with first, we have already noted
that the determinator must be dealt with before the determinable.
Consequently we must first descend under 'B'. If the rule that precedence be given to the determinator is violated invalid inferences can
be drawn. For example, if it were permissible to descend first under
'ass' in 'Of every man every ass is running' it would be possible to infer
'Of every man ass[1] is running'. But there is a model on which the
premiss is true and the conclusion false, namely, that according to
which there are several men each of whom owns asses, though no ass is
under joint ownership.

Hence, in analysing (8) we shall descend first under 'B'. The first stage of analysis is:

(8a) Of $B^1$ every A is C & Of $B^2$ every A is C

We descend now under 'A':

(8b) $(Of B^1 A^1 is C \& Of B^1 A^2 is C) \& (Of B^2 A^1 is C \& Of B^2 A^2 is C)$.

Finally descent is made under 'C':

(8c) $[(Of B^1 A^1 is C^1 \vee C^2) \& (Of B^1 A^2 is C^1 \vee C^2)] \&$
$[(Of B^2 A^1 is C^1 \vee C^2) \& (Of B^2 A^2 is C^1 \vee C^2)]$.

On this analysis, 'Of every man every ass is running' implies that each ass is under joint ownership – $A^1$ and $A^2$ are each owned by both $B^1$ and $B^2$. The sentence may, however, be understood not to imply joint ownership of all asses owned by anyone, but only to imply that of every man every ass, even the non-jointly owned ones (if any), is running. To secure symbolic expression of this weaker interpretation it is necessary to assign different names to the asses of $B^2$ from those assigned to the asses of $B^1$. That move allows the possibility of merely individual ownership while not excluding the possibility of joint ownership. On this interpretation (8) should be analysed as:

(8d) $[(Of B^1 A^1 is C^1 \vee C^2) \& (Of B^1 A^2 is C^1 \vee C^2)] \&$
$[(Of B^2 D^1 is C^1 \vee C^2) \& (Of B^2 D^2 is C^1 \vee C^2)]$.

We need not here consider the analysis of the remaining schemata in the list of eight, since the others present no additional problems of interpretation.

In addition to the standard quantifiers 'all' and 'some' Lokert makes extensive use of four further quantifiers which were the subject of close scrutiny by logicians in the first half of the sixteenth century. The quantifier expressions employed were the first four letters of the alphabet and each was taken to govern the immediately following term. Thus for example, Lokert discusses the validity of the syllogism 'Of every man every ass is running, and some white thing is $a$ ass; therefore of some man some white thing is running' [*De Sill.* 18v²]; and elsewhere he argues that 'A man is not an animal' is the only sentence contrary to 'Every man is $b$ animal' [*De Opp.* 5v²].

The function of each of the letters $a$, $b$, $c$ and $d$ is to affect the supposition of the term governed by the letter, and, without a grasp of the kind of effect each letter has, a good deal of what Lokert has to say, particularly on the relations of contradiction, contrariety and sub-contrariety, but on many other matters also, will be unintelligible.

Any term governed by '$a$' has merely confused supposition. Introducing the '$a$' into a sentence can have the effect of reversing its truth value. For example, 'A man is not an animal' (where the 'A' is the ordinary indefinite article) is analysed on the basis of the fact that

'man' has determinate supposition and 'animal' has distributive supposition, and hence that descent must be made under 'man' before it
can be made under 'animal'. This results in the following analysis:

(Man$^1$ is not animal$^1$ & Man$^1$ is not animal$^2$) ∨

(Man$^2$ is not animal$^1$ & Man$^2$ is not animal$^2$),

where, as previously, we assume there to be just two members in each
of the relevant classes. Clearly 'A man is not an animal' is false. But in
'*a* man is not an animal', 'man', which now has merely confused
supposition, must be replaced by singular terms after descent has
been made under 'animal' which still has distributive supposition.
Hence the first step in the analysis of '*a* man is not an animal' takes us
to:

*a* man is not animal$^1$ & *a* man is not animal$^2$

which itself is to be analysed as:

Man$^1$ ∨ man$^2$ is not animal$^1$ & Man$^1$ ∨ man$^2$ is not animal$^2$.

On this analysis what '*a* man is not an animal' says is that there is no
one animal that every man is, which is obviously true in a universe
containing more than one man.

We turn now to the second of the four special quantifiers. Any term
governed by '*b*' has determinate supposition. Thus, to return to
Lokert's example, mentioned above, 'Every man is *b* animal', since
man has distributive supposition and 'animal' has determinate supposition a proper analysis requires descent to singulars under 'animal'
before it is made under 'man'.

Thus, 'Every man is *b* animal' is equivalent, at the first stage of
analysis, to:

Every man is animal$^1$ ∨ Every man is animal$^2$,

which at the next and final step in the analysis is equivalent to:

(Man$^1$ is animal$^1$ & Man$^2$ is animal$^1$) ∨

(Man$^1$ is animal$^2$ & Man$^2$ is animal$^2$),

which says that there is some animal that every man is, which is
manifestly false. Had we, on the contrary, made the false step of
descending first under 'man' the result would have been a true sentence asserting that every man is some animal or other.

Whereas '*a*' and '*b*' can occur in sentences containing only two
terms, '*c*' and '*d*' cannot occur in sentences containing less than three
terms; they are commonly employed in sentences which accord with
the patterns (1) to (8) discussed above. Lokert describes '*c*' and '*d*' as
conferring mixed supposition on the terms they govern [*De Sill.*
23v$^1$],[7] for the term governed by '*c*' has confused supposition in relation to the first term in the sentence and determinate supposition in
relation to the second, while the term governed by '*d*' has determinate

supposition in relation to the first term and confused supposition in relation to the second. Let us consider, for example, 'Of some man every ass is $c$ white' (which conforms with pattern (6). 'White' has confused supposition in relation to 'man', and determinate supposition in relation to 'ass'. Hence in the analysis of the sentence descent is made first under 'man' since 'man' has determinate supposition which takes precedence over the distributive supposition of 'ass' and over the merely confused supposition of 'white'. Descent is next made under 'white' which has determinate supposition in relation to 'ass' which has distributive supposition. Reverting to 'A', 'B' and 'C', instead of 'ass', 'man' and 'white', in order to keep the formulae to manageable proportions, and also making the assumption that each of the relevant classes has only two members, the first step in the analysis of 'Of some B every A is $c$ C' takes us to:

Of $B^1$ every A is $c$ C $\vee$ Of $B^2$ every A is $c$ C.

Descent is next made under 'C', to reach:

(Of $B^1$ every A is $C^1$ $\vee$ Of $B^1$ every A is $C^2$) $\vee$

(Of $B^2$ every A is $C^1$ $\vee$ Of $B^2$ every A is $C^2$).

Finally descent is made under 'A' to reach:

[(Of $B^1 A^1$ is $C^1$ & Of $B^1 A^2$ is $C^1$) $\vee$ (Of $B^1 A^1$ is $C^2$ & Of $B^1 A^2$ is $C^2$)] $\vee$

[(Of $B^2 A^1$ is $C^1$ & Of $B^2 A^2$ is $C^1$) $\vee$ (Of $B^2 A^1$ is $C^2$ & Of $B^2 A^2$ is $C^2$)].

Ignoring the restriction on the number of men, asses and white things in the universe of discourse, this formula asserts that it is true of some man that there is some one white thing that all his asses are, which is clearly false so long as we suppose all men who have any asses to have at least two.

A further example will suffice to make the point. During his discussion of opposite propositions Lokert writes: 'These propositions are contraries: "Of every man an ass is not an animal" and "Of every man every ass is $c$ animal", as the "$c$" makes the predicate of the affirmative proposition have mixed supposition, since the predicate has merely confused supposition in relation to the determinator ['man'] and has determinate supposition in relation to the determinable ['ass']' [*De Opp.* 14v$^{1-2}$]. Thus descent is made first under 'man' which has distributive supposition and therefore should be taken before 'animal' which has merely confused supposition in relation to 'man', and 'man' should also be taken before 'ass' since in order of descent determinator has precedence over determinable. Next descent is made under 'animal' since it has determinate supposition in relation to 'ass'. Hence, using 'A', 'B' and 'C' instead of 'man', 'ass' and 'animal' respectively, and assuming once again that each relevant class has only two members, the first step in the analysis of 'Of every A every B is $c$ C' takes us to:

Of $A^1$ every B is $c$ C & Of $A^2$ every B is $c$ C.

Descent is next made under 'C' to reach:

(Of $A^1$ every B is $C^1$ ∨ Of $A^1$ every B is $C^2$) &

(Of $A^2$ every B is $C^1$ ∨ Of $A^2$ every B is $C^2$).

Finally descent is made under 'B' to reach:

$[($Of $A^1 B^1$ is $C^1$ & Of $A^1 B^2$ is $C^1) ∨ ($Of $A^1 B^1$ is $C^2$ & Of $A^1 B^2$ is $C^2)]$ &

$[($Of $A^2 B^1$ is $C^1$ & Of $A^2 B^2$ is $C^1) ∨ ($Of $A^2 B^1$ is $C^2$ & Of $A^2 B^2$ is $C^2)]$.

A final example may be given, this time illustrating the '$d$' operator. Lokert, while discussing the proposition 'Of every man every ass is $d$ animal', writes: 'The $d$ gives the predicate determinate supposition in relation to "man" and confused supposition in relation to "ass"' [*De Opp.* 14v$^2$]. Hence descent must be made under 'animal' before it is made under 'man', and under 'ass' before 'animal'. Using 'A', 'B', and 'C' as before, and again assuming only two-membered classes, the first step in the analysis of 'Of every A every B is $d$ C' takes us to a conjunction of singulars under 'B':

Of every A $B^1$ is $d$ C & Of every A $B^2$ is $d$ C.

Next descent is made to a disjunction of singulars under C:

(Of every A $B^1$ is $C^1$ ∨ Of every A $B^1$ is $C^2$) &

(Of every A $B^2$ is $C^1$ ∨ Of every A $B^2$ is $C^2$).

Finally descent is made under the distributed 'A':

$[($Of $A^1 B^1$ is $C^1$ & Of $A^2 B^1$ is $C^1) ∨ ($Of $A^1 B^1$ is $C^2$ & Of $A^2 B^1$ is $C^2)]$ &

$[($Of $A^1 B^2$ is $C^1$ & Of $A^2 B^2$ is $C^2) ∨ ($Of $A^1 B^2$ is $C^2$ & Of $A^2 B^2$ is $C^2)]$.

A last point may be made here. At numerous points Lokert warns that the general principles he formulates do not work in a straight-forward way if applied to the persons of the Trinity. His illustrations are therefore in the main restricted to the domain of created things. One example of this should clarify what is at issue. In his discussion of the quantifiers 'both', 'either' and 'neither' he says that the proposition 'Both animals are $b$ man' is impossible, and immediately adds 'at any rate for terms signifying creatures' [*De Opp.* 22v$^1$]. Since the $b$ renders 'man' determinate, and since 'both' gives 'animal' distributive supposition (it is taken to mean 'all two') descent to a disjunction of singulars must first be made under 'man'. But each disjunct is false since two animals cannot be any one man. But since in Catholic theology, the Father and the Son are both God, both are in some sense one; and in that case by replacing the matter of the 'impossible' 'Both animals are $b$ man' we could construct the perhaps not impossible 'Both persons are $b$ God' [*De Opp.* 23r$^1$]. In that case 'Both animals are $b$ man' cannot, it seems, be impossible on purely formal grounds, since material considerations (the nature of the significata of the categorematic terms) contribute to making it impossible. Lokert's approach is to say that membership of the domain of discourse is relevant, but that within the domain which he stipulates, namely that of all created things, the proposition 'Both animals are *b* man' is impossible.[8]

This account of the supposition of terms in non-standard sentences, including sentences containing the special quantifier expressions, takes us as far as we need to go for present purposes. When we come to consider Lokert's discussions of conversions of sentences and of contradictories, contraries and subcontraries, we shall see that extensive use is made of the kinds of sentence we have just been considering.

This account of the nature and taxonomy of supposition and the analysis of propositions will suffice to enable us to deal, at least in outline, with the medieval theory of truth conditions.

Truth conditions must first be specified for the simplest kind of proposition and then specified for successively more complex kinds. In this recursive procedure Lokert starts, as did medieval logicians in general, with the affirmative, categorical, non-modal and non-exponible proposition. His treatment of the simplest kind of proposition might suggest that such a proposition has just three components, namely, subject, predicate and copula. But what in that case should be said of Aristotle's dictum that the simplest kind has just two parts, namely, a subject and a verb, as in 'Socrates runs'? In fact Lokert treats propositions of this sort as virtually three-part, since the verb is treated as a copula plus predicate. Thus the foregoing proposition is understood as the formally three-part proposition 'Socrates is running' or 'Socrates is a runner'.

There are however also propositions that consist of a subject term plus a part of the verb 'to be', but lacking a predicate term. The verb 'is' in such a context is evidently not a copula since it does not couple subject and predicate terms. Nor is it helpful to say that the predicate 'being' is virtually present, so that 'Socrates is' means 'Socrates is being', although it would not be an error to translate 'Socrates is' in this way. The reason why it is unhelpful is that such a translation tends to conceal the distinctive role played by 'is' in the context where it is not followed by a predicate. Such an 'is' is called the '*secundum adiacens* is', and its role is to signal that what the subject term stands for now exists. If there is nothing such that one could point to, or otherwise indicate, it and say 'This is (an) A' then the proposition 'A is' would be false.

Where the 'is' couples a subject and a predicate term then it is called a '*tertium adiacens* is'. It is with propositions containing the latter sort of 'is' that Lokert starts his investigation of the truth conditions of categorical propositions (see appendix, no.15). How he deals with propositions which are non-present tense, negative, exponible, modal or hypothetical will be seen in the sequel; he starts with propositions which are none of these things. Different truth conditions must be specified for affirmative categorical propositions according as the propositions are singular, particular or universal, but one feature is common to all, namely, that for the proposition to be true it is necessary that the subject and predicate terms stand for the same thing in the context of the proposition. In 'Socrates is an animal' 'animal' must stand for what the subject term names (assuming, of course, as Lokert adds, that Socrates exists [*De Term.* 10v]). 'Every man is white' is true just if 'white' supposits for everything for which 'man' supposits. And 'Some man is white' is true just if there is something such that both the subject term and the predicate term supposit for it, that is, 'white' is true of something of which 'man' also is true.

It is not to be supposed however that on this account of the truth conditions of a categorical affirmative proposition, the proposition is a disguised proposition of identity, even though the subject and predicate terms are said to supposit for the *same* thing. Consider again the proposition 'Some man is white'. If this were translated into an expression employing quantifiers in the modern fashion, but retaining the basic 'stands for' relationship standardly invoked by medieval logicians in describing the relation between sign and significate, the result would be: 'There is an x such that "man" stands for x and "white" stands for x'. The identity in question is, then, the identity of the bound variable of which both subject and predicate terms are predicated. But that would be entirely insufficient ground for classifying 'Some man is white' as an identity proposition.

So far the truth conditions only of so-called 'propositions of inherence', that is, non-modal propositions, have been considered, but something should be said here about the truth conditions of modal propositions also.

While William of Ockham and others took the concept of a mode very broadly, regarding any term predicable of an entire proposition (including 'true', 'false', 'possible', 'known' and 'believed') as a modal term, Lokert restricted the list of modal terms to 'necessary', 'possible', 'contingent', 'impossible' and their adverbial forms. The standard medieval tactic for expounding the truth conditions of modal propositions was to remove the modal term from the proposition being investigated and to place the modal term in the metalanguage that is employed to talk about the resulting demodalised proposition.

For example, where $p$ is a proposition lacking a modal term, then 'It is necessary that $p$' is true just if the following proposition is necessary: $p$. In this kind of case the modality is said to be 'with composition' (*in sensu composito*) since the modal term is treated as taking within its scope a composite expression, namely, an entire proposition of inherence. But a modal term may be taken otherwise than *in sensu composito*. In particular the modal proposition can be treated as if the modal term divides the proposition in two and includes within its scope not the entire proposition but only the predicate. In this case the modality is said to be 'with division' (*in sensu diviso*). Two kinds of case may be mentioned here in anticipation of points to be made shortly in connection with past tense propositions. First, a modal proposition taken *in sensu diviso* may have a proper name or a demonstrative pronoun as subject, for example 'Socrates is possibly white'. This proposition is true if and only if 'Socrates is white' is possible. The procedure here is to rewrite the modal proposition by deleting its modal term, otherwise leaving the proposition intact, and employing the modal term in the metalanguage in which are stated the truth conditions of the demodalised proposition.

Secondly, a modal proposition taken *in sensu diviso* may have a subject which includes a common noun, for example, 'Every man is possibly mortal'. This proposition is true if and only if there is something of which 'man' can be truly predicated, and 'This is mortal' is possible where 'this' stands for anything which is a man.

Clearly in stating the truth conditions of a modal proposition a central procedural problem concerns the identity of the inherence proposition which remains after the modal proposition has been demodalised. In some cases (for example, those where the subject term is a proper name) the proposition of inherence is simply the modal proposition minus the modal term, whereas in certain other cases a more radical change has to be made.

We shall turn now to a consideration of the truth conditions of past tense propositions, and shall observe there to be close similarities between the way modal and past tense propositions are dealt with. The basic tactic in dealing with past tense propositions is the same as that employed in dealing with modal propositions. In the case of modal propositions no attempt was made to give an account of the supposition of subject and predicate terms in so far as they occur within the modal proposition, but instead a non-modal proposition corresponding to the modal one is constructed and the question of supposition of terms is raised only in connection with the non-modal proposition. And likewise no attempt is made to give an account of the truth conditions of a past tense proposition in terms of the supposition of subject and predicate as they occur within the past tense proposition; but instead a corresponding present tense proposition is constructed and the question of supposition is raised in connection with the latter proposition. Lokert states the position very briefly as follows: 'For the truth of a categorical affirmative past tense proposition . . . it is sufficient and required that at some time its present tense form was true, or that it was as signified through its present tense form' [*De Term.* 10v]. Thus where $p^2$ is the present tense proposition corresponding to the past tense proposition $p^1$, the truth condition for the basic kind of case is given simply as follows: $p^1$ is true if and only if $p^2$ was true at some past time. It is, then, necessary to establish what present tense proposition corresponds to a given past tense proposition, and to establish also the correct way of specifying the expression which indicates when in the past the present tense proposition was true. Thus for example, 'Socrates was running' is true if and only if 'Socrates is running' was true at some past time. If the time when Socrates was running is given more precisely in the past tense proposition then that greater precision should be reflected in the phrase which indicates when the corresponding present tense proposition was true. If the past tense proposition is 'Socrates was running last year' its truth condition is given as follows: 'Socrates is running' was true last year.

A good deal has to be added to the account so far developed if it is to be able to cope with the wide variety of past tense propositions, but Lokert does not pursue his discussion further in the *De Terminis*. However, one complicating factor should be mentioned here to indicate the direction in which development must take place.

Past tense categorical propositions in which the subject term is not a proper name but is instead a common noun are ambiguous, and the ambiguity has, of course, to be resolved before the truth conditions can be specified. For example, 'A white thing was running' can be understood to mean either 'A thing which was white was running' or 'A thing which is white was running'. It should be noted that this ambiguity, while it can affect the common noun subject terms of past tense propositions, cannot similarly affect the predicate. The pastness of the predicate is already determined by the past tense of the copula – a white thing, whether white now or in the past, *was* running. It is the possibility of the subject term suppositing for something which is now, while the predicate term supposits for what was, that prevents the standard medieval exemplar 'A white thing was black' from being contradictory. If we treated that proposition as we treated 'Socrates was running' the truth condition would be specified by saying that it is true if and only if 'A white thing is black' was true. And that truth condition can, of course, never be met. Rather, the way to deal with such a case as 'A white thing was black' is to introduce a singular proposition constructed by making the past tense proposition into a present tense one, and replacing the subject term by the demonstrative pronoun 'this' which points to something white. The truth condition for the past tense proposition can now be given as follows: 'A white thing was black' is true if and only if 'This is white' is true of something and 'This is black' (pointing to the same thing that is signified by the 'this' in 'This is white') was true. It should be noted that a precise modal parallel to this manoeuvre is found in medieval logic. 'A white thing is possibly black' was said to be true if and only if 'This is white' is true of something and 'This is black' (pointing to the same thing that is signified by the 'this' in 'This is white') is possible.

Lokert deals with future tense propositions in the same way that he dealt with past tense propositions; he did not regard the identification of the truth conditions of future tense propositions as presenting additional difficulties.

After his discussion of past and future tense propositions Lokert turns from consideration of affirmative propositions to consideration of negative ones. As regards a negative present tense categorical proposition which is non-modal, non-exponible and lacking particularity the truth condition is simply stated: 'It is sufficient and required that the subject and predicate do not supposit for the same thing' [*De Term.* 11r]. Thus 'No man is an ass' is true just if there is nothing for which 'man' and 'ass' both supposit. This condition gives a sufficient requirement for a particular negative proposition but not a necessary requirement, since for the latter sort of proposition it is necessary merely that there be something for which 'man' supposits for which 'ass' does not supposit. Lokert here points out the relationship between the necessary and sufficient conditions for universal affirmative propositions and for particular negative ones. He writes: 'For the truth of a negative proposition in which particularity occurs it is not necessary that the subject and predicate do not supposit for the same thing just as for the truth of an affirmative proposition in which universality occurs it is not sufficient for the subject and predicate to supposit for the same thing' [*De Term.* 11r]. Thus, for 'Every A is a B' to be true it is necessary but not sufficient that there be something for which A supposits for which B also supposits, while for 'Some A is not a B' it is sufficient but not necessary that there be nothing for which A supposits for which B also supposits.

We shall not pursue here this analysis of negative propositions, though it should be noted in passing that introduction of negation operators creates the possibility of interesting lines of research on logical relations between modal and past and future tense propositions. For example, the truth condition of 'Socrates is possibly running' is that 'Socrates is running' is possible, and the truth condition of 'Socrates is possibly not running' is that 'Socrates is not running' is possible; and evidently both conditions might be satisfied simultaneously even though the two non-modal propositions are mutually inconsistent. And a parallel case arises for past tense proposition. For example, the truth condition of 'Socrates was running' is that 'Socrates is running' was true at some time, and the truth condition of 'Socrates was not running' is that 'Socrates is not running' was true at some time. And both of these conditions can be satisfied now even though the two present tense propositions are mutually inconsistent. For Socrates might have been running at one time and not at another.

Thus modalising or past-tensing a pair of mutually inconsistent present tense propositions can result in a pair of propositions which are not mutually inconsistent. But of course whether that is the result depends on how the propositions are modalised and on how the past tense is specified. Had the modality chosen been 'necessarily' instead of 'possibly' then the modalised version of the mutually inconsistent propositions would also have been mutually inconsistent. And had the time specification been as precise as possible, for example 'noontime yesterday' then again the past tense version of the mutually inconsistent propositions would have been mutually inconsistent – for 'Socrates is running' and 'Socrates is not running' could not both have been true at noontime yesterday, even though each could have been true at some time or other.

After considering categorical propositions, Lokert turns to the question of the truth conditions of hypotheticals. The three kinds of hypothetical in question are the disjunction, conjunction and conditional. The first two are dealt with in a straightforwardly truth functional way. 'As regards the truth of a hypothetical affirmative, if it is disjunctive it is sufficient and necessary that one of its principal parts be true; and if it is conjunctive it is necessary and sufficient that each part be true' [*De Term.* 11r]. The disjuncts or conjuncts may themselves, of course, be conjunctions or disjunctions, in which case, as Lokert points out, the truth of the proposition is affected by whether the whole proposition is conjunctive or disjunctive. He gives the example: 'Man is an animal or Socrates runs and a man is an ass' [*De*

*Term.* 11v], which is true if it is a disjunction, since the first disjunct
('Man is an animal') is true; and is false if it is a conjunction, since the
second conjunct ('a man is an ass') is false.

Lokert expressly excludes from his discussion of conjunctive and
disjunctive propositions an account of those cases where the principal
connective is governed by a modal operator. But since he subsequently employs such modal propositions in his discussion of syllogistic
validity it is in order to mention here certain standard medieval propositions, to which it is likely in the highest degree that Lokert sub-
scribed, on modalised conjunctions and disjunctions.

'Possibly ($p$ or $q$)' is true just if $p$ is possible or $q$ is possible. 'Necessarily ($p$ or $q$)' is true just if (1) $p$ is necessary or (2) $q$ is necessary or (3)
$p$ and $q$ are either a pair of contradictories or a pair of subcontraries.
The relationships invoked in condition (3) will be considered at length
in chapter five. The point that is of immediate concern is that even if
neither $p$ nor not-$p$ is necessary, the disjunction '$p$ or not-$p$' is necessary; and while neither 'Some S is P' nor 'Some S is not P' need be
necessary, 'Some S is P or some S is not P' is necessary for otherwise
there could be an S of which neither the predicate P nor its negation
could be truly predicated, and that is impossible.

Modalised conjunctions are systematically related, and in interesting ways, to modalised disjunctions. We shall not follow here detailed
comparisons but will merely note the following two points:

(1) 'Possibly ($p$ and $q$)' is true just if each of $p$ and $q$ is possible, and $p$
and $q$ are neither mutually contradictory nor mutually contrary;

(2) 'Necessarily ($p$ and $q$)' is true just if each of $p$ and $q$ is necessary.
Once the truth conditions of modalised conjunctions and disjunctions
are stated in terms of modalised categoricals, the way is then open,
along the lines discussed earlier, to giving the truth conditions of
modalised conjunctions in terms of non-modal categoricals.

Unlike disjunctions and conjunctions, the kind of hypothetical
called the conditional is not straightforwardly truth functional. Lokert's account of the truth condition of a conditional proposition is
briefly stated: 'If it is a conditional it is sufficient and required that it
be a good consequence' [*De Term.* 11r]. Earlier in the *De Terminis* the
following definitions are given:

> An antecedent is a sentence from which, it is denoted, a con-
> sequent is inferred. A consequent is a sentence which is denoted
> to follow from an antecedent . . . The mark of inference is the
> 'therefore' by reason of which the consequent is denoted to be
> inferred from the antecedent, and the whole consequence results
> from the antecedent, the consequent and the mark of inference . . .

Some consequences are called good. One is good if it is of such a nature that things cannot be as are signified by the antecedent and yet not be as are signified by the consequent. A bad consequence is one where it is possible for things to be as they are signified by the antecedent and yet not be as are signified by the consequent. [3v–4r] (see appendix, no.16)

Clearly, then, the 'therefore' in a consequence signifies a modal relation between antecedent and consequent – the conjunction of the antecedent and the negation of the consequent in a good consequence is an impossibility; and hence the conditional proposition should be understood not as a material implication but, rather, as a strict implication.

Lokert refers to two kinds of conditional for which he gives the truth conditions. First: 'If it is a rational conditional it is sufficient and required that it be a good consequence and also that the antecedent and consequent be true' [*De Term.* 11r]. These truth conditions are appropriate in English usage for a pair of propositions conjoined by the connectives 'since' or 'therefore'; 'Since $p$, $q$' and '$p$, therefore $q$' both say more than 'If $p$, $q$', and in each case the more is that $p$ and $q$ are both true.

Secondly: 'If the conditional is a causal conditional it is sufficient and required that it be a good consequence, and that the antecedent and consequent be true, and that the antecedent refer to the cause of an effect referred to by the consequent' [*De Term.* 11r]. As regards the kind of cause which is of relevance to causal conditionals, medieval logicians took the term broadly, to include not only natural causes, but also what may be called logical or mathematical causes. Thus, for example, the fact that triangles have three sides was regarded as the cause of isosceles triangles having three sides.

It is evident that causal conditionals are logically on a quite different footing from conditionals as such, for causal conditionals do not fit into a system of formal logic. What rules them out is the fact that their truth conditions cannot be stated without introducing strictly material factors, such as natural causal nexus, into what should be a purely formal account. However, Lokert was following a long-standing tradition in listing causal conditionals under the general heading of conditionals.

At this stage we shall, however, not pursue further Lokert's discussion of sentential connectives and other syncategorematic terms. A sufficient conceptual framework has now been provided in terms of which topics investigated by Lokert in the second half of the *De Terminis* can be discussed.

## IV

Following his discussion in the first half of the *De Terminis*, in which attention is focused on the notions of signification and supposition of terms and on the analysis of certain syncategorematic terms, Lokert turns, in the second half, to an exposition, for which the ground has by now been prepared, of six principles of division of terms. The six divisions are into (1) mental, spoken and written terms [21v et seq.], (2) categorematic and syncategorematic terms [24v et seq.], (3) ultimate and non-ultimate mental terms [27r et seq.], (4) absolute and connotative terms [29v et seq.], (5) common and singular terms [31r et seq.] and (6) first intention and second intention terms [34v ad fin.].

The division into mental, spoken and written terms is, of course, made on the basis of the different ways by which the terms come to be known: 'A term is called "written" if it can be perceived by the bodily eye; a spoken term is one which can be perceived by bodily hearing; and a mental term is one signifying by itself and with nothing else mediating' [21v] (see appendix, no.17). As we know, unmediatedness was claimed for mental terms because they were regarded as themselves modifications of the cognitive faculty – there was, so to say, no room for a mediator between the term and the power which it modified. But a question can be raised, and Lokert duly raises it, whether any modification, of whatever sort, of the cognitive faculty can serve as a mental term. He writes: 'It is not necessary that every quality existing in the cognitive faculty should be a notion or mental term . . . In the cognitive faculty there are emotions and dispositions, but such things are not notions or mental terms, for they cannot actually represent [anything] to the cognitive faculty by themselves and without other things mediating' [23v] (see appendix, no.18). Acts of will are also ruled out, this time on the ground that such an act could not be a part of a proposition. That emotions, dispositions and volitions are excluded from the class of mental terms, and indeed are excluded for the reasons provided by Lokert, need come as no surprise, though it is perhaps surprising that he considered them to be in the cognitive faculty. The notion of a cognitive faculty, as understood in this context, is so wide that it is hardly distinguishable from the notion of the psyche of a rational being.

It is however clear that emotions, dispositions and volitions are distinguishable from mental terms, despite the fact that the first three mentioned are modifications of a psychological faculty and are, at least emotions and volitions are, possible objects of unmediated awareness;

whether we can have unmediated awareness of a psychological disposition would require additional argument. But emotions and volitions are more similar to mental terms than to either spoken or written terms. What spoken and written terms crucially share is the mediateness of our awareness of them – they can exist without impinging on our consciousness. This suggests that the tripartite division is unsatisfactory in that the three parts are not all on the same logical level. Lokert does indeed suggest at one point (though he does not pursue the suggestion further) that: 'It is safer to posit a two-part division in this way: of terms some are mental and others are non-mental' [*De Term.* 22r]. The merit of this suggestion lies in the fact that the division is clearly exhaustive of the possibilities. Once the bipartite division is granted, spoken and written terms can be placed under the heading 'non-mental'. But this latter division of the non-mental is more problematic, for whereas the division into mental and non-mental is manifestly exhaustive, the division into spoken and written is not, as Lokert was aware. For granted that some terms can be known by sight and others by sound, it is difficult to see why we should rule out the possibility of terms being known by the remaining senses. He writes: 'Qualities perceptible to other senses than hearing and sight, such as the primary qualities of tastes and smells, can be terms by imposition . . . and yet no such quality could be a mental, spoken or written term or perceptible by the intellect alone. Nor would it even be a mixed term made up of such parts' [*De Term.* 22r] (see appendix, no.19). Lokert appears to allow in the end that stimuli designed to give us olfactory or gustatory sensations could be imposed to signify something, or even in some way. Perhaps it was a reluctance on his part to consider such means of linguistic communication at all likely that prevented him developing this line of thought further.[9]

Whatever his reason for ignoring smells and tastes after apparently allowing that such things could be terms, Lokert in fact attends only to the visible and the audible variety of non-mental terms. These latter are distinguished not only with respect to the different sensory receptors by which they are known but also, we are told, with respect to the time when they can be grasped. He writes: 'It is required of a spoken term that it be immediately perceptible by bodily hearing . . . and as regards the written term it is said that it is not required that it be immediately perceptible by bodily vision' [*De Term.* 24r] (see appendix, no.20). What Lokert appears to have in mind here is that a word, once written, is then available to be read long after the scribal performance, whereas a word, once spoken, must be heard when it is spoken or else that performance is lost. The natural reply to make to this distinction is that Lokert lived before the days of sound record-ing; otherwise he would have recognised that just as we can read and re-read what was written just once, so we can hear and re-hear what was said just once. But there remains a difference between the two cases, namely, that to hear the sound a second time that sound has to be repeated, that is, re-sounded, for it is a repetition of the sound that is heard the 'second' time, not the original sound, however similar the second might be to the first. But the letters of the written word do not have to be reshaped for the word to be read again. This remaking of the sound, which is not paralleled by a remaking of the marks on paper, points to a logical distinction between vocal and written terms that would enable Lokert to reject as irrelevant to his point the refer-ence to sound recording.

V

In his discussion of the second division of terms, namely, that of categorematic and syncategorematic, Lokert takes up a variety of topics. We have already noted that both sorts of term signify, but do so differently: 'A categorematic term is a term signifying something and a syncategorematic term is a term signifying in some way' [*De Term.* 24v]. The latter kind of term, unlike the former, signifies nothing. But to say that it signifies nothing is not a way of saying that it does not signify; it is to say merely that whatever way it may be that such a term signifies, it does not at any rate signify in such a way that the term can be truly predicated of a demonstrative pronoun which points to a thing. Syncategorematic terms are not fitted by their nature to serve as predicates or as subjects. This fact about them serves as an essential part of their syntactic characterisation.

Lokert is, however, concerned to stress the point that not all categorematic terms can serve as either subject or predicate. The distinction is drawn between those categorematic terms which have signification merely and those which have signification and function (*officium*). Lokert writes (see appendix, no.21): 'A categorematic term with signification merely is said to be a term which, in accord-ance with a signification that it has, signifies something but is not, in accordance with that signification, able to have a function in a propos-ition' [*De Term.* 24v]. The notion of a 'function' is immediately clari-fied: 'A term is said to have a function in a proposition in accordance with some signification that it has when, in accordance with that signification, it is able to be a principal part of a proposition'. Hence a categorematic term with signification but no function cannot serve as either subject or predicate of a categorical proposition. The first kind of non-functional significative categorematic term that Lokert mentions is the noun which occurs in an oblique (i.e. non-nominative) case. The oblique case most commonly signalled morphologically in English is the possessive, for example, the word 'man's' in 'The man's ass is white'. The term 'man's', no less than the term 'man', signifies all men, but not in such a way that the term can be predicated truly of a demonstrative pronoun which points to a man. A sentence thus formed out of such materials would not be false so much as ungrammatical.

As has already been made plain a syncategorematic term cannot be placed as a predicate in a proposition, and in this respect a word such as 'man's' behaves syntactically like a word such as 'not' or 'every'. But there remains the semantic difference that 'man's' is a term that can stand in the relation of sign to thing signified, where what is signified is not the term itself but men. 'Not' and 'every' naturally stand for themselves – everything is a natural sign of itself – but they were not imposed to signify themselves; they were imposed to signify in some way, namely, in such a way as to have a certain kind of effect on the term to which they are added. Lokert refers to a common way of describing the kind of signification that a syncategorematic term has, namely: 'By reason of the syncategorematic term's way of signifying, the term to which it is added is taken otherwise than it would be taken if the syncategorematic term did not have that mode of signifying' [*De Term.* 25v]. But this description of the way syncategorematic terms function prompts the question of whether all terms said to be syncategorematic really are such (see appendix, no.22). Lokert offers two problematic examples, namely, the quantifiers 'every' and 'some'. He writes:

> Against [this description] it is argued that it would follow that the term 'every' in this proposition: 'Every man who is Socrates runs' does not signify in some way, since the complex 'man who is Socrates' is not taken otherwise on account of the occurrence of the sign 'every' than it would be taken without such a sign, for with or without the sign the complex is a singular term. In the same way the word 'some' in 'Some man is running' would not be a syncategorematic term, for it does not make the word 'man' understood otherwise than it would be understood without the sign 'some'. [*De Term.* 25v]

The point being made about the role of 'every' has some plausibility; the complex term 'man who is Socrates' is a singular term since it can signify only what the singular term 'Socrates' signifies. And even if 'every' were added to that complex term the resulting term would still be a singular term uniquely signifying Socrates. And if it is impossible for a syncategorematic term to be added to a term without affecting the way that the latter term is taken then 'every' cannot after all be syncategorematic. The argument regarding 'some' is pursued along the same lines.

Furthermore, if what makes a term syncategorematic is its effectiveness in changing the way in which that to which it is added is taken, then many terms normally thought of as plainly categorematic would have to be classified as syncategorematic after all. To take Lokert's example: 'The word 'man' would signify in some way and would be a syncategorematic term since by its addition to some term the latter term is taken otherwise than it would be taken without the word 'man'. This is obvious in the proposition 'An animal which is a man runs' where the complex 'an animal which is' is taken otherwise than in this proposition 'An animal which is [i.e. exists] runs'. And likewise the word 'man's' results in the word 'ass' being taken otherwise in the proposition 'A man's ass runs' than it would be taken without the determination 'man's'.

However, Lokert is not inclined on the basis of such examples to alter his account of categorematic and syncategorematic terms. He affirms that if a term is to signify in some way: 'it is required that the term have a signification by which it signifies no thing or things, but by reason of its signification it could make the term to which it is added be taken in some other way' [*De Term*. 26r]. He immediately applies this point to the arguments concerning the signification of 'every' and 'some':

> When it is said that the word 'every' in the proposition 'Every man who is Socrates runs' is not a syncategorematic term, and neither is 'some' in 'Some man runs', that is denied. And for proof, when it is said that the term to which 'every' is added in the first proposition is not taken otherwise than it would be taken without that sign, and likewise with the term to which 'some' is added in the second proposition, that is denied. The term which is the subject of the first proposition is taken universally on account of the 'every', and the subject of the second proposition is taken particularly by reason of the sign of particularity, though it is granted that the second proposition is equivalent to the prejacent form in which the sign of particularity is not placed.

Thus Lokert's argument as regards both 'every' and 'some' is that the fact that the exemplary *sentence* containing 'every' is equivalent to that sentence with the 'every' deleted does not prove that the *term* to which the 'every' is added is not taken differently in consequence of the addition of the 'every'. And likewise with 'some'. The argument thus amounts to the unexceptionable principle that terms shared by different sentences can be taken differently though the different sentences are equivalent. The situation here is similar to one discussed earlier where Lokert argued that each negation in a double negated sentence signifies negatively although the proposition which is doubly negated is equivalent to that very sentence without the two negation signs.

As regards what should be said about the term 'man's' in 'A man's ass runs', it has to be granted that the term does affect the way that 'ass' is taken; but that a term has an effect on the way another term is taken is not sufficient ground for classifying that term as syncategorematic. Two related reasons are adduced by Lokert in support of the view that 'man's' is not syncategorematic (see appendix, no.33). The first is expressed as follows: 'As regards a term in an oblique case and with oblique signification, it should probably be said that such an oblique term, which is able to refer to a suppositum with an impersonal verb or an infinitive verb, is a categorematic term with a function and not with signification merely' [*De Term.* 26v]. What he is saying is that in certain kinds of sentence a word in an oblique case should 'probably' be seen as functioning as a principal part of a categorical sentence yet not as a copula, from which it would follow that the term must be categorematic. An example of such categorematic terms is the dative term 'to me' in the sentences 'It is pleasing to me' and 'It is offensive to me'.

The second reason Lokert has for wishing to deny that 'man's' is syncategorematic is simply that the term signifies something, namely, the same thing that 'man' signifies. Indeed, he classifies 'man' and 'man's' (and also any other two terms of which one is an oblique form of the other) as synonyms [*De Term.* 26v]. But distinctions have to be noted here:

> Terms are called synonymous in two senses, first as regards essential signification merely, when, namely, terms signify the same thing and in the same way with respect to signifying absolutely or connotatively. In this sense a nominative term and its oblique form are called synonymous terms. But it does not follow from this that it is necessary that whatever belongs to one of the synonymous terms also belongs to the other. In a second sense terms are called synonymous, namely, in respect of essential signification and also accidental or grammatical signification. In this case the notion corresponding to the one term also corresponds to the other. In this [second] sense a nominative term and its oblique form are not called synonymous. [*De Term.* 26v–27r]

Thus two terms which are synonymous in both senses have a shared corresponding mental term. But 'man' and 'man's' do not share a corresponding mental term. If they did it would be possible to replace one by the other in a proposition without affecting the truth value of that proposition. But replacing 'man' by 'man's' in a true proposition will result in something which is not true, at least if the two terms are used with their normal significative function (and do not, say, supposit materially); it will indeed result in something which is not grammatically well formed and which will therefore not have a truth value at all.

VI

Unlike the second division of terms, that into categorematic and syncategorematic, which is a division of terms whether mental, spoken or written, the third division is of mental terms only, namely, into those which are ultimate and those which are non-ultimate (see appendix, no.24). The distinction between the categorematic and the syncategorematic is, however, invoked by Lokert at an important juncture in the argument.

The distinction between the ultimate and the non-ultimate mental term is based on distinctions already familiar to us. Lokert writes: 'The significate of a term which the term signifies strictly is called its *ultimate significate*; and that which a term non-strictly signifies is called its *non-ultimate significate*' [*De Term.* 27r]. For example, the term 'man' strictly signifies all men; that is, the term was imposed to signify all men. In virtue of this relation in which men stand to the term 'man' any man is said to be an ultimate significate of the term 'man'. But 'man' also signifies non-strictly. It does so when it is used to signify not men, but itself, as when it is said that 'man' is triliteral. The term is not, of course, imposed to signify itself, but so signifies naturally, and when it does signify in this way it signifies its non-ultimate significate. Hence whether a significate is or is not ultimate depends on whether the term signifying it is signifying strictly. For example, that the term 'man' is the significate of a term does not imply that the term 'man' is a non-ultimate significate, for if it is being signified by the term 'term' or 'noun' or 'monosyllable', say, then it is an ultimate significate. Only if it is being signified by itself is it a non-ultimate significate.

Given the notions of an ultimate and a non-ultimate significate, two further pieces of terminology can be introduced: 'The *ultimate signification* of a term is that signification by which the term signifies strictly, and the *non-ultimate signification* of a term is that signification by which it signifies non-strictly' [*De Term.* 27r]. 'Man', for example, is being used in accordance with its ultimate signification when it is being used to signify Socrates and any other man, and in accordance with its non-ultimate signification when it is used to signify itself (as when it is used with material supposition as in '"Man" is monosyllabic'). The two main heads of division can now be introduced: 'An *ultimate mental term* is a [mental] term corresponding to another term according to the ultimate signification of the other term, and a *non-ultimate mental term* is a mental term corresponding to another term according to the latter's non-ultimate signification'. The distinction can be expounded as follows: any non-mental sign whatever has a mental correlate since a sign is something that represents something, or in some way, to the cognitive faculty. The mental term thus associated with a non-mental term can be classified, on the basis of the foregoing distinctions, according to whether that term to which the mental term corresponds is being taken in accordance with its ultimate signification or in accordance with its non-ultimate signification. Thus the mental term corresponding to the term 'man' taken in its ultimate signification is quite different from the mental term corresponding to that term taken in accordance with its non-ultimate signification. The mental term is said to be ultimate if it corresponds to a term taken in accordance with the latter's strict signification, and the mental term is non-ultimate if it corresponds to a term which is taken in accordance with its non-strict signification.

One corollary is stated as follows: 'Of the foregoing division, the divisum is not just this complex "mental term", but this whole "mental term of another term" or this whole "mental term corresponding to some other term". I mean that no mental term is called ultimate or non-ultimate except relationally, that is, in relation to some other term' [*De Term.* 27v]. Thus if there were no term 'man' imposed to signify all men there could be no ultimate mental term 'man'. This is not to say that if there were no conventional term 'man' there could be no mental term 'man'; on the contrary, as we know, it was held that the mental term had to exist before the conventional term, signifying conventionally, could exist. It is to say merely that since 'ultimate' and 'non-ultimate' are always in relation to, or in respect of, some other term, the mental term 'man', though it could exist in the absence of a conventional term strictly signifying all men, could not be either ultimate or non-ultimate. Lokert states the position as follows: 'If there were a natural similitude of Socrates, with no other term signifying Socrates in existence (whether that signification be conventionally strictly or in some other way non-strictly) then that natural likeness of Socrates would not be an ultimate mental term or a non-ultimate mental term. And consequently it is conceded that it is possible for there to be a mental term which is neither ultimate nor non-ultimate. This is sufficiently proved by arguing that before terms were imposed to signify conventionally strictly there were mental terms which were neither ultimate nor non-ultimate' [*De Term.* 28v].

It is evident from what has been said that a conventional term cannot strictly signify unless it is subordinate to an ultimate mental term. But it should be added that, as Lokert states the matter, 'Not every term which strictly signifies has an ultimate mental term in accordance with its strict signification . . . This is obvious as regards mental terms which naturally strictly signify, and not conventionally strictly. Such terms are not subordinate to ultimate mental terms, since they are subordinate to no terms at all in accordance with their strict signification. But any spoken or written term which strictly signifies has an ultimate mental term' [*De Term.* 27v]. The strictly signifying mental term 'man' does not require a further mental term to which it must be subordinate for it to be able to signify men strictly, since it has the signification that it has by its very nature.

Although the example we have been using (following Lokert) is of the simple term 'man' this is not because it was thought that there could be an ultimate or non-ultimate mental term only of a simple term. Lokert asks the question: 'whether just as to a simple term there corresponds an ultimate mental term and a non-ultimate mental term, so also to a complex term and likewise to a whole proposition there corresponds an ultimate mental proposition and likewise also a non-ultimate mental proposition' [*De Term.* 29r]. His position on this matter is that the arguments that there must be ultimate and non-ultimate mental terms of strictly signifying spoken and written terms have no less force where the spoken or written terms are complex categorematic terms; and they also apply to spoken or written propositions. He writes:

> If a term, whether complex or incomplex, is subordinate to a mental term according to its strict signification then that mental term is called an ultimate mental term in respect of the other term. And if the term is subordinate to the mental term in accordance with its non-strict signification that mental term is called non-ultimate in relation to that term. And thus a spoken or written proposition, such as 'Man is an animal', according as it signifies conventionally strictly propositionally is subordinate to an ultimate mental proposition. And according as it signifies non-strictly it is said to be subordinate to a notion which is called a

non-ultimate mental proposition, and so the natural likeness of a proposition is called a non-ultimate mental proposition.
[*De Term.* 29r]

What Lokert has in mind here is that a proposition, no less than a simple categorematic term, signifies strictly, though it does so in a different way since its signification is a product of the signification of the terms of which it is composed, and given the way the terms are arranged in the proposition. A proposition can also signify non-strictly, since, like everything else, it signifies itself naturally. Corresponding to these modes of signification of spoken or written propositions there are mental correlates which are modifications of the cognitive power, and the modification which is produced by the spoken proposition being taken in accordance with its propositional signification is entirely different from that produced by the spoken proposition being taken for the particular kind of natural object that it is. In the latter case the proposition is being treated as if it had no propositional signification, but were just a sound sequence. In the former case the modification of the cognitive power is a mental proposition which is an ultimate mental proposition of the spoken proposition taken as signifying strictly, that is, propositionally. The non-ultimate mental proposition of that proposition is the mental correlate of that proposition taken as signifying non-strictly, that is, non-propositionally.

What has just been said about mental propositions can be applied in answering the question raised by Lokert: 'whether just as there are ultimate mental categorematic terms and non-ultimate ones, so likewise there are ultimate mental syncategorematic terms and also non-ultimate ones' [*De Term.* 29r] (see appendix, no.25). Lokert answers his question as follows:

> Just as there can be terms which strictly or non-strictly signify some thing or things, so also there can be terms which conventionally strictly and likewise non-strictly signify in some way. And in consequence there are syncategorematic terms which are non-ultimate mental terms in relation to other terms, and hence the syncategorematic act which is a mental term of the word 'every' is a non-ultimate mental term with a natural likeness to the word 'every', since a natural likeness to that word signifies conventionally non-strictly in the way in which the spoken word signifies conventionally strictly. [*De Term.* 29r–v]

The following position emerges from this account. A syncategorematic term has two kinds of signification. According to its strict signification it signifies *in some way*, and of course it has to be imposed for such a role. But like everything else it signifies itself without imposition, that is, naturally. In so far as its signification is of the latter kind, namely, non-strict, the term does not signify syncategorematically at all; it signifies categorematically for it signifies itself as a thing. In the proposition 'If he comes he is brave', when that proposition is taken as signifying propositionally, the 'if' is being taken syncategorematically. It signifies no thing, but instead signifies in some way. If, on the other hand, the proposition were taken to be signifying non-strictly then the 'if' must also be signifying non-strictly, and in that case it signifies in such a manner that it can be truly said of its significate that it is biliteral, that it is monosyllabic, and so on. If we translate these points into the recently introduced terminology, what is being said is, first, that the mental term to which a strictly signifying syncategorematic term is subordinate is an ultimate mental term in relation to that syncategorematic term, and secondly, that a mental term to which a syncategorematic term signifying non-strictly is subordinate is a non-ultimate mental term in relation to the syncategorematic term.

## VII

Unlike the division just considered, the fourth division presented by Lokert is explicitly a division of categorematic terms, though it is immaterial whether the terms are mental, spoken or written. The division in question is that into absolute and connotative terms (see appendix, no.26). He writes:

A connotative term is a categorematic term with a material significate, referring to some thing or things and formally denoting that something else or that same thing (or those same things) exist in some way. And an absolute term is said to be a categorematic term referring to nothing beyond its material significate and not denoting that its material significate exists in some way . . . The material significate of a term is said to be that for which a term is fitted to be taken because of its mode of signifying. This is clarified: the word 'man' is an absolute term whose material significates are men. The aforesaid term refers to nothing else beyond those significates. Nor does it denote that those significates exist in some way. And the word 'white' is a connotative term whose material significate is a white thing, and beyond its signifying white things it connotes that whiteness belongs to that material significate. For that reason whiteness is its formal significate. Likewise 'sitting' [or 'seated'] is a connotative term with a material significate, signifying a seated thing, and beyond that it refers to no other thing but connotes that the same thing exists in some way, viz. in such and such a manner. [*De Term.* 29v–30r]

To focus briefly on Lokert's examples: the term 'seated' materially signifies everything of which it is true to say 'This is seated' and hence the material significates of the term are all seated individuals. And the term formally signifies the way in which the material significates exist; the formal significate may be termed 'sedentariness'. Likewise, the term 'white' materially signifies all white things, and its formal significate is whiteness. In virtue of possessing both a material and a formal significate the terms 'seated' and 'white' are connotative terms.

There is clearly a sense in which 'white' primarily signifies white things and secondarily signifies whiteness, for it is true of white things that they are white, but not true of whiteness that it is white. 'White', we might say, signifies whiteness only indirectly, for 'white' signifies whiteness through white individuals. What signifies whiteness directly is the term 'whiteness' itself. Thus 'whiteness' has a material significate, but unlike 'white' it lacks a formal significate, for the term does not indicate the way in which anything exists. 'White' might signify a marble statue in virtue of the statue's existing 'whitely', but 'whiteness', though it signifies a certain colour, does not indicate the manner in which that colour, or anything else, exists. Since 'whiteness' has a material significate while lacking a formal one it is classified as an absolute term.

The importance of the distinction between absolute and connotative terms is due most especially to its connection with a metaphysical problem which Lokert does not discuss in the specifically logical treatise which we are here primarily concerned with. But to grasp the significance of Lokert's discussion brief mention should be made of the metaphysical problem in question. A basic distinction extensively discussed by medieval logicians is that between concrete and abstract terms. One common way employed to distinguish between these two kinds of term was on the basis of a syntactic consideration, namely, the consideration that many terms which appear in the predicate position in a proposition can occur in that same position with or without a certain kind of suffix. The suffixes, which can be identified simply by enumerating them, include most commonly '-hood', '-ity' and '-ness'. Thus the following pairs can be used as our exemplars: 'bachelor/bachelorhood', 'white/whiteness' and 'rapid/rapidity'. In each case the first of the pair of terms is concrete and the second is abstract. Now, the syntactic distinction between the members of the pairs marks also a semantic distinction, for the members of a pair are not thought of as signifying precisely the same thing. The concrete term signifies concrete entities, namely, things which are bachelors, or are white or rapid, and the abstract terms signify abstract entities, namely, those qualities that the concrete things have in virtue of which the concrete terms truly signify them. This way of speaking sets the scene for the medieval dispute between the nominalists and realists who argued precisely over the question of whether there are, or are not, individuals which are named by the abstract terms. The distinction between connotative and absolute terms is central to this fundamental issue because the way the distinction between concrete and abstract terms is drawn leads to the conclusion that concrete terms are connotative and abstract terms are absolute.

## IX

The fifth division of terms discussed by Lokert is that into common and singular (see appendix, no.27). He begins by identifying the divisum:

> Of this division the divisum is this whole: 'term fitted by its strict mode of signifying to be taken for some thing or things', so that as 'term' is equivalent to this complex, by reason of this no syncategorematic term is a singular or a common term according to its syncategorematic signification; and hence neither is a whole proposition or a propositional complex according as it is of this kind, and thus neither is some other term which is not fitted by its mode of signifying to be taken for some thing or things.
>
> [De Term. 31r–v]

The division applies, then, only to the class of categorematic terms signifying categorematically. Lokert defines the heads of division in these terms: 'A common term is a term which can without contradiction be taken, univocally and separately, for several things, according to its mode of signifying, for example, such terms as "man", "animal" and so on. A singular term is a term fitted to be taken for something by its strict mode of signifying and not for many things univocally and separately, as for example the term "Socrates" and such like'.

Parts of these definitions require elucidation. Lokert tells us that: 'In the foregoing statement "to be taken" is taken for "supposit" or "be true of". And in the foregoing definitions it is said "by its strict mode of signifying" since it is not necessary that every common term or singular term simply be fitted to be taken for something' [De Term. 31v]. That is to say, Lokert wishes to ensure that certain terms are classified as common or singular despite the fact that there is nothing for which they can be taken tout court. The example he gives is 'chimera'. The phrase 'taken according to its strict mode of signifying' helps to make the point that the failure of the term to signify is not due to a defect in the term's mode of signifying, for if there were creatures answering to a given description then the term 'chimera' could be taken for them. The failure or 'defect' (Lokert's term) lies simply in the non-existence of things answering to that description.

This is no less true of singular terms than it is of common terms. For there may not be anything for which a singular term may be taken, and Lokert wishes to argue that failure of a singular term to be taken for anything may not be due to the fact that something has gone wrong with the mode of signification of the term but be due instead simply to the non-existence of the appropriate object. The example given is 'this chimera'. The expression is well fitted to be taken for a unique individual, and it is merely the absence of any chimera which can be pointed to by the speaker that prevents the term signifying something.

Just as a term may be singular though there is nothing that it signifies, so also a term may be common though there is just one thing which it signifies. This follows from Lokert's position though he does not give any examples. Major, who discusses this point, offers several (see Appendix no.28). He argues that 'sun', 'world' and 'phoenix' are common terms although each signifies only one thing, for if we grant the physical possibility of, say, another sun being produced no new term would need to be imposed to signify it. 'Sun' would signify the new sun as well as the old [*Terminorum* 10v¹]. Another example furnished by Major is the following: 'Superlative nouns affirmatively expounded are common terms since, granted that they cannot be taken for several things at the same time (as is said in the fifth book of the *Physics*), they are, or can be, taken for several things in temporal succession' [*Terminorum* 11r¹]. (I discuss superlatives in chapter three. Here it need only be said that the difference between expounding a superlative affirmatively and negatively is the difference between, say, expounding 'A is the highest hill' as 'Every hill other than A is not as high as A' and as 'No hill is higher than A'. The second exposition allows for the possibility that other hills are as high as A, and the first exposition blocks this possibility).

The crucial difference between common and singular terms lies in the fact that a common term, employed univocally, can be taken for a number of things 'separately' and a singular term cannot. Lokert enlarges on two key terms in this distinction: 'A term is said to be taken univocally for many things (1) when it is a mental term taken for those things which it naturally strictly signifies or (2) when it is a term which is taken for those things with that same mental term mediating. The word "separately" appeared in the definitions since it is not unsatisfactory for a singular term to be taken univocally for many

things conjointly, as "Socrates" is taken conjointly and separately for
the matter and form of Socrates' [*De Term.* 31v]. Thus the two separate things, the matter and the form of Socrates, taken conjointly can
be signified by 'Socrates', but the name cannot be taken for the matter
of Socrates separately, and for his form separately. For then there
would be at least two things that were Socrates. Nevertheless Lokert
clearly considered that the claim that 'Socrates' was a singular term
was not entirely uncontentious, and he presents various arguments for
the view that the name is, after all, a common term, before producing
counter arguments to that claim. Aspects of his discussion have a very
modern ring.

The first argument he presents is this: '"Socrates", in accordance
with one signification that it has, univocally signifies all who are called
by the name "Socrates", and it cannot, given that signification, be
called a singular term' [*De Term.* 31v]. The term must therefore be
common. One might put the point by saying that according to one
signification that the term has, 'Socrates' admits of a plural, according, that is, to that signification in virtue of which we can truly say that
there are many Socrateses.

Lokert deals with this point by saying in effect that while it is true
that in accordance with one signification that the term 'Socrates' has,
that term is common, it is in fact a quite different signification that is at
issue when it is said that it is singular. In logic, especially in the area
presently under consideration, the precise signification of terms has to
be clearly grasped. After all, on one signification, as Lokert points out
[31v], every categorematic term, including every 'common' one, is
singular, namely, on the signification it has in virtue of which it
signifies itself; and on another signification every categorematic term,
including every 'singular' one, is common, namely, on that signification in virtue of which it signifies every term similar to itself, that is,
all tokens of the one type. Now, 'Socrates' is significative in several
ways. In accordance with one signification that it has it is equivalent to
the complex term 'what is called by the name "Socrates"',[10] and when
so taken the name is a connotative term which has as a material
significate anything which has the name 'Socrates'. But, Lokert adds,
there is a second way to take the term, for: 'the name "Socrates" is
generally taken so that it is an absolute singular term, not signifying
several things univocally and separately, and it is customarily conceded that in accordance with this further signification Socrates was
Socrates before he was called "Socrates", and thus the term signifies
someone while connoting nothing, not even in some way'[11] [*De Term.*
32r] (see appendix, no.29).

Granted, then, that the name 'Socrates' is, according to one signification that it has, a singular term, what should be said of the negative term 'non-Socrates' (see appendix, no.30)? The answer given is that: '"Non-Socrates" is a common term and not a singular one; I have in mind the signification by which it signifies strictly' [*De Term.* 32v]. The reason for maintaining this is that: 'The term is fitted to be taken, univocally and separately, for many things, since it is fitted to be taken for anything other than Socrates'. Lokert draws the following conclusion: 'There is a complex, whose signification arises formally from the signification of its parts, signifying something which is not signified by a part of the said complex. Nor even is a part of the thing signified by a part of the complex. This is obvious as regards the negative term "non-Socrates". As the argument proves, it is fitted by its nature to be taken, and to supposit, for anything other than Socrates, and in consequence signifies every such thing. But no part of it signifies such a being, nor signifies a part of it' [*De Term.* 33r].

Clearly the negation operator, when operating upon a categorematic term to form a negative term, functions syncategorematically just as it does when operating on a proposition to form a negative proposition, for 'non', operating on 'Socrates' to form the negative term 'non-Socrates', does not itself signify anything, but instead signifies in some way, in such a way, namely, that the term upon which it operates signifies anything whatever except what it signifies when unnegated. This negation operator is in one crucial logical way quite different from the propositional operator 'not' in that the introduction of the former negation operator into an affirmative proposition does not result in a negative proposition. Neither Lokert, nor medieval logicians generally, treated, say, 'This is not Socrates' as falling under the same mental proposition as 'This is a non-Socrates'. An important consequence of the distinction thus drawn between the two uses of the negation operator is that the syllogistic rule that no valid syllogism can have two negative premisses is not violated by a syllogism one of whose premisses is negative only in the sense that it contains a negative term.

Although the example used above is of a singular term which combines with a negation operator to form a common term, this is not the exclusive pattern. In the course of his discussion of negative terms Lokert presents the following proposition: 'A negative term whose negated term is fitted to be taken for anything other than Socrates is taken only for Socrates, and such a negative term could be called singular; for so far as an affirmative term is taken for more things, by that amount its negative term is taken for less, and vice versa. And from this it is obvious when a negative term is a singular or a common term' [*De Term.* 33r]. Thus, granted that 'Socrates' is a singular term, 'non-Socrates' is a common term, and 'non-non-Socrates', which signifies the same thing that 'Socrates' signifies, for the law of double negation applies to negation operators operating on terms, is a singular term. But negating a negative term does not in all cases result in a singular term; if the original, unnegated term is a common term, then its negation results in another common term, and the negation of the negative term is also common.

A further doctrine concerning negative terms is presented by Lokert:

> If an affirmative term supposits for something with the mediating copula 'are', the corresponding negative term does not supposit for the same thing with the same mediating copula and with respect to just the same tense. This is obvious from this fact, that an affirmative term and its negative term are *contradictory terms*, and such terms never supposit for the same thing in respect of the same copula and in relation to just the same tenses, even allowing that one or other member of a pair of contradictory terms is true of any entity whatever. Just as a transcendental term is true of anything whatever with any mediating copula, any disjunction of contradictory terms is true of the same thing with the same mediating copula. And that means a common rule of contradictory terms, namely, that of anything at all one of a pair of contradictories is true, and of nothing both are. [*De Term.* 33r]

This last mentioned rule holds in virtue of the nature of negation, and independently of whether either of the terms in the pair is singular. But it should be added that though a pair of contradictories can consist of two common terms, it cannot consist of two singular terms, for if the negated term is singular the negative term, that is, the one composed of the negated term plus the negation operator, cannot be construed as a singular term amounting to the name of the totality of things which are other than the significate of the negated term. For the negative term is not to be understood as signifying the conjunction of all things other than the significate of the negated term, but as signifying the disjunction of all those other things. Were it the sign of a conjunction it would indeed be a singular term, but since it is to be understood as signifying a disjunction it is a common term truly predicable of any term signifying any disjunct in that disjunction.

## X

We turn now to a brief discussion of the sixth and final division of terms expounded in the *De Terminis*, the division into terms of first intention and of second intention (see appendix, no. 31). The divisum of this division is 'categorematic term'. The definitions are stated as follows: 'A term of second intention is a term signifying something qua sign or qua significate; and a term of first intention is a term signifying something not qua sign or qua significate' [34v]. Lokert proceeds with a short exposition of this statement:

It is obvious from the foregoing definitions that a term can be taken in two ways as a term of second intention; in one way when it signifies something qua sign, as with 'name', 'proposition', 'sign (strictly taken)'; and in a second way a term is said to be of second intention, viz. when it signifies something qua significate, as with such terms: 'definitum', 'negated', 'equivocation', 'equivocal'. 'Significate' is understood here strictly. Hence a term can be understood in two ways to signify something qua sign. In the first way a term so signifies that thing that if the thing is not a sign, the term, in accordance with that signification, will not supposit for it. (I assume a present tense mediating copula and no ampliation). Thus, this term 'noun' signifies this spoken or written word 'man' such that if 'man' were not a sign then 'noun' would not supposit for it with the assumed kind of copula mediating. A term can be understood in a second way to signify something qua sign. Such a term signifies that thing while connoting formally or equivalently as 'sign' connotes. Thus 'noun' connotes equivalently to 'sign' because there is in the definition of 'noun' the term 'sign' or 'signifying' or 'significative' or some other term including in its connotation the connotation of the term 'sign'. And correspondingly it is possible for 'A term signifies something qua significate' to be understood in two ways; in one way since such a term would not supposit for that thing, with a mediating present tense copula, unless the thing were signified strictly by some term. And a term can be understood, in a second way, to signify something qua significate, since it signifies the thing while connoting formally or equivalently just as 'significate' connotes. And in the proposition [i.e. the definitions] it is better to take 'signify something qua sign or qua significate' according to the last senses. [34v]

Since the 'last senses' refer explicitly in each case to the connotation of the terms of second intention, it is plain that any second intention term must be connotative, and that accordingly any absolute term must be of first intention. These two corollaries are drawn [35r] by Lokert directly from the passage just quoted. He adds a third corollary: 'Each head of division of the foregoing division is a term of second intention. From this it is obvious that some terms of second intention are true only of terms of first intention (I assume a present tense mediating copula); that is obvious in the case of this complex: term of first intention' [35r].

Following these corollaries Lokert discusses a series of questions concerning the syntactic limits on what can be classed as terms of second intention. For example he discusses whether negative, conjunctive and disjunctive terms can be of second intention. But this final section of *De Terminis* has less material of interest to modern logicians than have the earlier sections of the book. Rather than pursue topics into which new life can perhaps no longer be breathed we shall instead turn, in the next chapter, to an examination of an important aspect of the theory of terms which contains a good deal that would be of interest to modern logicians but to which, since the middle ages, attention has hardly been given. The aspect in question is the theory of exponible terms.

CHAPTER THREE

# Exponibilia

## I

In the *De Terminis* [8r] Lokert asks what is required for the truth of a categorical proposition, whether affirmative or negative, and says that to answer this a distinction must first be made between different kinds of proposition. One kind is the exponible proposition or, more briefly, the 'exponible'. We are told that such a proposition is: 'one in which an exponible sign is placed, namely, an exclusive, exceptive, reduplicative or collective sign, a comparative or superlative term, "begins", "ceases", "mediately", "differs", and so on[1] for any other term which obscures the sense of a proposition. Propositions in which such signs are not placed are called "non-exponibles"' [*De Term.* 10r] (see appendix, no.32). Thus both a proposition and a term can be classified as exponible; what makes a proposition exponible is that it contains an exponible term[2] and what makes a term exponible is that it obscures the sense of the proposition it is in.[3] Since the exponible proposition is, as it stands, obscure, clarification requires that it be expounded in such a way that the obscurity caused by the presence of the exponible term is removed. Once the exposition has been given the truth value of the proposition can be ascertained.

The introduction of the psychological criterion of obscurity is in a sense unsatisfactory. An exclusive proposition, such as 'Only animals are men' is not more obscure than, say, 'All men are animals', which, according to Lokert is equivalent to the exclusive proposition. What underlies the reference to obscurity is the fact that exponibles were seen as being, in an important respect, more complex than the non-exponible propositions in terms of which they were expounded. The basic categorical proposition was of the form 'A is B'. This could be universal, particular or singular and it could be affirmed or denied.[4] Next, such propositions could be conjoined by one or other of a variety of connectives, such as the conjunctive, disjunctive or conditional connective. And it was in terms of such categorical propositions and their conjunctions and disjunctions that propositions containing exponible terms, such as 'only', 'except' and 'in so far as', were expounded. Thus in order of exposition of the system, exponibles are introduced as propositions which, though apparently categorical, are to be understood in terms of hypotheticals. And on the grounds that the more complex is likely to be more difficult to grasp than the less complex, exponible propositions could be seen as more obscure than the non-exponible propositions in terms of which the exponibles were expounded.

Now, it was in response to a question about the truth conditions of categorical propositions that Lokert introduced the notion of an exponible proposition, and a hint is thereby given that he classified exponibles as categoricals. Indeed, it may seem reasonable to treat the exclusive exponible 'Only A is B' as a categorical if 'Every B is A' is a categorical, for 'Only A is B' is formally no more complex than the universal affirmative to which it is equivalent. But the fact that 'Only A is B' is expounded as a conjunction of categorical propositions (namely, to anticipate: 'A is B & Every non-A is non-B') prompts the suggestion that the exclusive may look like a categorical but is in reality a hypothetical, namely, a conjunction of categoricals. That is to say, the exclusive is formally a categorical, but virtually a hypothetical.

On the basis of this consideration it might be argued that while exponible terms occur in spoken or written propositions, such terms do not really exist for they do not exist in mental propositions. In our discussion, in the previous chapter, of mental language it was pointed out that just as equivocal terms in spoken language are terms which fall under different mental terms, so synonymous terms are terms with perhaps different physical properties which nevertheless fall under the same mental term. The same holds for propositions. For example, to take Lokert's model, 'Socrates runs' and 'Socrates is running' are subordinate to the same mental proposition. But it is a further feature of the theory of mental language that the mental proposition displays in its very form the logical form which a spoken proposition may have only virtually. Thus, of the two equivalent spoken propositions 'Socrates runs' and 'Socrates is running' the second one, not the first, corresponds term for term with the mental proposition to which both propositions are subordinate. Thus there is no mental term 'runs' understood as the conflation of 'is running', for 'runs' does not show its copula-plus-predicate form. This same move can be made to show that exponible terms do not really exist, that is, do not exist in the basic language to which spoken and written language are subordinate. For the exposition of 'Only A is B', which reveals the logical form contained virtually in the exponible, does not itself contain the exponible term 'only'. But it is the exposition of the exponible that corresponds term for term with the corresponding mental proposition, and hence the term 'only' does not exist in the mental proposition.

It can thus be argued that two aspects of the one point are being presented when it is said that exponible propositions are really, that is, virtually hypothetical, and that exponible terms do not exist on that level of language in relation to which spoken and written language is merely secondary and subordinate.

Lokert did not address himself directly to this line of argument, but it should be noted that John Major did discuss the problem, raising it first in the opening page of his *De Exponibilibus*,[5] and it can hardly be expected that Lokert did not know his teacher's answer. For Major the answer was apparent once the precise relation between an exponible and its exposition was identified. It was generally agreed that the two were mutually equivalent, but the point had to be made that the equivalence was not due to the two having the same signification, but to having the same inferential power; that is, an exponible and its exposition had the same truth value and each was inferable from the other.[6] The reason that this distinction resolves the problem of whether exponibles are virtual hypotheticals is that two expressions do not fall under the one mental expression unless the two have the same signification. Hence despite their equivalence an exponible and its exposition fall under different mental expressions, from which it follows that it cannot be validly argued that since an exponible and its exposition are equivalent they do not both exist at the primary linguistic level, namely, at the level of mental language. The way was thus open to treat exponibles as genuine categoricals, and hence to say that their subject plus copula plus predicate structure in spoken and written language reflected the true logical state of affairs, and therefore they were categorical virtually as well as formally. Adding 'only' to a proposition of the form 'A is B' no more decategorises it than does adding 'every'.

An exponible proposition, then, must be understood as a categorical proposition which is equivalent to a hypothetical proposition which displays more perspicuously the truth conditions of the exponible. In the *De Exponibilibus* Lokert discusses eleven exponible terms. They are, in order of discussion, 'only', 'except', 'insofar as' (or, 'in as much as'), 'immediately', 'begins', 'ceases', 'is X-er than' (i.e. the comparative form of the adjective), 'is the X-est' (i.e. the superlative form of the adjective), 'differs', 'whole' and 'infinite'. This list, as has been mentioned, does not include all the terms that were ever treated by medieval logicians as exponible. In other sources

'always', 'eternally' and 'just as' are classified as exponible terms. But
in the present chapter we shall confine ourselves to a brief consideration of salient points in the *De Exponibilibus*. In that substantial
work, running to seventy-two double columned pages, Lokert has a
great deal of interest to say that we shall not be able to refer to at all.
Our order of exposition of Lokert's exponibles will follow his own
order, though in view of the brevity with which the final three exponible terms are dealt with in the *De Exponibilibus* we shall not
consider those here. Nearly half of the treatise (fols. 1r–16v) is devoted to an exposition of 'only'. That I give more space to 'only' than
to the other exponibles merely reflects Lokert's own apportionment.

## II

Lokert distinguishes two main kinds of exclusive proposition, namely, exclusives of otherness and exclusives of plurality. The latter kind,
which characteristically contain a number term within the scope of the
'only', as in 'Only four men are running', will be considered later. For
the present we shall deal with exclusives of otherness, which are, for
Lokert, in effect those exclusives which are not exclusives of plurality.

First he introduces some terminology (see appendix, no.37). He
writes:

> 'Commonly, four orders or genera of exclusives are posited. In
> the first are propositions in which neither the exclusive sign nor
> the principal copula is negated.[7] In the second are propositions in
> which the exclusive sign is affirmed and the principal copula is
> denied. Propositions of the third order are the contradictories of
> propositions of the first, and propositions of the fourth order are
> the contradictories of propositions of the second' [*De Ex.* 1r[1]].

The four orders are represented by the following schemata:

(1) Only A is B
(2) Only A is not B
(3) Not only A is B (i.e. the negation of (1))
(4) Not only A is not B (i.e. the negation of (2))

Two more technical terms should here be introduced. First the
'prejacent' of an exclusive proposition is that proposition with the
'only' deleted (and in general the prejacent of an exponible proposition is that proposition with the exponible term deleted). Secondly,
an 'exponent' is a categorical proposition which forms part of the
hypothetical proposition which is the exposition of the exponible. We
can now quote in full Lokert's preliminary exposition of the four
orders of exclusive. He presents two propositions:

*First proposition:* exclusives of otherness of the first and second orders should be expounded conjunctively with two exponents, where the first exponent will be the prejacent, and the second will be the opposite of the prejacent in quantity and quality with the contradictory of the subject if the opposite of the whole subject is excluded, and if the opposite of just a part of the extreme is excluded then just that part, from whose opposite the exclusion is made, is negated . . . This proposition is clarified: this exclusive 'Only a man is an animal' is expounded as 'A man is an animal & No non-man is an animal'. And 'Only a man is not an animal' is expounded as 'A man is not an animal & Every non-man is an animal'.[8] Propositions in which the opposite of just a part of an extreme is excluded are expounded correspondingly.

*Second proposition:* exclusives of the third and fourth order are expounded with two disjoined exponents in a contradictory way to the exclusives of the first and second orders which contradict them. 'Not only a man is an animal' is expounded as 'No man is an animal ∨ A non-man is an animal'. 'Not only a man is not an animal' is expounded as 'It is not the case that a man is not an animal ∨ A non-man is not an animal'. [$1r^{1-2}$]

The examples given above do not contain quantifier expressions, but at numerous points Lokert discusses exclusives which consist of 'only' operating on universal propositions. He does not unfortunately give a systematic exposition of such exclusives, but his position is clear from his practice. The first-order universal affirmative exclusive 'Only every man is an animal' is expounded as 'Every man is an animal & No non-man is an animal'. The second-order universal affirmative exclusive 'Only every man is not an animal' is expounded as 'No man is an animal & Every non-man is an animal'. The exposition of the third-order proposition 'It is not the case that only every man is an animal' is the negation of the exposition of the first-order proposition, and the exposition of the fourth order 'It is not the case that only every man is not an animal' is the negation of the exposition of the second-order exclusive.

Lokert describes a square of opposition of exclusive propositions, deriving the square from the consideration that: 'An affirmative exclusive sign is universal and a negated exclusive sign is particular' [*De Ex.* $1r^2$]. That is, he treats 'Only A is B' as equivalent to 'every B is A', and 'Not only A is B' as equivalent to 'Some B is not A'. This permits the schemata of the four orders of exclusive to be displayed as shown at the top of the next page. That is to say, of (1) and (2) both can be false and not both can be true; of (4) and (3) both can be true and not both can be false; of (1) and (3) one must be true and one false; of (2)

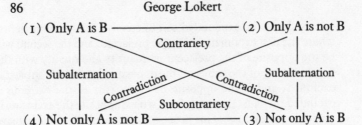

and (4) one must be true and one false; of (1) and (4) (4) must be true
if (1) is; and finally, of (2) and (3) (3) must be true if (2) is.

A related, but different justification to that given by Lokert can be
provided for the arrangement of the above square of opposition. The
exposition of the first-order exclusive is a conjunction of exponents of
which the first is a particular affirmative proposition and the second a
universal negative; the exposition of a second-order exclusive consists
of a conjunction whose first conjunct is a particular negative and
whose second is a universal affirmative; the exposition of the third-
order exclusive is a disjunction whose first disjunct is a universal
negative and whose second disjunct is a particular affirmative; and
finally the exposition of the fourth-order exclusive consists of a disjunction whose first disjunct is a universal affirmative (since 'It is not
the case that a man is not an animal' is identified with 'Every man is an
animal'), and whose second disjunct is a particular negative. Following tradition and symbolising the universal affirmative proposition by
the letter 'A', the particular affirmative by 'I', the universal negative
by 'E' and the particular negative by 'O', the foregoing square of
opposition can be rewritten as:

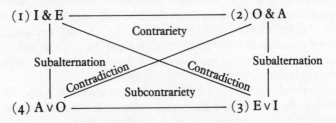

It is clear that (1) and (3) are contradictories, for if (1) is true then both
conjuncts are true in which case both disjuncts in (3) are false, since
the 'I' of (1) contradicts the 'E' of (3), and the 'E' of (1) contradicts the
'I' of (3); and likewise, if (3) is true then one of its disjuncts must be
true, in which case one of the conjuncts in (1) is false, from which it
would follow that (1) would be false. Likewise, (1) and (2) are con-

traries, for if (1) is true then both conjuncts are true, but the second conjunct of (1) contradicts the second conjunct of (2), and hence if (1) is true (2) is false; and similarly if (2) is true then (1) is false. But furthermore, both might be false, for the second conjunct in each case might be false, as would be the case if some but not all A's were B. Thus the square of opposition for exclusives can be justified in terms of the standard logical relations between the non-exponible quantified propositions that form the exponents of the four kinds of exclusive.

Of course, Lokert secures the same effect by taking as his starting point the equivalence of 'Only A is B' and 'Every B is A'. It should be noted that he nowhere offers a proof of this equivalence, though it was provable within the resources of medieval logic. For example, the following proof was constructed by Domingo de Soto,[9] pupil of Lokert's great Spanish contemporary Francisco de Vitoria (who gained his doctorate in theology at Paris just two years after Lokert):

(1) Only an animal is a man

   (1) is assumed. From it 'Every man is an animal' will be proved.

(2) An animal is a man & No non-animal is a man

   (2) is the exposition of (1)

(3) A man is an animal & No man is a non-animal

   The first conjunction of (3) follows by simple conversion from the first conjunct of (2), and the second conjunct of (3) follows by simple conversion from the second conjunct of (2)

(4) No man is a non-animal & Some man is [i.e. exists]

   The first conjunct of (4) is a repetition of the second conjunct of (3), and the second conjunct of (4) follows from the first conjunct (3) (for if a man is an animal then there exists a man who is animal)

(5) Every man is an animal

   (5) follows from (4). It cannot follow from just the first conjunct of (4) since that conjunct does not imply that any man exists whereas (5) does (in medieval logic). Hence the second conjunct is required if (5) is to be proved.

   Hence (5) is a formally valid inference from (1). QED

(6) Some man is an animal & No man is a non-animal

   The first conjunct of (6) follows by subalternation ('all' implies 'some') from (5). And the second conjunct of (6) follows from (5) 'from affirmation to negation with varied predicate' – i.e. 'Every A is B' implies 'No A is a non-B'. (We saw in the move from (4) to (5) that the reverse implication does not hold unless the existence of some A is already granted)

(7) Some animal is a man & No non-animal is a man

The first conjunct of (7) is a simple conversion of the first conjunct of (6), and the second conjunct of (7) is a simple conversion of the second conjunct of (6)

(8) Only an animal is a man

(8) is the exponible of which (7) is the conjunction of exponents. Hence (8) (which = (1)) follows by a formally valid argument from (5). QED

Lokert presents his square of opposition as a first corollary of his account of the exposition of the four orders of exclusive proposition. This is followed by a tersely worded second corollary: 'An exclusive proposition, in which an undistributed common term is placed before an affirmed exclusive sign, should be resolved first on the side of the common term before it is expounded conjunctively on account of the affirmed sign. But if the common term [is distributed and] is placed in front of the affirmed exclusive sign then the proposition can be expounded conjunctively in the usual way or after the resolution of the distributed term' [De Ex. IV[1]]. It is worth considering these two rules in some detail.

(1) Of some man only his ass runs

is an exclusive proposition in which an undistributed common term ('man') is placed before an affirmed exclusive sign. According to the first of the two rules just quoted it is necessary to descend under 'man' before expounding the exponible. Since 'man' has determinate supposition descent must be made under it to a disjunction of singulars. We shall assume, for the sake of keeping the formulae brief, that there are just two men. The descent from (1) takes us, therefore, to:

(2) Of man[1] only his ass runs v Of man[2] only his ass runs.

The exclusives can now be expounded:

(3) (Of man[1] his ass runs & Of man[1] every non-ass of his
does not run) v
(Of man[2] his ass runs & Of man[2] every non-ass of his
does not run).

The second of the foregoing two rules asserts that if a common term placed before an affirmed exclusive sign is distributed, as in

(4) Of every man only his ass runs,

the logical outcome is the same whether a descent to singulars is made under 'man' before the exclusive sign is expounded or after it is expounded. Thus, if the exclusive is expounded first, the result is:

(5) Of every man his ass runs & Of every man every non-ass of

his does not run.

Descent can now be made under the distributed term 'man' to a conjunction of singulars:

(6) (Of man$^1$ his ass runs & Of man$^2$ his ass runs) & (Of man$^1$ every non-ass of his does not run & Of man$^2$ every non-ass of his does not run).

Had descent been made under 'man' prior to the exposition of the exclusive the sequence of formulae would have been as follows:

(7) Of man$^1$ only his ass runs & Of man$^2$ only his ass runs.

(8) (Of man$^1$ his ass runs & Of man$^1$ every non-ass of his does not run) & (Of man$^2$ his ass runs & Of man$^2$ every non-ass of his does not run).

The four conjuncts which compose (6), where the exclusive is expounded first, are identical to the four conjuncts which compose (8), where descent was made first under the distributed term. But the order in which a set of conjuncts are arranged in a conjunction does not affect the truth value of the conjunction. Hence (6) and (8) are equivalent formulae, from which it follows that, as Lokert said in his second rule, the logical outcome is the same whether, in expounding a proposition in which a distributed term precedes an affirmed exclusive sign, we first descend under the distributed term or first expound the exclusive sign.

The explanation given by Lokert for the difference in logical behaviour of (1) and (4) above is that if (1) were expounded before descent were made under 'man' a crucial logical point would be lost, for an immediate exposition of (1) yields:

(9) Of some man his ass runs & Of some man every non-ass of his does not run.

What (1) makes clear and what is at the same time not expressed in (9) is that it is the *same* man whose ass runs and whose non-asses do not run. It is for this reason that Lokert asserts that (1) is not expoundable in the strict way 'unless in the second exponent the relative of identity is added to the determinator [i.e. to 'of a man']' [*De Ex.* iv$^1$]. Thus in the resolution of (1) if we wished to expound the exclusive before descending under 'man' it would be necessary to depart from the standard procedure for constructing exponents and write instead:

(10) Of some man his ass runs & Of the same man every non-ass of his does not run.

The same problem does not arise in the case of the analysis of (4) since there is no need for the same man to be picked out again for every man is being referred to.

Immediately following the pair of rules just considered, Lokert

adds a second pair to deal with the kind of case where the exponible
following a common term is negated. He writes: 'An exclusive which
can be expounded disjunctively [i.e. third and fourth order exclu-
sives], in which a distributed term precedes the exclusive sign, is not
immediately expounded, but first the distributed term should be resolved into singulars, unless the relative of identity be added to that
term in the second exponent. But if an undistributed common term
precedes the exclusive where the exponible term is expounded disjunctively, the proposition can be expounded strictly or by resolution
of the common term' [*De Ex.* iv$^1$]. In other words the first two rules
are reversed to deal with the case where the exponible term is immediately preceded by a negation sign. Hence, in resolving 'Of every man
not only his ass runs' it is necessary to descend conjunctively under
the distributed term 'man' before expounding the exclusive, whereas
in resolving 'Of some man not only his ass runs' it is immaterial
whether descent is first made under 'man' or whether the exponible is
first resolved.

Lokert turns next to a series of conversion rules (see appendix,
no.38), rules, that is to say, concerning the way to rewrite a subject
predicate proposition so that its subject and predicate terms are in
reverse order while the truth of the proposition is preserved. We have
already observed that Lokert accepted that 'Only A is B' and 'Every B
is A' are mutually convertible (though he added that this conversion
worked only where the 'only' operated on the entire subject term, for
'Of some man only his ass runs' is not convertible with 'Every runner
is some man's ass' but rather with 'Of some man every runner is an
ass'). Lokert also held that if two sentences are equivalent then
their negations are equivalent. From this principle together with the
equivalence of 'Only A is B' and 'Every B is A' we can derive the
equivalence of 'Not only A is B' and 'Not every B is A'. But 'Not every
B is A' is itself equivalent to 'Some B is not A'. Hence it comes as no
surprise to find Lokert accepting as a further conversion principle
the following: 'Not only A is B' is convertible with 'Some B is not A'
[*De Ex.* iv$^2$].

Conversions of such quantified exclusives as 'Only every A is B'
were also recognised. Granted the equivalence of (1) 'Only A is B' with
(2) 'Every B is A', it might be expected to follow that 'Only every A is
B' is false unless there exists not more than one A and one B. For (3)
'Only every A is B', on the model of the relation between (1) and (2),
would be equivalent to (4) 'Every B is every A'. Given that the subject
term in (4) supposits distributively, a descent to a conjunction of
singulars is permissible under 'B'. Hence if (4) is true then B$^1$ is every

A & B$^2$ is every A & . . . and so on for every B. But one individual thing cannot be every A unless there is only one A. And if there is only one A, then it cannot be the case that many B's can separately be that A. Hence there is only one B. In view of the logical relation between (1) and (2) we should therefore expect that 'Only every A is every B' would be true only if there is not more than one A and one B. But in fact (3) does not stand to (4) as (1) stands to (2). That Lokert could not allow the equivalence of (3) and (4) is clear from the exposition of (3), namely, 'Every A is B & No non-A is B', for that exposition carries no implication that there is only one A or one B. But he does not tell us how he thinks 'Only every A is B' should be converted.

Lokert does however present a number of rules of conversion where both the converted proposition and its convertent are exclusives. For example, he asserts: 'An exclusive of the first order with constancy of the contradiction of the subject implies an exclusive of the same order with the terms transposed and with the affirmative terms changed into negative ones' [1v$^2$–2r$^1$]. This rule can be represented schematically as:

If only A is B & there is a non-A then only non-B is non-A.

Lokert hints at a proof of this rule, but the steps can readily be supplied. He accepts the following rule of quantification:

(1) If every B is A & there is a non-A then every non-A is non-B.

(The second conjunct in the antecedent of (1) is required because the consequent implies – in medieval logic – that non-A's exist.) He also accepts, as we know:

(2) 'Every B is A' is equivalent to 'Only A is B'.

By replacing the universal affirmative propositions in (1) by their exclusive equivalents as expressed in (2), we can derive:

(3) If only A is B & there is a non-A then only non-B is non-A.

QED

The rule just given concerns exclusives of the first order. A rule of conversion for second-order exclusives is also given. Lokert writes: 'As regards a second-order exclusive it is said that, granted the constancy of the extremes, such an exclusive can be converted, though not simply, into an exclusive of the same order, with the terms transposed' [*De Ex.* 2r$^1$]. What Lokert has in mind here is that from 'Only A is not B & There exists an A' there follows 'Only B is not A', and from 'Only B is not A & There exists a B' there follows 'Only A is not B'. Lokert does not offer a proof of this rule, but one is provided by his Scottish colleague at Paris, Robert Caubraith. We shall give only the first half of the proof since the second half is almost identical (see appendix, no.39).

(1) Only an animal is not a man & There exists an animal
  (1) is the basic assumption from which 'Only a man is not an animal' is to be proved.

(2) An animal is not a man & There exists an animal
  Follows from (1) since the first conjunct of (2) is the first exponent of the exclusive in (1)

(3) An animal is a non-man
  Follows from (2) by contraposition, i.e. If A is not B and A exists then A is non-B.

(4) A non-man is an animal
  Follows from (3) by simple conversion

(5) Every non-animal is a man
  Follows from (1) since (5) is the second exponent of the exclusive in (1)

(6) There exists a non-man
  Follows from (4) (from the *tertium adiacens* 'is' in a particular affirmative proposition to the *secundum adiacens* 'is' is a valid inference).

(7) Every non-man is an animal
  Follows from (5) and (6) by contraposition and conversion ((6) is required since in medieval logic a universal affirmative is not true unless its subject term succeeds in referring).

(8) A non-animal is a man
  Follows from (5) by subalternation ('All' implies 'some').

(9) A man is a non-animal
  Follows from (8) by simple conversion.

(10) A man is not an animal
  Follows from (9) by contraposition.

(11) Only a man is not an animal
  Follows from (10) and (7) which are the exponents of (11).

The formal inference of (11) from (1) is the first half of Lokert's thesis. The second half, beginning with (11), plus 'There exists a man' (which is derived from (9)), goes through in a similar way.

Following his lengthy discussion of exclusives of otherness Lokert gives a brief account of a different kind of exclusive, namely, an exclusive of plurality (see appendix, no.40). The distinctive feature of exponible propositions containing an exclusive term of plurality is that they contain an 'only' followed by a term standing for a number, as in 'Only two men are running' [17r¹]. Lokert asserts that: 'Like exclusives of otherness, exclusives of plurality have four orders' [16v²].

Once again, the order to which a given exclusive of plurality must be assigned depends upon whether, and if so then how, it is negated. The two kinds of exclusive are also the same in that they each have two exponents, which are conjoined in the first two orders, and disjoined in the second two. They are thirdly the same in that in each case the first exponent is the prejacent of the exclusive proposition. But the second exponent is, in the two cases, crucially different: 'In place of the infinitising negation [i.e. the 'not' operating on a name] which occurs in the second exponent of an exclusive of otherness, in the second exponent of an exclusive of plurality there is placed a "more than"' [*De Ex.* 16v²]. Thus, for example, where the exponible asserts that only two men are running the second exponent asserts that not more than two are running.

But not more than two what? Lokert points out that the foregoing exponible is ambiguous: 'If the "only" denotes the exclusion of what the term to which the "only" is added stands for, then the second exponent of the exponible is "Not more men than two men are running"; but if all the entities other than the two men are excluded then the second exponent will be "Not more entities than two men are running"' [*De Ex.* 17r¹]. These two versions of the second exponent are clearly quite distinct logically, for the second version implies the first but the first does not imply the second. Put otherwise, the second version, like the exclusive of otherness 'Only men are running', contradicts the claim that anything of a species other than man is running, whereas the first version of the second exponent is consistent with that claim. Nevertheless, in whatever way we choose to resolve the ambiguity mentioned by Lokert, it is at least reasonably plain how the first and third orders of exclusive of plurality should be expounded. Staying with his examples, the first and third orders are expounded as follows:

(1) Only two men are running = Two men are running & Not more than two men are running.

(3) Not (only two men are running) = Not (two men are running) ∨ More than two men are running.

The exposition of (3) states that either fewer than, or more than two men are running. All it excludes is that just two are running.

However, Lokert gives no clear guidance on the question of how the second and fourth orders of exclusive of plurality should be expounded. For example, if Lokert's rule for constructing the second exponent is followed, then the second exponent of the second-order exclusive of plurality 'Only two men are not running' must be 'All men more than two are running', but it is not clear that that sentence means 'Not more than two men are not running', though the latter sentence is the one we should naturally aim for if we are to capture the sense of the exponible of the second order that we are trying to expound. However, if we allowed that 'All men more than two are running' has the same sense as 'Not more than two men are not running', we can construct the exposition of the second and fourth orders of exclusive of plurality as follows:

(2) Only two men are not running = Two men are not running & Not more than two men are not running.

(4) Not only two men are not running = Not (two men are not running) ∨ More than two men are not running.

The exposition of (4) states that the number of men not running is either smaller or greater than two.

Following his discussion of the exposition of exclusives of plurality, Lokert turns to an account of the convertibility of such propositions, though he concerns himself solely with exclusives of the first order. In the course of his account he invokes a kind of supposition with which we have not yet met. That a further kind is at least describable can be shown, even though it would still remain to be established that it was useful. Determinate supposition involves descent to a disjunction of singular propositions, distributive supposition involves descent to a conjunction of singular propositions, and merely confused supposition involves descent to a disjunction of singular terms. A further kind of supposition can be invoked, its distinguishing feature being that it permits descent to a conjunction of singular terms. Such a kind of supposition, which is called 'merely confused conjunctive [or 'copulative'] supposition', is rarely referred to in medieval logic, but one place where it is used is in the field of exclusives of plurality. Lokert writes:

> An exclusive of plurality of the first order converts with an affirmative proposition with the extremes transposed where the subject term is taken with a collective sign. Just as the collective sign makes the term to which it is immediately added stand merely confusedly conjunctively, and has no power as regards the term mediately following the sign, so also the sign of an exclusive of plurality has no power as regards the immediately following term, but it makes the mediately following term stand merely confusedly conjunctively. For example, 'Only twelve are the apostles of God' converts with 'All the apostles of God are twelve', taking the 'all' collectively. [De Ex. 17r¹]

Thus 'Only twelve are the apostles of God' is converted by transposing the subject and predicate terms and replacing the 'only' which is an exclusive sign of plurality by 'all' taken collectively. In both the convertent proposition and its converse 'the apostles of God' is taken to have merely confused conjunctive supposition. Hence, under that phrase, which is governed immediately by 'all', from

(1) All the apostles of God are twelve

it is possible to descend to a conjunction of singular terms. That is, (1) yields:

(2) $A^1$ & $A^2$ & ... & $A^{12}$ are twelve

though it is not possible to descend to any one of the conjuncts. And likewise in

(3) Only twelve are the apostles of God

under the term governed mediately by 'only', namely, 'the apostles of God', it is possible to descend to a conjunction of singular terms. Thus, (3) yields:

(4) Only twelve are $A^1$ & $A^2$ & ... & $A^{12}$.

It is because it is not possible to descend to any one of the conjuncts though it is possible to descend to the entire collection of conjuncts that the 'all' in (1) is said to be taken collectively as opposed to distributively. It should be noted that the syllogism: 'All Bs are C & All As are B, therefore all As are C' is valid only if the three occurrences of 'all' are taken distributively. Hence 'All the apostles of God are twelve, and all the sons of Zebedee are apostles of God, therefore all the sons of Zebedee are twelve' is invalid since it is based on an equivocal use of 'all'.

It may be noted, for the sake of completeness, that it is not only in cases where a number is explicitly referred to that merely confused conjunctive supposition occurs. It occurs, for example, in 'These are all the disciples', for though that proposition does not permit descent to a conjunction of singular propositions, it does permit descent to a conjunction of singular terms. Likewise the 'all' in 'All men are numerous' (assuming we are allowed to construct that proposition) must be understood collectively, for descent can be made under 'men' to a conjunction of singular terms, whereas descent to a conjunction of singular propositions under 'men' would result in a set of propositions which did not make sense.

### III

The second kind of exponible proposition discussed by Lokert is the exceptive (see Appendix no.41). An exceptive proposition contains the word 'except' (usually the Latin *preter*)[10] though Lokert does not treat all propositions containing 'except' as exponibles. Thus, for

example, he refers to 'additive' and 'subtractive' exceptings, which
are instanced in '10 are 2 except for 8' (an additive exceptive) and '10
except for 5 are 5' (a subtractive exceptive),[11] but which are not
treated as exceptive exponibles since there is a rule that: 'to be an
exceptive it is required that the term from which the exception is made
should be taken with a universal sign, whether it be affirmative or
negative' [De Ex. 21r²]. Clearly neither the additive nor the subtractive exceptive just quoted follows this rule.

Lokert gives a full description of the kind of proposition he has in
mind. First, it must satisfy the rule just stated. Secondly, it must also
contain the following four elements: 'First, the exceptive sign;
secondly, the term excepted, which immediately follows the exceptive
sign;[12] thirdly, the term from which the exception is made, which is
the term (the categorematic term) immediately preceding the exceptive phrase; and fourthly, the principal predicate, or the other extreme
from that in which the exceptive sign is placed' [De Ex. 21v¹⁻²]. Thus,
'Every man except Socrates is running' (Lokert's standard example)[13]
is an exceptive exponible. It has the four elements just referred to, and
also, in accordance with the foregoing rule, the term from which the
exception is made (the 'man') is taken with the sign of universality.
'Some man except Socrates is running' would not count as an exceptive exponible, since, though it has the four elements it does not accord
with the rule concerning universality.

A second rule laid down by Lokert is the following: 'The term
excepted [i.e. the term immediately following the exceptive sign]
should not be either superior to, or disparate in relation to, the term
from which the exception is made' [De Ex. 21v²]. 'A is superior to
B' means 'Every B is A but not every A is B'. Hence, given the first
half of this rule, 'All men except animals are rational' cannot be
classified as an exceptive exponible since the excepted term 'animals'
is superior to the term from which the exception is made ('men').
Furthermore, given the second half of the rule, 'Every man except a
stone is rational' also cannot be classified as an exceptive exponible,
for 'man' and 'stone' are disparate terms, since two common terms are
not disparate only if it is possible for one to be truly predicated of the
other.

Lokert is obviously correct in finding something wrong with such a
proposition as 'Every man except a stone is rational'. But his concern
to rule it out of court as a non-exceptive sits uneasily with the fact,
which will shortly become plain, that that proposition and all others
which are acceptable except for falling foul of the disparity rule, are
false since, (assuming we expound them) of their three exponents

one, namely, the second, is false. But it is not clear why a proposition which otherwise looks like an exceptive should not be called one merely because it is necessarily a false proposition. The more obvious line to take is to say that an exceptive which infringes the disparity rule is an exceptive, and that that is a harmless fact to accommodate since such an exceptive cannot occur as a premiss in an argument in which truth is inferred from truth. But Lokert does not, unfortunately, give us guidance on how he would deal with such a line of criticism.

Prior to describing the exponents of exceptives, Lokert describes what he refers to as four orders of exceptive, though at first sight he appears to be describing eight. He writes: 'There are four orders of exceptive proposition, as there are of exclusives. In the first order are such propositions as [1a] "Every man except Socrates is running", [1b] "Not every man not except Socrates is running", and the contradictories of these are in the third order. In the second order are such propositions as [2a] "Every man except Socrates is not running", [2b] "Not every man not except Socrates is not running", and in the fourth order are the contradictories of these' [*De Ex.* 21r¹]. The second proposition in each of these pairs hardly looks like an exceptive at all, since 'Not every man not except Socrates is running' seems to be merely a way of saying that not every man is running, and 'Not every man not except Socrates is not running' seems to be merely a way of saying that not every man is not running. However, Lokert did treat such propositions as exceptives and he placed them in the order that he did because of their relation to the other kind of exceptive in each order. In particular, apart from a different quantifier in one of the exponents each of the propositions which occurs as second in the pairs given by Lokert has the same exponents as has the proposition which is given as the first in the pair.

We can now list the eight sorts of exceptive that Lokert describes, and give their expositions. He himself states in full the expositions of only four of the kinds of exceptive (namely, 1a, 2a, 3a and 4a) but the remaining four are readily constructible.¹⁴ We shall consider first the case where both the term from which the exception is made and also the excepted term is a common noun.

(1a) Every A except B is C = Every A which is non-B is C & Every B is A & No B is C.

(1b) It is not the case that every A not except B is C = Some A which is non-B is C & Every B is A & No B is C.

(2a) Every A except B is not C = No A which is non-B is C & Every B is A & Every B is C.

(2b) It is not the case that every A not except B is not C = Some

A which is non-B is not C & Every B is A & Every B is C.

(3a) It is not the case that every A except B is C = Some A which is non-B is not C ∨ Some B is not A ∨ Some B is C.

(3b) Every A not except B is C = No A which is non-B is C ∨ Some B is not A ∨ Some B is C.

(4a) It is not the case that every A except B is not C = Some A which is non-B is C ∨ Some B is not A ∨ Some B is not C.

(4b) Every A not except B is not C = Every A which is non-B is C ∨ Some B is not A ∨ Some B is not C.

It is clear from these expositions why Lokert wished to place 'Every man except Socrates runs' and 'It is not the case that not every man not except Socrates runs' together in the first order, for the only difference between their expositions is that the first exponent of the first of those propositions has a universal quantifier whereas the first exponent of the second of them has a particular quantifier. The same sort of difference exists between (2a) and (2b). A similar change in quantifier is the only thing which distinguishes the expositions of (3a) and (3b), and (4a) and (4b).

The kinds of exposition just given do not work if the excepted term is a proper name. Thus, to take Lokert's example, 'Every man except Socrates is running' cannot take as its second and third exponents 'Every Socrates is a man & No Socrates is running'. Taking 'A' and 'C' as common terms, as before, and 'B' as a proper name rather than as a common term, (1a) and (2a) are expounded, in accordance with Lokert's analysis [21r²] as follows:

(1a) Every A except B is C = Every A which is non-B is C & B is A & B is not C.

(2a) Every A except B is not C = No A which is non-B is C & B is A & B is C.

The exponents of (3a) and (4a) are the negated and disjoined exponents of, respectively, (1a) and (2a).

It is clear from the construction of the four orders of exceptives that it is possible to construct a square of opposition with an exceptive proposition at each corner. For (2a) and (3a) are, respectively, a contrary and a contradictory of (1a), while (4a) is the contradictory of (2a). (4a) and (3a), which are subcontraries, are, respectively, subalternates of (1a) and (2a). Since each of the exponibles from (1a) to (4a) has three exponents, which are universal or particular, affirmative or negative, and conjoined or disjoined, the square of opposition for those four exceptives can be set out as shown (top of next page).

The standard relations between the corners in the square of opposition can be seen to hold in this schema. For example, given the three

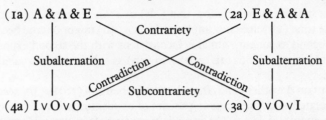

exponents of (1a), which are, in order, an A, an A and an E proposition, at least one of the disjuncts in (4a) must be true, for since the first exponent of (1a) is an A proposition the first exponent of (4a), which is the corresponding I proposition, is implied by that A proposition, and hence the first disjunct is true if (1a) is true. By the same line of reasoning the third disjunct of (4a) is true if (1a) is true, since a universal negative proposition implies the corresponding particular negative. And to consider one more relation represented in the foregoing square: the first, second and third conjuncts of (1a) are respectively the contradictories of the first, second and third disjuncts of (3a). Hence if all three conjuncts of (1a) are true it follows that none of the disjuncts of (3a) is true, and if any of the disjuncts of (3a) is true (from which, of course, it would follow that (3a) itself is true) then one of the conjuncts of (1a), and hence the conjunction as a whole, would be false. And also one or other of (1a) and (3a) must be true since each exponent in (1a) is the contradictory, and not a contrary, of the corresponding exponent in (3a). Thus (1a) and (3a) must be contradictories.

It would seem at first sight that a similar square of opposition can be set up for the exceptives (1b) to (4b) as follows:

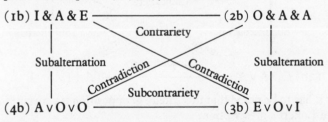

For example, (1b) and (2b) are contraries, for though their first exponents are mutually consistent, and their second exponents are the same, their third exponents are contraries, and hence both might be false, in which case both conjunctions (1b) and (2b) might be false. Also (4b) is the subalternate of (1b), since if (1b) is true then its third conjunct is true, in which case the third disjunct of (4b) is also true, from which it would follow that (4b) as a whole is true; and at the same time (4b) does not imply (1b) since (4b) might be true because its second exponent, which is inconsistent with the second exponent of (1b) is true. Thus (1b) relates to (4b) as subalternant to subalternate.

But on the other hand, though the exponents of (1b) to (4b) seem to be related as in the foregoing square of opposition, their corresponding exponibles do not. On an obvious reading of the exponible propositions themselves (1b) and (3b) are indeed contradictories, as are (2b) and (4b). But (3b) and (4b) appear to be contraries, and (1b) and (2b) to be subcontraries. Thus it might seem that our square of opposition for exponibles with negated exceptive signs is upside down.

If the square under discussion were inverted this would have the further advantage of bringing out the fact that the exponible of (4b) is the subalternant of the exponible of (1b), and that the exponible of (3b) is the subalternant of the exponible of (2b). However, it is clear that the exposition of (1b) implies the exposition of (4b), and that the exposition of (2b) implies the exposition of (3b), even though the sense of the exponibles would suggest that the implication relations are in the opposite direction. This conflict between the evident logical relations between the exponibles and the relations Lokert subscribes to between their expositions can perhaps be resolved satisfactorily only by revising the account of those expositions. The simplest change would involve making the expositions of (1b) and (2b) disjunctive, and making the expositions of (3b) and (4b) conjunctive, thus yielding the following square of opposition:

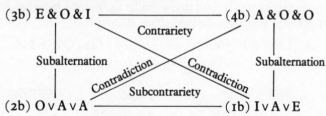

(3b) E & O & I ——— (4b) A & O & O

Contrariety

Subalternation          Subalternation

Contradiction          Contradiction

Subcontrariety

(2b) O ∨ A ∨ A ——— (1b) I ∨ A ∨ E

But it has to be noted that this square of opposition is very far indeed from Lokert's prescription.

Following his account of the exposition of exceptives, Lokert presents certain rules. The first one is this:

A universal proposition which is partly true and partly false can be made true by the excepting of those things by which the proposition is falsified. For example, 'Every animal is a man' is partly true and partly false since under the distributed subject some singulars are true and some are false. For that reason the proposition 'Every animal is a man' is made true by excepting as follows: 'Every animal except a beast is a man'. To the distributed term 'animal' in 'Every animal is a man' is added the exceptive sign and the excepted term which is taken for those things by which 'Every animal is a man' is falsified. A true exceptive results from this procedure. [*De Ex.* 21v¹].

This rule is surely correct; if 'Every A is C' is false only because B's which are A are not C, then 'Every A except B is C' must be true.

Lokert continues:

From this rule a second one is derived as a corollary, namely, that two subcontrary propositions, that is, a conjunction composed of such propositions, implies an exceptive of the first order and, as in many cases, also an exceptive of the second order. An exceptive of the first order is derived by excepting [from the affirmative subcontrary] those things by which, it is denoted, the negative subcontrary is verified, and an exceptive of the second order is derived by excepting [from the negative subcontrary] those things by which, it is denoted, the affirmative subcontrary is verified . . . This is clarified. The following is a good consequence: 'Some animal is a man & Some animal is not a man. Therefore, every animal, except an animal which is a man, is not a man'. Likewise, from the same subcontraries this first order exceptive follows: 'Every animal, except an animal which is not a man, is a man'. And thus it should be said regarding the universal proposition: 'Every animal is a man', which is partly true and partly false, that by turning it into an exceptive it is made true in the following way: 'Every animal, except an animal which is not a man, is a man'. And this negative universal: 'Every animal is not a man', if it be partly true and partly false, can be made true by turning it into an exceptive in this way: 'Every animal, except an animal which is a man, is not a man'. [*De Ex.* 21v¹⁻²]

The implicational relations mentioned above, between exceptives and non-exceptive quantified propositions suggest possible lines of investigation on relations between different kinds of exponibilia. For example, (1a) 'Every A except B is C' implies its first exponent (2) 'Every A which is non-B is C'. But Lokert held, as we have seen, that a universal affirmative converts with an exclusive. Hence, (2) is equivalent to (3) 'Only C is A which is non-B'. Thus an exceptive implies an exclusive. Also (4) 'Every thing except A is not B' implies (5) 'Only A is B', which, given constancy, in turn implies (4). Lokert has little to say about these further matters, but granted the teaching on the relation between, on the one hand, universal propositions, and, on the other, exclusives and exceptives, it should not be ground for surprise that the latter two types of exponible stand in a complex network of formal relations.

## IV

The third kind of exponible proposition discussed by Lokert is the reduplicative (see appendix, no.44). This kind of exponible is distinguished by the presence in it of the term 'in so far as' (*inquantum*) or a synonym,[15] as in, to take Lokert's (and Major's) stock example, 'Socrates in so far as he is rational is risible [i.e. capable of laughter]'. But not every proposition containing 'in so far as' was classified as a reduplicative properly speaking. Lokert writes: '"In so far as" is sometimes taken specifically so that it impedes the appellation of reason which would be made in the absence of that sign, as in the proposition "Socrates knows Plato in so far as he [Plato] is a man"' [*De Ex.* 26v[1]]. The point being made here is that whereas 'Socrates knows Plato' would be taken to imply that Socrates knows that it is Plato, that is, to imply that he knows Plato *as* Plato, the addition of 'in so far as he is a man' impedes this understanding of the first half of the sentence, for the second half implies that it is as a man merely, and not as Plato, that Socrates knows Plato. Plato is thus known merely as a member of the species (he is known 'specifically').[16] When 'in so far as' occurs in the kind of context just mentioned it has no causal significance; there is no implication that Plato's being a man is a cause of Socrates' knowing him. But the reduplicative sign strictly understood does have such causal significance. 'Socrates in so far as he is rational is risible' is strictly reduplicative because it states (following an Aristotelian doctrine) that the ability to laugh (not just to make laughter noises like a jackass) is grounded in an ability to secure a rational grasp of a situation, and hence being rational is a cause of being risible.

Lokert lists certain elements which must be present in a reduplicative proposition: '(1) the reduplicative sign, (2) the reduplicated term, which immediately follows the reduplicative sign, (3) the term immediately preceding the reduplicative sign, which some people call the principal subject, and (4) the other extreme from that in which the reduplicative sign is placed' [*De Ex.* 25v[1]].

Just as with exclusives and exceptives, reduplicatives can be placed in four orders, where the order to which a reduplicative is assigned is determined by the way the proposition is negated. The orders are:

(1) Every A in so far as it is B is C.
(2) Every A in so far as it is B is not C.

(3) It is not the case that every A in so far as it is B is C.

(4) It is not the case that every A in so far as it is B is not C.

But unlike exclusives, which have two exponents, and exceptives, which have three, reduplicatives have four. Lokert describes the expositions as follows:

> The first exponent is the prejacent, which is the residue [from the exponible proposition] after the removal of the reduplicative sign and the reduplicated term. The second exponent, in propositions of the first and second order, should be affirmative, and negative in the third and fourth orders. The reduplicated term is predicated of the term preceding the reduplicative sign. The third exponent will be of the same quality as the exponible. In it the other extreme from that containing the reduplicative sign is predicated of the reduplicated term. And the fourth exponent will be an affirmative condition in propositions of the first and second order, and negative in the others. Its antecedent will likewise be an affirmative in which the reduplicated term will be predicated of its synonym or of a transcendental term, and the consequent will be of the same quality as the exponible in which the other extreme will be predicated of the reduplicated term or of a relative pronoun of identity referring to the reduplicated term in the antecedent . . . This is clarified. The proposition 'Every man in so far as he is rational is risible' is expounded as follows: '(1) Every man is risible & (2) Every man is rational & (3) Every rational thing is risible & (4) If a rational thing is rational it is risible'. And this proposition of the second order 'Every man in so far as he is rational is not an ass' is expounded as follows: '(1) Every man is not an ass & (2) Every man is rational & (3) Every rational thing is not an ass & (4) If a rational thing is rational it is not an ass'. And reduplicatives of the third and fourth orders should be expounded in the opposite way. [25v$^{1-2}$]

Several aspects of Lokert's exposition of reduplicatives are puzzling. For the sake of simplicity we shall focus on his exposition of first-order propositions. But the same puzzling features are to be found in the expositions of the other orders also. Of the four exponents taken separately the most unexpected is the fourth, for though it is not unreasonable to employ a conditional sentence to capture the fact that risibility is conditional upon rationality, the antecedent in Lokert's conditional seems to be a mere tautology, in which case surely the consequent alone need be asserted. The immediate reply to this criticism is that for Lokert, and for late medieval logicians in general, the sentence 'A rational thing is rational' is not a tautology, for in one circumstance it is false, namely, when there is no rational thing. For, as already noted, it was a standard doctrine that if a term in an affirmative sentence lacks supposition the sentence is false. But the question remains as to why Lokert adopted the particular curious formulation that he did adopt for the fourth exponent. The explanation lies in the fact that that formulation blocked a line of criticism that it was thought could be levelled at the more obvious formulation 'If something is rational it is risible'. Let us consider the false reduplicative 'Every man in so far as he is rational is white'. This reduplicative is false because rationality cannot be a cause of a man's whiteness. But if we suppose all men to be white then all four exponents would be true if the fourth exponent were 'If something is rational it is white'. Since 'something' can supposit for anything it can supposit for an ass. Hence the fourth exponent can be replaced by 'If an ass is rational it is white', which is a true conditional in virtue of having an impossible premiss.

On Lokert's account of the matter the fourth exponent should read 'If a rational thing is rational then it is white', and if this is not true the exponible is not true. Assuming there to be rational things the antecedent is true, but it is not true of a rational thing that if it is rational then it is white, for rationality is not a cause of whiteness, and hence the fourth exponent (as Lokert formulates it) of the false exponible 'Every man in so far as he is rational is white' is itself false.

An important point about terminist logic, which emerges from the explanation for Lokert's formulation of the fourth exponent, is the unsatisfactoriness of the quantifier plus bound variable notation of modern logic as a means of capturing what the terminists understood by 'something' (and also by 'everything'). For them 'Something is white' and 'Everything is white' have the form, respectively, 'Some A is B' and 'Every A is B'. That is, 'Something is risible' is true if the subject and predicate terms (respectively, 'thing' and 'risible') supposit for the same thing; and 'Everything is risible' is true if the predicate term supposits for everything for which the subject term supposits. Hence, for a medieval logician 'Something is rational' has the same logical form as 'Some man is rational', whereas in modern logic the two have very different forms, namely, 'For some x, x is rational' and 'For some x, x is a man and x is rational'.

It is, then, reasonably clear why Lokert should think that the fourth exponent was required, and was required with his formulation. But, as he was aware, there were other difficulties also. He sets up an argument against his own position: 'There is a superfluity of exponents of reduplicatives. This can be proved as follows: such a proposition [as 'Every man in so far as he is rational is risible'] could be expounded with the first two exponents and the last conditional, and thus it seems that the aforementioned [three] exponents are sufficient. Indeed of the first three exponents the first is syllogistically implied by the other two. Hence the exponible proposition is sufficiently expounded without the exponent which is implied by the other exponents' [25v²–26r¹].

In fact Lokert goes on to reject both of these criticisms. As regards the claim that the first exponent is syllogistically implied by the second and third he says merely that the fact that the claim is false 'is obvious on consideration' [26v¹]. But since the claim certainly looks true it is a pity that Lokert does not spell out the considerations that would lead us to recognise it as false.

Also his argument that the third exponent is not after all superfluous leaves questions unanswered. It might be argued that the third exponent follows from the second and the fourth. For if 'Every man is rational' (the second exponent of Lokert's stock reduplicative example) is true, then there are rational things, since, as we noted, an affirmative proposition was held to be false if either its subject term or predicate term failed to refer. And given both that there are rational things, and also that the fourth exponent (that if a rational thing is rational it is risible) is true, it would seem to follow that every rational thing is risible, from which it would follow that the third exponent is superfluous.[17] Lokert thinks that the exponent is, however, required, but he does not say what is wrong with the argument to the effect that it is superfluous. Instead he sets up an example of what he claims to be a false reduplicative whose only false exponent is the third. If the example is valid then clearly that argument for the redundancy of the third exponent is unsatisfactory. But it is not at all clear whether the example Lokert sets up is valid or not. He writes: 'Neither is the third exponent superfluous, as is obvious from this proposition: "Every god in so far as he is a being necessarily is a being", which is rendered false by the third exponent alone' [*De Ex.* 26v¹].

The chief problem with this reduplicative is to know how the modal term is to figure in the exponents. The problem arises from the ambiguity of the reduplicative itself. If it is taken to mean 'Every god in so far as he is a being is, necessarily, a being' then the proposition is true so long as a god exists, but the example does not work unless the reduplicative is false, for the whole point of the example is to show that the reduplicative is false by virtue of the falsity of the third exponent. The likeliest interpretation is 'Every god in so far as he is a being is a necessary being' which might be thought to be false on the ground that only one god (*the* God) is a necessary being, and other gods are not. On this interpretation the four exponents are (1) Every god is a necessary being, (2) Every god is a being, (3) Every being is a necessary being, and (4) If a being is a being it is a necessary being. It is clear that the third exponent in this list is false, as Lokert said it was, but the first also is false, and contradicts our interpretation of the reduplicative; and even the fourth exponent is false. So his example fails, at least on the interpretation we gave it, to make the point he had intended. On the other hand it is not at all obvious what other interpretation would save his argument.

Given the way that the second, third and fourth orders of reduplicative are constructed by negating first-order reduplicatives, it is clear that, as with the kinds of exponible already discussed, reduplicatives can be placed in a square of opposition. On the other hand, whereas exclusives and exceptives could be organised into squares of opposition in terms of their conjunctions or disjunctions of exponents, that is not quite so straightforward a procedure in the case of reduplicatives since there the fourth exponent is a conditional proposition and hence is not classifiable in the ordinary way as an A, I, E or O proposition. However it is possible here to invoke the convention that a negated conditional with a negated consequent is an A proposition (a conditional analogue of a universal affirmative), a conditional with no negation sign is an I proposition, a negated conditional is an E proposition, and a conditional with a negated consequent is an O proposition (this convention is not merely *ad hoc*; there is clearly a syntactic relation between (A) 'Every A is B' [ = Not(Some A is not B)] and 'It is not the case that if something is A it is not B'; between (I) 'Some A is B' and 'If something is A it is B'; between (E) 'No A is B' and 'It is not the case that if something is A it is B'; and between (O) 'Some A is not B' and 'If something is A it is not B'). Interpreting the conditional fourth exponents as analogues of categoricals in the way just described, the following square of opposition for reduplicatives can be constructed:

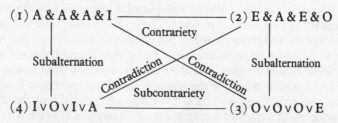

(1) A & A & A & I —————————— (2) E & A & E & O

Contrariety

Subalternation ⟍ Contradiction ⟋ Subalternation

Subcontrariety

(4) I ∨ O ∨ I ∨ A —————————— (3) O ∨ O ∨ O ∨ E

(1) and (2) are contraries in virtue of their first and third exponents.

They have the same second exponent, but since the first and third exponents of (1) are universal affirmatives and the first and third exponents of (2) are the corresponding universal negatives, the first and third exponents of (1) and (2) could all be false, in which case (1) and (2) could be false together. And since either (1) or (2) could be true, so long as the other is false, (1) and (2) are contraries. The disjunctions (3) and (4) share a second exponent, and hence both can be true, and since their first exponents are mutually subcontrary, as are their third exponents, they cannot both be false, and hence (3) and (4) are subcontraries.

Lokert has little to say about the convertibility of reduplicatives or about the kind of supposition that terms in reduplicatives have, but in one difficult passage both of these matters surface. He puts forward, for the sake of argument, the suggestion that (1) 'Every man in so far as he is rational is risible' is convertible with (2) 'Only a risible is a man in so far as he is rational'. But, he argues, since (2) is false (1) must also be false. His reason for rejecting (2) is stated cryptically as follows: 'its falsity is obvious by taking singulars under the subject of the first exponent. Pointing to anything whatever, this is false: "This risible thing is a man in so far as he is rational". That it is false is evident from its last exponent, namely, "If a rational thing is rational, a rational thing is this risible thing"' [*De Ex.* 26r¹]. Laid out more explicitly, the argument appears to run as follows:

(1) Every man in so far as he is rational is risible
  (1) is the basic assumption
(2) Only a risible thing is a man in so far as he is rational
  Follows from (1) by conversion
(3) A risible thing is a man in so far as he is rational
  (3) is first exponent of (2)
(4) This (risible) is a man in so far as he is rational v
  That (risible) is . . .
  Follows from (3) by descent under 'risible'
  which has determinate supposition
(5) If a rational thing is rational it is this risible
  (5) is fourth exponent of one of the disjuncts of (4).

But (5) is clearly false. Hence if it does follow validly from (1) then (1) also must be false. Lokert denies that (5) does follow validly from (1). He accepts the truth of (1) and also the falsity of (5) and argues that the invalid move is the very first one, that from the reduplicative to its alleged exclusive converse, for he denies that (2) is the converse of (1). Owing to the position of 'risible' in (1) and (2) those two propositions are of a quite different logical character from each other. This is due to

the different order in which they should be analysed out. The rule that
has to be applied here is that a term which follows the reduplicative
sign should not be resolved until the reduplicative has been expounded, whereas a term which precedes the reduplicative sign can be
resolved before the exposition of the reduplicative. In (1) the term
'risible' follows the reduplicative sign and hence it should not be
resolved until after the exposition of the reduplicative; but in (2)
'risible' precedes the reduplicative sign and should be resolved before
the proposition is expounded. The different order in which the propositions are to be analysed results in propositions which have different truth conditions – hence Lokert's insistence that the exclusive is
not the converse of the universal reduplicative.

## V

Following his discussion of reduplicatives, Lokert turns to a consideration of propositions whose main verb is a part of the verb 'to begin' or
'to cease', but he does not proceed directly to an exposition of such
propositions. He states his reason succinctly: 'The term "immediately" taken syncategorematically occurs in the exponents of propositions about "begin" and "cease" so that it denotes immediateness of
time or duration, as in "Immediately after this instant Socrates will
exist" . . . For that reason it should first be seen how propositions of
immediateness should be expounded' [De Ex. 26v²]. As with the
previous three types of exponible discussed, propositions of immediateness are first placed in four orders (see Appendix no.46) where the
order to which a proposition is assigned is determined by the way, if
any, that it is negated. As with exclusives, propositions of immediateness are expounded with two exponents: 'Propositions of the first and
second order are expounded conjunctively with two exponents, and
the contradictories of these, which are of the third and fourth order,
should be expounded disjunctively' [De Ex. 27r¹]. But Lokert does
not present his exposition at once, preferring instead to begin by
offering solutions which had been canvassed by others:

There are various opinions about how the exponents are to be
assigned, at any rate as regards the second exponent since every-
body agrees that the first exponent should be the prejacent. This
proposition 'Immediately after this instant Socrates will exist' is
commonly expounded in this way: 'After this instant Socrates
will exist & There will be no instant after this one but that between this instant and that one Socrates will exist'. And this
following proposition: 'Immediately after this instant Socrates
will not exist' is commonly expounded in this way: 'After this

instant Socrates will not exist & There will be no instant after this one but that between this instant and that one Socrates will not exist'. And one would expound the contradictories of these propositions in the opposite way. [27r$^1$]

Since Lokert regards the relation of 'immediately after' as being formally the same whether applied to temporal or spatial contexts,[18] he shows how the foregoing analysis would apply to the exposition of a sentence about points laid out in space: 'A corresponding account would be given of propositions in which the "immediately" refers to spatial immediateness, as in this proposition: "Immediately after point A is point B", if it were expounded as: "After point A is point B & There is no point after point A but that between that and point A is point B"' [27r$^1$].

However, Lokert rejects the foregoing account of the second exponent, but his arguments are not compelling, for all depend upon the acceptance of models which in fact appear to be incoherent. For example, he argues:

> Assuming that the present instant is reproduced after one year and Socrates will exist for one hour or a certain period of time around the middle of the year of which the aforesaid instant is both the start and the finish, and assuming also that Socrates will not exist at another time, then the following proposition would be false: 'Immediately after this instant Socrates will exist' as is agreed; and each exponent, taken in accordance with the foregoing interpretation, would be true. As regards the first exponent there is no doubt. And the second exponent is obvious from the fact that, at any designated instant whatever after the present instant, between that instant and this one Socrates will exist. [27r$^{1-2}$].

Lokert appears to be arguing as follows: let us suppose that the present instant, which we shall call 'A', is repeated in a year's time. Hence we can call the terminal point of the year 'A' also. For some period between the initial A and the terminal A Socrates exists and he does not exist at any other period. Let us call the period of his existence 'S'. This model represented geometrically would be as follows:

$$\overset{\bullet}{A} \quad \underline{\quad S \quad} \quad \overset{\bullet}{A}$$

On this model, the proposition 'Immediately after this instant Socrates will exist' is false. But both exponents are true. The prejacent of the exponible is true; it simply says that after instant A Socrates will exist, which is true, granted that it is the first A that is at issue. And the second exponent is also correct. It states that there is no instant after A but that between that instant and A Socrates will exist. Let us pick any instant, say B which is located between the first A and the period S, thus:

A      B      <u>S</u>      A

But B is such that between it and A, namely, the second A, Socrates exists. And if we pick a different instant, call it 'C', which is located between the period S and the second A, thus:

A      <u>S</u>      C      A

then C is such that between it and A, namely, the first A, Socrates exists. There are thus two models at least on which the original proposition of immediateness is false and both exponents are true. Lokert draws the conclusion that we should reject the account of the exposition of propositions of immediateness which is under consideration. But the obvious response to make to Lokert's criticism is that his model relies on the incoherent notion of an instant being 'reproduced'. In the absence of any possible criterion of identity for an instant, so that we could identify 'something' as the same instant again, that is, next time it occurred, Lokert's model does not make sense, and therefore cannot be used to establish the unsatisfactoriness of the exposition at issue.

Lokert produces a further argument against the kind of exposition of propositions of immediateness presently under discussion. He writes:

> Assuming that the first instant of a future hour is A and the final instant is B, and Socrates will exist just for the middle third of that hour, then the truth of the following proposition would follow: 'Immediately after instant A or instant B Socrates will exist', since after instant A or instant B Socrates will exist, and there will be no instant after A or B but that between that instant and instant A or instant B Socrates will exist. But that should not be conceded. Neither immediately after instant A will Socrates exist nor immediately after instant B will Socrates exist [*De Ex.* 27r²]

Lokert is arguing here as follows: let us suppose some future hour whose first instant and terminal instant we shall call, respectively, 'A' and 'B', and we shall suppose that Socrates will exist just for the middle third of that hour, for a period we shall call 'S'. This model represented geometrically is as follows:

A      <u>S</u>      B

But, the argument continues, the exponible 'Immediately after instant A or instant B Socrates will exist' is false, since Socrates will not exist immediately after instant A or immediately after instant B, for he does not start to exist till a third of an hour after A, and he never does exist after B. Yet both exponents are true. The prejacent is clearly true, for it states that after A or B Socrates will exist, and according to the model Socrates does exist after instant A. And the second exponent also is true. That states that there will be no instant after A or B but that between that instant and A or B Socrates will exist. Let us pick an instant, call it 'C', which is between A and the start of S. The model represented geometrically is as follows:

$$\overset{\bullet}{A} \quad \overset{\bullet}{C} \quad \underline{\quad S \quad} \quad \overset{\bullet}{B}$$

But C is an instant such that it is after A-or-B, namely, after A; and Socrates will exist between C and A-or-B, since he will exist between C and B. Alternatively, we could place C between B and the termination of S, in which case C is an instant such that it is after A-or-B; and Socrates will exist between C and A-or-B, since he will exist between C and A. As can readily be established, even if C is placed after B the second exponent is verified. And since, the argument concludes, the exponible is false whereas both its alleged exponents are true the conjunction of those exponents cannot constitute a correct exposition of that exponible.

In the face of this argument Lokert proceeds: 'On account of some of these reasons some people give "After the present instant it will never be but that Socrates is or was" as the second exponent of "Immediately after the present instant Socrates will exist"; and for the second exponent of this: "Immediately before this instant Socrates existed", they give this second exponent: "Before the present instant it never was but that Socrates is or will be". But it is known that such a way of expounding [propositions of immediateness] is not valid' [*De Ex*. 27r²].

Lokert gives several reasons for rejecting this exposition. We shall for the present rehearse just one of them. He writes: 'Assuming that Socrates existed in the past and will not exist in the future until the last instant of the hour of which the present instant is the beginning, the truth of this would follow: 'Immediately after this instant Socrates will exist' indicating [with the 'this'] the present instant, as is obvious from the aforesaid exponents. But its falsity is sufficiently obvious from the model' [*De Ex*. 27v¹]. Lokert is arguing here as follows: let us suppose that at some past time, call it 'A', Socrates existed, that he does not exist at the present instant, call it 'B', and that he will not exist again until the last instant, call it 'C', of the hour of which B is the start. The exponible 'Immediately after the present instant Socrates will exist' is false, since an hour will elapse after the present instant before Socrates will exist. But both exponents are true. The first exponent, the prejacent, is clearly true, that is, 'After the present instant [viz. one hour after] Socrates will exist'. And the second is true. To show this let us pick an instant 'D' which falls between B (which is now) and C (which is in an hour); then Socrates exists either at or before C since he existed before, namely, at A. If D is placed after C it is still true then that Socrates then exists or had existed, since he had previously existed both at C and at A. Hence the conjunction of the two exponents constitutes a false exposition of the exponible.

As regards the above model constructed by Lokert a question might be raised concerning the assumption of the coherence of the notion of Socrates ceasing to exist, and starting, after a duration, to exist again. But Lokert does not himself question this matter. Instead he turns to a third account of how propositions of immediateness might be expounded. He writes: 'Others give the second exponent of propositions of immediateness in terms of a proposition about the infinite, so that they give this: "Infinitely soon after this instant Socrates will exist" as the second exponent of "Immediately after this instant Socrates will exist"' [*De Ex.* 27v[1]]. But Lokert rejects this exposition, though his reasons for doing so are unclear. He makes a distinction, a common one of the period, between 'infinite' understood categorematically and understood syncategorematically,[19] and argues that however it be understood the above exposition must be rejected. Taken categorematically 'infinitely soon' signifies a period whose shortness is without end. Taken syncategorematically 'infinitely soon' signifies either 'no soonness but that sooner' or 'soon, and doubly soon and triply soon, etc.' [28v[2]]. Lokert argues that where 'infinitely soon' is taken categorematically then according to its exposition 'Immediately after this instant there will be an instant', though 'commonly' accepted as true, will in fact be false. 'And', he continues, 'that the exposition would not be valid with the 'infinitely' taken syncategorematically is obvious, since then this would be false: "Immediately after this hour this instant will exist" indicating [by the occurrences of 'this'] the future hour and its terminating instant. But that is false since between that hour and the given instant nothing will mediate'. The point being made here is that where 'infinitely soon' is taken syncategorematically (on either of its definitions) the second exponent of the exponible proposition is false, whereas the exponible itself would be regarded as true. Lokert provides, unfortunately, too few details to permit a full reconstruction of the argument by which he reaches this conclusion.

All that is clear is that in the face of the unacceptability of the exposition of propositions of immediateness given in terms of infinite soonness, he turns to a further exposition, a fourth (see appendix, no.47).

'It seems more probable that the second exponent of a proposition of immediateness should be given in terms of 'earlier' and 'later', where immediateness of duration is denoted . . . So this proposition "Immediately after this instant Socrates will exist" is expounded thus: "After this instant Socrates will exist & It is not possible for anything to exist sooner after this instant than Socrates will exist after this instant". And of this: "Immediately before this instant Socrates existed" this second exponent is given: "It was not possible for something to exist before this instant later than Socrates existed before this instant"' [*De Ex.* 28r¹]. This exposition does not contain explicit reference to infinity, as did the last one, but has the merit, from Lokert's point of view, of being in accord with his view of time as continuous. Most especially, it was not open to Lokert to give an exposition of propositions of immediateness in terms of the notion of 'the very next instant', since for him the notion of the very next instant is incoherent. He writes: 'between any parts of time there mediates something indivisible in respect of duration which is called an instant . . . And thus in any time whatever however small there are infinite intrinsic instants mediating between the parts of time itself just as there is one initial instant and one terminal instant of the same thing. And from this it follows that in no time are there two unmediated instants; granted any instants whatever, between them time mediates and in consequence an infinity of instants' [*De Ex.* 28r¹] (see appendix, no.48). But there is no suggestion in Lokert's writings that he wanted to hold that an instant was, in virtue of its indivisibility from the point of view of duration, a minimal period of time. For him, an instant does not last long enough to have even minimal duration, for an instant has no duration whatever. Hence, two successive instants, each of which has no duration, would between them also have no duration, and the second of the two would be no later than the first. It was in order to avoid the incoherence just described, which arises when time is taken to be composed of a succession of durationless instants, that Lokert formulated the second exponent in the way that he did.

## VI

Lokert expounded propositions of immediateness because he intended to employ such propositions in his exposition of propositions of inception and cessation, that is, propositions whose main verbs are, respectively, 'begins' and 'ceases'. We turn now to a consideration of his discussion of the exposition of the latter two sorts of exponible. The notion of an instant continues to loom large, as it did when the analysis of 'immediately' was at issue.

Lokert starts his discussion by making a distinction between kinds of instant: 'It should be noticed that for the exposition of propositions about "begins" and "ceases" four instants are commonly attributed to things with respect to inception and cessation, namely, the first instant of existence and the last instant of non-existence (these concern inception), and the first instant of non-existence and the last instant of existence (these concern cessation)' [*De Ex.* 28v$^{1-2}$] (see appendix, no.49). This short passage contains the framework within which Lokert's discussion takes place. In saying that something, call it 'A', begins to exist, we make reference, explicitly or otherwise, to two instants, namely, the last instant of A's non-existence and the first instant of A's existence – the last instant of A's existence and the first of its non-existence are irrelevant. And in saying that something, B, ceases to exist, we make reference, explicit or otherwise, to two instants, namely, the last instant of B's existence and the first instant of its non-existence – the first instant of B's existence and the last of its non-existence are irrelevant.

It is in terms of these four types of instant that Lokert describes the correct way to expound propositions of inception and cessation. He writes (see appendix, no.50):

Something can begin to be in two ways. For that reason an affirmative proposition which is exponible in virtue of containing the term 'begins' is expounded disjunctively with each disjunct being a conjunction, one of which contains an affirmative proposition about the present and a negative about the past with the determinator 'immediately' mediating, and this conjunction deals with inception in terms of the first instant of existence [i.e. it says that now is the first instant of existence]. And the other conjunction contains a negative about the present and an affirmative about the future with the determinator 'immediately' mediating, and this conjunction deals with inception in terms of the last instant of non-existence [i.e. it says that now is the last instant of non-existence]. So anything beginning to exist in either of these ways, begins to exist through the first instant of existence or the last of non-existence. And likewise a thing can cease to exist in two ways. And for that reason an affirmative proposition about 'ceases' should similarly be expounded disjunctively with each disjunct being a conjunction, one of which contains an affirm-

ative proposition about the present and a negative about the future with 'immediately' mediating, and this conjunction deals with cessation in terms of the last instant of existence [i.e. it says that now is the last instant of existence]. And the other conjunction contains a negative proposition about the present and an affirmative about the past, and this conjunction deals with cessation in terms of the first instant of non-existence [i.e. it says that now is the first instant of non-existence]. So it is not the case that something ceases to exist, unless it ceases to exist through the last instant of existence or the first of non-existence. This is clarified by example. This proposition: 'Socrates begins to be a man' is expounded in this way: 'Socrates at the present instant is a man & Not immediately before the present instant was Socrates a man, *or* Socrates at the present instant is not a man & Immediately after the present instant Socrates will be a man'. And this proposition: 'Socrates ceases to be a man' should be expounded in this way: 'Socrates at the present instant is a man & Not immediately after the present instant will Socrates be a man, *or* Socrates at the present instant is not a man & Immediately before the present instant Socrates was a man'. In the negative exponent of past or future the determinator 'immediately' should be negated.
[*De Ex.* 28v²]

No doubt for the sake of lucidity of exposition Lokert has picked an example in which the terms preceding the exponible term in the exponibles of inception and cessation are singular terms (in each case the name 'Socrates'). But a complication not present in the kind of case used by Lokert arises if a quantified expression precedes the 'begins' or 'ceases', for the presence of such an expression raises the question of whether the exponible should be expounded before descent is made to singulars under the quantified term, or whether the quantified term should be resolved before the exponible is expounded. Lokert states the order of procedure briefly: 'In such propositions the terms preceding the "begins" or "ceases' should be sufficiently resolved before they are expounded' [*De Ex.* 29r¹].

The point at issue can be illustrated by the following schematic example. Consider (1) 'Every A begins to be B'. If (1) is expounded before the 'A' is resolved, the exposition is: (2) (Every A is now B & Not immediately before now was every A B) ∨ (Every A is now not B & Immediately after now every A will be B). According to (2) one or other of 'Every A is now B' and 'Every A is now not B' is true, and one false. But this is only one possible interpretation of (1) and, at least in Lokert's view, not the most plausible, since (1) could be true even though it is not the case either that every A is B or that every A is not B. For some A's might be beginning to be B in virtue of the fact that at the instant immediately before now they were not B, and now they are B, while other A's are beginning to be B in virtue of the fact that now they are not B and immediately after now they will be B. This latter interpretation is captured by adopting the order of procedure stipulated by Lokert, that is, by descending to singulars under 'A' before expounding the exponible. Assuming for the sake of brevity that there are just two A's, that is, $A^1$ and $A^2$, descent to singulars under A, which has distributive supposition, leads to the following formula:

(3) $A^1$ begins to be B & $A^2$ begins to be B.

These two exponibles should now be expounded. Therefore:

(4) $((A^1$ is now B & Not immediately before now was $A^1$ B$) \vee$
$(A^1$ is now not B & Immediately after now $A^1$ will be B$)) \&$
$((A^2$ is now B & Not immediately before now was $A^2$ B$) \vee$
$(A^2$ is now not B & Immediately after now $A^2$ will be B$))$.

This formulation clearly captures the notion that every A begins to be B, without at the same time making the stronger claim that each A comes into existence at the same moment as every other.

Having laid down the principle that terms preceding 'begins' and 'ceases' should be resolved before the propositions are expounded, Lokert immediately adds a further principle of order of procedure, namely, that modal propositions and non-present tense propositions of inception and cessation should be reduced to non-modal present tense propositions before the exponibles are expounded [*De Ex.* 29r$^1$]. Thus for example (5) 'A began to be B at noon yesterday' should not be expounded as it stands, but should first be reduced to: (6) '"A begins to be B" was true at noon yesterday'. 'A begins to be B' can next be expounded within the propositional context '– was true at noon yesterday'.

The foregoing account of how past tense propositions of inception should be handled does not, it should be noted, apply to propositions which contain a past tense verb, but where the principal verb 'begin' is in the present tense. Thus (7) 'Socrates begins to have existed' does not require to be rewritten before it can be expounded. Lokert expounds the proposition straightforwardly in this way:

(8) (At the present instant it is the case that Socrates existed & Not immediately before the present instant was it the case that Socrates had existed) $\vee$ (At the present instant it is not the case that Socrates existed & Immediately after the present instant it will be the case that Socrates existed)
[*De Ex.* 30r$^{1-2}$].

'Socrates ceases to be about to exist', which Lokert also discusses, is dealt with in a parallel way.

Lokert offers a number of criticisms of his account of the exposition of propositions of inception and cessation. For example, the claim that a thing begins to exist either through the last instant of non-existence or the first instant of existence, was treated as though what began did so in its entirety immediately after some instant of its non-existence. But Lokert points out that there are things which are by their nature temporally successive, for example, an hour. It, in its entirety, cannot begin to exist at an instant, for that would imply that it could *be* at an instant, which, as Lokert says, is impossible [*De Ex.* 29v²]. Hence the exposition of propositions of inception and cessation appears to fail for things which are in their nature temporally successive. Lokert does not, however, see the foregoing problem case as grounds for rejecting the kind of exposition which he has put forward, but merely for tightening up the formulation in order to accommodate that sort of case.

Maintaining, then, his original analysis he draws out certain of its implications. He considers, for example, the question of whether propositions of inception are convertible. The question is raised whether:

(1) Some man begins to exist

is convertible with:

(2) There begins to exist some man.

But once raised it is not definitely answered. The first suggestion [32r²] is that these propositions are not mutually equivalent and hence are not simply convertible. One ground for this is based upon a principle already stated by Lokert, namely, that a term preceding 'begins' should be resolved before the exponible is expounded, and if no term precedes the 'begins' then the exponible should be expounded before terms are resolved. It follows that the order of procedure for (1) is different from that for (2), since in the analysis of (1) the term 'man' must be resolved before the proposition is expounded. Since in (1) 'man' has determinate supposition, descent is made to a disjunction of singulars under 'man'. Assuming, for the sake of brevity, that there are just two men, man¹ and man², (1) is equivalent to:

(3) Man¹ begins to exist ∨ Man² begins to exist.

(3) can now be expounded as:

(4) (Man¹ now exists & Not immediately before now did man¹ exist ∨ Man¹ now does not exist & Immediately after now man¹ will exist) ∨ (Man² now exists & Not immediately before now did man² exist ∨ Man² now does not exist & Immediately after now man² will exist).

On the other hand (2) can be expounded straightaway. Its exposition is:

> (5) (A man now exists & Not immediately before now did
>       a man exist) ∨ (A man now does not exist & Immediately
>       after now a man will exist).

It is clear from these expositions that (1) and (2) do not make the same point, for (2) implies that either immediately before now no man existed or no man now exists, whereas (1) does not imply this but instead implies merely that there is some man of whom it is true that *he* did not exist immediately before now though now does exist, or else *he* now does not exist but will exist immediately after now.

But subsequently Lokert writes: 'It would not be entirely improbable to say that these are equivalent: "There begins to exist some man" and "Some man begins to exist", and that they ought to be proved in the same way' [*De Ex.* 32v²]. He does not state explicitly why the equivalence of the two propositions 'would not be entirely improbable', but the explanation surely lies in the evident ambiguity of (2). For though proposition (5) above represents one way of taking (2) another way is to hand, which involves a linguistic device to which Lokert payed a good deal of attention, namely, the relative pronoun of identity. That is, (2) could be expounded as:

> (6) (A man now exists & Not immediately before now did the
>       same man exist) ∨ (A man now does not exist & Immediately
>       after now the same man will exist).

If, once again, we assume there to be just two men, man¹ and man², and descend to singulars under 'man' in (6), we reach a formula demonstrably equivalent to (4). Lokert's doubt about whether 'Some man begins to exist' and 'There begins to exist some man' are convertible is, then, clearly justified.

It should be noted that had the two propositions just mentioned contained, instead of a quantifier plus common noun, a singular term, for example, a proper name, the convertibility of the two propositions could readily be established. The convertibility of such propositions is due to two things, first, the fact that if the subject of the sentence is a proper name preceding the 'begins' the subject does not need to be resolved before the proposition is expounded, and secondly, the relative pronoun of identity is implicitly present in the exposition. For example:

> (7) Socrates begins to exist, and
> (8) There begins to exist Socrates

are both expounded as follows:

> (9) (S now exists & Not immediately before now did S exist) ∨

(S now does not exist & Immediately after now S will exist). (7) and (8) are, therefore, straightforwardly convertible, unlike (1) and (2), despite the structural similarities between the two pairs of propositions.

The doubts which beset Lokert in considering whether (1) and (2) were convertible did not trouble him in the least in dealing with other pairs of propositions of inception and cessation. He writes: 'It is not valid to argue from a conjunction to a proposition concerning the coupled extremes, or to a proposition concerning a term of a plural number placed before the conjunction complexively taken, nor vice versa' [*De Ex.* 33r¹]. He provides as an argument of the kind with which he is here concerned the following: 'Socrates begins to exist & Plato begins to exist. Therefore Socrates and Plato begin to exist'. He does not give an example of a proposition with a term of plural number illicitly inferred, but it is clear that he has in mind an argument such as: 'Man¹ begins to be white & Man² begins to be white. Therefore two men begin to be white'.

The exposition of 'Socrates and Plato begin to exist' is: (S and P now exist & Not immediately before now did S and P exist) ∨ (S and P do not now exist & Immediately after now S and P will exist). Hence 'Socrates and Plato begin to exist' implies that either immediately before now neither Socrates nor Plato existed or else neither of them now exists. But 'Socrates begins to exist & Plato begins to exist' does not have this implication. This conjunction can be true because Socrates now does not exist and immediately after now will exist, and Plato now exists and immediately before now did not exist. Hence, 'Socrates begins to exist and Plato begins to exist' could be true though 'Socrates and Plato begin to exist' is false. By the same sort of reasoning it can be shown that 'Man¹ begins to be white & Man² begins to be white' can be true while 'Two men begin to be white' is false.

## VII

Lokert discusses propositions of inception and cessation together because of the very close logical relation between the two sorts of proposition. The next section of the *De Exponibilibus* is also taken up with an investigation of a pair of exponible terms, or rather with the investigation of a pair of classes of exponible terms, for following his discussion of 'begins' and 'ceases' he turns to two kinds of term, not to two terms in particular. The one kind is the adjective in its comparative form, and the other is the adjective in its superlative form. And these are taken together because of their close logical relation. Indeed, as we shall see, superlatives are expounded by Lokert in terms of comparatives. And though at one point he shows that superlatives can be expounded in terms of the positive form of the relevant adjective on condition that that positive is imbedded in a certain syncategorematic phrase, that phrase itself is then treated as an exponible which requires for its exposition reference to the comparative form of the adjective which appears as a superlative in the original exponible proposition.

We are, then, concerned with the exposition of propositions such as 'Socrates is stronger than Plato' and 'Socrates is the strongest of men', and the relation of these to each other and to the positive form 'Socrates is strong'. Lokert begins by distinguishing between the non-strict employment of the comparative and the strict employment (see appendix, no.51). He writes: 'A comparative is taken non-strictly when the positive of the comparative is not denoted to belong to each of the things being compared' [De Ex. 33v¹]. He gives the example 'A man is more rational than an ass',[20] which is evidently to be regarded as a comparative only non-strictly in view of the fact that asses lack rationality.

But it is not clear why this kind of case should not count as a comparative strictly speaking, even though admittedly a comparative which is false. But Lokert does not delay over this sort of case.[21] He proceeds to a description of the exponents of a comparative strictly speaking:

> Taking the comparative strictly renders the proposition exponible. If that proposition is affirmative it should be expounded conjunctively, and if negative then it should be expounded disjunctively, [in both cases] with three exponents. In the first two exponents, which should be of the same quality as the exponible, the positive of the comparative should be predicated of the terms referring to the things being compared, namely, the thing which exceeds (the 'exceedent') and the thing which is exceeded. The third exponent is of the opposite quality to the exponible and to the other two exponents. In it the subject is a term referring to the exceeded thing, and the predicate is a complex composed of the term for the exceedent plus the expression 'as . . . as' with the positive form of the comparative mediating between the two occurrences of 'as'. [De Ex. 33v¹⁻²]

Lokert furnishes the following example: 'Socrates is stronger than an ass' is expounded as 'Socrates is strong & Every ass is strong & No ass is as strong as Socrates'. It is in the light of this exposition that it is puzzling that Lokert described 'A man is more rational than an ass' as not strictly speaking a comparative. For evidently its second exponent should read: 'Every ass is rational' which is merely false from which it would follow that the exposition, which is conjunctive since the exponible is affirmative, must also be false. Perhaps the point behind Lokert's remark is that on any interpretation according to which 'A man is more rational than an ass' is true, that proposition could not be taken as a comparative strictly speaking. But a comparative cannot be any less a comparative for having a false second exponent.

Before discussing certain aspects of this exposition, we shall turn first to Lokert's account of superlatives. He writes (see appendix, no. 52):

> A proposition about a superlative is also exponible through three exponents. In the first two the positive of the superlative will be denoted to belong to each of the things being compared, if the proposition [the exponible] is affirmative. And the third exponent could be affirmative or negative according to different ways of taking the superlative, with one of the compared things predicated of the other with the comparative of the superlative mediating. For example: 'Socrates is the strongest of men' is expounded affirmatively as: 'Socrates is strong & Every man other than Socrates is strong & Socrates is stronger than every man other than Socrates'. And taking the superlative negatively, the first two exponents are the same as before and the third one is: 'No man other than Socrates is stronger than Socrates'.
>
> [*De Ex.* 33v²]

Lokert spells out the difference between the affirmative and the negative interpretation in these terms: first, 'A superlative, or a complex whose superlative is the more principal part, with the superlative taken affirmatively cannot at the same time be true of more things' [33v²]. That is, taken affirmatively 'Socrates is the strongest of men' implies that there is no man, other than Socrates, of whom it is true that he, as well as Socrates, is the strongest of men. But taking that sentence negatively, it is consistent that someone other than Socrates is the strongest of men, granted also that if there is another who is the strongest he is no stronger than Socrates; the two are equally the strongest. The other is as strong as Socrates, but not stronger.

It is for this reason that, as in his discussion of comparatives, Lokert introduces the 'as . . . as' construction, and suggests that the third exponent of the superlative exponible negatively interpreted should be 'Socrates is as strong as any man other than Socrates'. In the light of this it might seem that comparatives and superlatives are theoretically redundant, since both can be expounded in terms of the positive plus the 'as . . . as' construction, and a question could then be raised as to whether comparatives and superlatives occur in the mental language. But the situation is untidy. Lokert treats a sentence containing the 'as . . . as' construction as an exponible, and says that 'according to some people' it should be expounded in terms of the comparative. Thus, for example, 'Socrates is as strong as Plato' should be expounded as: 'Socrates is strong & Plato is strong & Plato is not stronger than Socrates'. It should be noted that on this interpretation the 'as . . . as' relation is not symmetrical, for given the third exponent it is not possible to infer 'Plato is as strong as Socrates' from 'Socrates is as strong as Plato' for the third exponent is consistent with Plato being less strong than Socrates. Hence on this interpretation 'Socrates is as strong as Plato' does not mean or even imply 'Socrates is exactly as strong as Plato'. Lokert adds: 'Consequently it should be conceded that just as, in expounding a proposition with a comparative, 'as . . . as' is placed in one exponent, so in one of the exponents of an 'as . . . as' proposition a comparative is placed. And hence exponents of such propositions would not be better known and clearer than their exponibles' [*De Ex.* 34r[1]] (see appendix, no. 53).

This point, as Lokert must have realised, has immediate implications for his definition of 'exponible', discussed at the start of this chapter, in which reference is made to a term which 'obscures' the sense of a proposition, for clarification of the obscure is not secured by expounding one exponible in terms of another, at any rate if all exponibles are seen as obscuring the sense of the proposition they are in. It might, of course, be argued that while all exponibles are obscure some are more so than others, and that therefore it makes sense to expound some exponibles in terms of exponents which themselves contain other, less obscure, exponible terms. And this might be the justification for expounding superlatives in terms of comparatives. But it cannot be the justification for expounding comparatives in terms of the positive plus the 'as . . . as' construction, if that latter construction is then treated as an exponible which is expounded in terms of the comparative. In the light of the way the definition of 'exponible' given in terms of 'obscurity' comes under such pressure from the alleged relation between the comparative and the 'as . . . as' construction, there seems particular merit in the suggestion of William Manderston's accuser, Jerome Hangest, that the notion of obscurity should not be brought into the definition of 'exponible'. He writes: 'Hence I say that an exponible proposition is a proposition to which is attached an exponible sign. An exponible sign is a sign implicitly denoting hypothetically . . . And a sign is said to denote hypothetically if its denotation has to be explicated, mediately or immediately, by a hypothetical proposition' [*Problemata Exponibilium* Paris, 1507 (also 1511, 1515, 1519, all in Paris)].

The comparative and the 'as . . . as' construction are not the only kinds of exponible relevant to the exposition of the superlative. The exceptive, which we have already considered in an earlier section of this chapter, is also involved. The point emerges clearly if we take up Lokert's question of the kind of supposition possessed by 'men' in 'Socrates is the strongest of men' [*De Ex.* 35r²]. He mentions, only to dismiss, the idea that the term has confused conjunctive supposition. That idea would amount to saying that under 'men' descent could be made to a conjunction of singular terms referring successively to all men. That is, it would imply 'Socrates is the strongest of $A^1$ & $A^2$ & . . . (and so on for all men)'. While Lokert does not find this analysis convincing he does say that 'Socrates is the strongest of men' 'could not be verified unless some true singular is given under the term ['man'] [35r¹]. Nor, as he immediately adds, does the term have distributive supposition. He does not even mention the possibility that the term has merely confused or determinate supposition, since these alternatives are clearly false.

The solution to the problem is to expound the superlative before descent to singulars is made. Taking the superlative on its affirmative interpretation for the time being (though the same point could be made *mutatis mutandis* if the negative interpretation were taken) the exponible is, as we know, expounded as follows: 'Socrates is strong & Every man is strong & Socrates is stronger than every man other than Socrates'. Instead of asking the unanswerable question of the kind of supposition possessed by the term immediately following the superlative term in the original exponible, we can now ask about the kind of supposition possessed by the term following the comparative term in the third exponent of the exposition of the superlative. How, in other words, should descent to singulars be made under 'every man other than Socrates'? Since that term has distributive supposition, the answer to the new question is that descent is made to a conjunction of singulars as follows: 'Socrates is stronger than man¹ & Socrates is stronger than man² & . . . (and so on for all men except Socrates)'. Hence superlatives can be understood in terms of positives, comparatives and exceptives.

In the kind of case just discussed no exceptive term appears in the original superlative. But there are cases where a single proposition contains two or more kinds of exponible term, and a question can then be raised as to the order of exposition of the exponibles. Lokert raises just that question in connection with propositions which are comparatives or superlatives and are also propositions of inception or cessation. The example he takes is 'Socrates begins to be stronger than an ass' [34r$^2$], and his reply is: 'Such propositions should be resolved in respect of the terms "begins" and "ceases" before the comparative and superlative are dealt with'. That Lokert's rule of precedence is correct, at least for a certain class of cases, can be seen if we try to expound 'Socrates begins to be stronger than an ass' while infringing that rule. The exposition would then be, at the first stage, 'Socrates begins to be strong & Every ass begins to be strong & No ass begins to be as strong as Socrates'. Clearly the exponible could be true while the exposition is false, for it may be false that Socrates begins to be strong and also that every ass begins to be strong. Socrates and every ass may, after now, be strong, and may also have been strong for some time past, even though it is now true that Socrates begins to be stronger than every ass. On the other hand the exposition of 'Socrates begins to be stronger than an ass' is readily acceptable when carried out in the order laid down by Lokert. The first stage of the exposition takes us to: (Socrates is now stronger than an ass &Not immediately before now was Socrates stronger than an ass) ∨ (Socrates now is not stronger than an ass & Immediately after now Socrates will be stronger than an ass). Each of the four propositions in the exposition is a comparative which can now be expounded in the way already described. The result is a compelling analysis of the doubly exponible proposition with which we started.

## CHAPTER FOUR
# Consequences

### I

Near the start of the *De Terminis* Lokert presents a series of definitions of terms associated with the notion of inference. In chapter two brief reference was made to the passage. Since that passage provides the conceptual framework within which our discussion will proceed in the present chapter, we shall, for the sake of convenience, quote it here in full:

> An antecedent is a sentence from which, it is denoted, a consequent is inferred. A consequent is a sentence which is denoted to follow from an antecedent[1] . . . The mark of inference is the 'therefore'[2] by reason of which the consequent is denoted to be inferred from the antecedent, and the whole consequence results from the antecedent, the consequent and the mark of inference . . . Some consequences are called good. One is good if it is of such a nature that things cannot be as are signified by the antecedent and yet not be as are signified by the consequent. A consequence is bad if it is possible for things to be as they are signified by the antecedent and yet not be as they are signified by the consequent. [*De Term.* 3v–4r] (see appendix, no. 54)

This account of consequence says nothing about the number of premisses or about the structure of the propositions in the premisses or in the conclusion. It specifies merely that there must be a propositional antecedent, a propositional consequent, and a mark of inference, a 'therefore', between them. This is a purely syntactical definition of 'consequence', and applies irrespective of whether the consequence is good or not.[3] What in addition is required if the consequence is to be good is that a certain modal relation holds between antecedent and consequent, namely, that it is impossible for things to be as signified by the antecedent and not as signified by the consequent.[4] Correspondingly a bad consequence is simply a consequence which is not a good one. The relation envisaged between antecedent and consequent in a good consequence is therefore not one of material implication but, instead, of strict implication however precisely the latter relation is defined.[5]

That this account of what constitutes a good consequence is made without reference to the internal properties of the propositions that occur in the antecedent and the consequent is important, for although most of what Lokert wrote on the theory of consequences was concerned with relations between analysed propositions, he displayed a lively awareness of the priority of what would now be termed the propositional calculus, that is, the area of logic which deals with rules of valid inference for unanalysed propositions. Numerous rules of purely propositional logic are invoked by Lokert, at appropriate points in his discussion. For example, he refers [*De Sill.* $4r^2$] (see appendix, no.55) to the valid inference (1) from a whole disjunction and the denial of one of its parts to the affirmation of the other part, and the valid inference (2) from a whole conditional and the affirmation of the antecedent to the affirmation of the consequent, and the valid inference (3) from a whole conditional and the denial of the consequent to the denial of the antecedent, three rules which in modern form may be expressed respectively as: $(1) (P \vee Q) \& \sim P \vdash Q$; $(2) (P \rightarrow Q) \& P \vdash Q$; $(3) (P \rightarrow Q) \& \sim Q \vdash \sim P$. He also discusses the law of double negation, that 'an even number of negatives renders a proposition affirmative' and 'an odd number of negatives renders a proposition negative' [*De Sill.* $2r^2$] (see appendix, no.56).

But though Lokert was aware of numerous laws of propositional logic and recognised their crucial role in the development of the logic of analysed sentences he makes no attempt at a systematic investigation of the laws of propositional logic. His systematic work is entirely within the field of the logic of analysed propositions, and when laws of propositional logic are invoked the reason is, almost always, that Lokert has to justify a move from one proposition to another within the logic of terms, within, that is to say, a logic in which the arrangement of terms within the propositions has an effect on the validity, or otherwise, of the argument. Thus, for example, the move from 'No A is B' to 'Some B is not A' is valid within the logic of terms but is proved within that logic with the aid of a law of propositional logic, the law, namely, that whatever is implied by a consequent is implied by the antecedent, i.e. $(Q \rightarrow R \& P \rightarrow Q) \rightarrow (P \rightarrow R)$.

The logic of terms is the systematic presentation of inferential relations between propositional schemata (we shall for the sake of brevity speak just of propositions *tout court*) where the order of the terms and their relation to the syncategorematic elements in the propositions contribute to the validity of the inferential relations. Lokert seeks, in various places, to establish the validity within the logic of terms of alleged inferential relations between propositions of great syntactic complexity, where, for example, both the subject and the predicate terms are highly complex, and the copula is a disjunction of parts of the verb 'to be', one past, one present and one future and not all affirmative. But the starting point for most of his discussions is a quantified proposition containing a subject, a copula and a predicate where the three are not complex. This starting point contains two, or perhaps three, syncategorematic terms, and two categorematic ones. The syncategorematic terms are the copula, a universal or particular quantifier, and perhaps also a sentence-negating operator.

A proposition with a simpler type of structure is often invoked though it does not receive separate treatment, namely, that consisting of a subject term followed by a part of the verb 'to be', as in 'An A is [i.e. exists]'. This type of proposition is often invoked because of the need to rely on a so-called *constantia* requirement. To say that a term in a proposition has *constantia* is to say that a proposition, consisting of that term plus the part of the verb 'to be' occurring in the first proposition, is true. Thus, in 'Some ass is white' 'ass' has *constantia* if 'An ass is [i.e. exists]' is true. The especial importance of the notion of *constantia* in late medieval logic lies in the requirement that each term in an affirmative proposition must have *constantia* if that proposition is to be true (this is a requirement but is not sufficient); and the obverse of this doctrine was also accepted, namely, that a negative proposition is true if one of its terms does not have *constantia*. 'No white thing is a chimera' is then true, so long as no chimera exists, and precisely because no chimera exists.

The doctrine of *constantia* can be seen to lead to paradoxes, for the apparently inviolable schemata 'Every A is A', 'Some A is A' and 'An A is A' are false if 'A' is replaced by 'chimera' or 'unicorn' or 'anti-Christ' or any other term which does not signify an existing thing. But Lokert did not regard these paradoxical implications as sufficient ground for rejecting the doctrine of *constantia*, nor indeed is it clear that he found these implications paradoxical.

However, though making extensive use of the notion of *constantia*, and though propositions of the form 'A is' are the simplest kind of proposition of relevance to the logic of terms, Lokert worked mainly with propositions containing a predicate term after the 'is'. Such propositions, as we know from a consideration of the square of opposition, were classified as falling under one or other of four heads, namely, universal affirmative, universal negative, particular affirmative and particular negative, or, as they are commonly called, respectively, *a*, *e*, *i* and *o* propositions. But there are grounds, some of them obvious, for wondering whether this quadripartite division is complete or is, at least, as clear cut as it looks.

One point to note, already considered in the discussion of exponibles, is that Lokert dealt extensively with propositions in which quantifier expressions appear not only before but also after the copula, as in the proposition 'Every white thing is every ass', where the second 'every' does not deform the proposition but merely ensures that it is not true unless there is just one thing for which both the subject and the predicate terms supposit. Should one say here that the proposition is a universal affirmative in virtue of the two quantifiers? And in the case of 'Some white thing is every ass' should the proposition be said to be both particular and universal? In fact the practice invariably adopted by Lokert was to classify a proposition on the basis of the quantifier immediately preceding the subject term. In the case of the latter example, then, the proposition is to be classified as a particular affirmative despite the presence of the 'every'.

Lokert's position in the case of propositions with complex subjects containing more than one quantifier is not so easily established. The problem arises for propositions such as 'Of every man some ass is running' and 'Every ass of some man is running'. But it seems to have been Lokert's practice to classify a proposition whose subject is a complex consisting of determinator plus determinable, each being quantified, on the basis of the quantifier which appears first. The situation is not, however, entirely clear. But it is at least clear that an important logical issue is at stake. To anticipate a point we shall be discussing later in this chapter, Lokert, following standard practice, held that a syllogistic argument could not be valid if both of its premisses were particular. And there has therefore to be some means of determining just which propositions are particular.

The kind of example so far considered raises a question as to whether the quadripartite division into *a*, *e*, *i* and *o* propositions is unsatisfactory, on the grounds that a single proposition can be a combination of several of these simultaneously, perhaps *a* with respect to the determinator of the subject, *i* with respect to its determinable, and *o* with respect to the predicate. But it may also be questioned whether there are not categorical propositions which fall entirely outwith this classificatory scheme. In particular, singular propositions, such as Socrates is running' and indefinite ones, such as 'A man is running', which lack both an 'every' and a 'some', seem to fall under heads of division not so far mentioned, and perhaps 'singular' and 'indefinite' should be added to 'particular' and 'universal' if the classificatory scheme is to be complete. But Lokert responded differently. He regarded the singular and the indefinite proposition as kinds of particular proposition, giving as his reason [*De Sill.* 3r²] that with respect to their role in syllogisms they behave no differently from particulars. It may be noted that in this, Lokert was going against the authority of William of Ockham who had argued that since in a singular affirmative proposition the predicate is understood to supposit for everything for which the subject term supposits, the singular subject term is in fact being treated as a universal.

A further problem that arises in the classification of propositions concerns the identification of those which are negative, for unless a proposition is negative it cannot be either an *e* or an *o* proposition. The problem arises in the first instance because of the distinction between those negation terms which negate 'negatively' (*neganter*) and those which negate 'infinitely' (*infinitanter*). The former kind of negation term negates a proposition, and the latter type negates a term. A distinction can, then, be drawn between, say, 'Some man is not white' (which is the negation of the sentence 'Every man is white') and 'Some man is a non-white' which is not classed as a negative proposition but, instead, as an affirmative proposition with a negated term. This distinction will be seen to be of crucial importance for the development of validity-deciding procedures for syllogistic theory in view of the rule, which we shall be examining, that a conclusion cannot be drawn syllogistically from two premisses both of which are negative.

Lokert refers not only to negations which negate 'negatively' or 'infinitely', but also, and often, to negations which negate 'implicitly' (*pregnanter*). Such a negation might also be said to be present 'virtually', though not 'formally'. Some exclusive propositions are implicitly negative, since one of the exponents is straightforwardly negative. Thus, the second exponent of 'Only A is B' is 'No non-A is B'. Exceptives likewise are implicitly negative. For example, the third exponent of 'Every A except B is C' is 'No B is C'. However, a proposition was not considered negative in the relevant sense, merely on account of having a negative exponent. To be negative in the relevant sense a proposition had to contain a negation formally, and not just virtually, and the negation had to negate the proposition and not merely a term in the proposition. Consequently it was possible to have a syllogism with a validly drawn conclusion following from two exclusive premisses, or from two exceptive premisses, without infringement of the rule that a conclusion cannot validly be drawn from two negative premisses. Lokert writes: 'The rule [that two negative premisses imply no conclusion] concerns purely negative propositions, since from implicitly negative premisses, or from premisses of which one is implicitly negative, a conclusion can follow validly, as is obvious in the case of exclusives and exceptives' [*De Sill.* 4v[1]].[6] He subsequently provides numerous examples of syllogisms with exponible premisses.

Proofs of valid syllogistic arguments are based on logical laws concerning unanalysed propositions, and on certain kinds of logical relation which hold between single categorical propositions. In the *De Sillogismis* Lokert has little to say about unanalysed propositions, but devotes considerable space (10r–17v) to a consideration of logical relations which can obtain between two categoricals. In order to understand the proof procedures for syllogistic arguments we shall turn to a brief consideration of certain relevant relations which can obtain between two categorical propositions.

## II

Lokert makes extensive use of the subalternation relation displayed in the verticals of the square of opposition, but does not do so without giving a general description of the relation (see appendix, no. 57). The law of subalternation is stated as follows: 'One of a pair of subaltern propositions implies the other formally and as regards the form of acceptance of the terms, and not vice versa' [*De Op.* 33v[2]], and we are then reminded of the two main technical terms involved: 'Of the two propositions the one which implies the other is called the "subalternant" and the other is the "subalternate"'. Two conditions of subalternation are then given, though it is clear from the sequel that they apply to what may be thought of as the basic sort of case only, and ought otherwise to be held lightly, since some relations which Lokert would wish to classify as relations of subalternation do not in fact satisfy each, or indeed either, condition.

He writes:

> First condition: subaltern propositions ought to be of the same quality and share the same terms in the same order . . . Second condition: a universality in the subalternant proposition ought to be changed into particularity in the subalternate proposition.

The basic pair of affirmative subalterns, namely, 'Every S is P' and 'Some S is P', and the basic pair of negative subalterns, 'No S is P' ( = 'Every S is not P') and 'Some S is not P', clearly conform with the law and satisfy the two conditions. A rider is added:

> It is not necessary in propositions which are thus opposed (*sc.* as subalternant to subalternate) that every universality in one should be changed into particularity in the other, or vice versa.

This is obvious in the case of these two: 'Of every man every ass is an ass' and 'Of some man every ass is an ass' [*De Op.* 34r¹]
Hence the second condition laid down must be understood as saying that it is sufficient if just one universality, out of however many there may be in a proposition, should be changed into particularity.

Elementary considerations discussed in an earlier chapter can be brought to bear in justification of the principle that 'From subaltern-ant to subalternate is a valid consequence'. In the case of a universal affirmative proposition, descent is made to a conjunction of singulars under the distributed subject term, and in the case of a particular affirmative descent is made to a disjunction of singulars under the determinate subject term. Thus for affirmatives the inference from subalternant to subalternate is based upon, or indeed amounts to, the principle that a conjunction of singular propositions implies a disjunction of the same singular propositions. This principle is simply a special case of the more general principle formulated by Lokert as: 'A disjunctive affirmative is the subalternate of a conjunctive affirmative composed of the same parts' [*De Op.* 35r¹⁻²]. Precisely the same considerations can be brought to bear in justification of the inference from a universal negative to the corresponding particular negative.

Intuitively the point at issue is that assent to a universal proposition is riskier than to the corresponding particular; there is, so to say, more to go wrong with the universal. As Lokert puts the point: 'Universality conduces more to the falsity of a proposition than does particularity, on account of the fact that for the truth of a proposition in which universality occurs more is required than for the truth of a proposition in which particularity replaces the universality, other things being equal' [*De Op.* 5r¹] (see appendix, no.58).

The reverse move, that from subalternate to subalternant, is not formally valid, though there may be material factors, in particular the meanings of the relevant categorematic terms in the propositions, which make such a move materially valid. What is however clearly true is that if a subalternate is false then so also must be its subaltern-ant. This holds on account of the propositional law enunciated by Lokert that from a conditional and the denial of its consequent to the denial of its antecedent is a valid consequence. In view of this it is perhaps surprising to find him arguing in one place [*De Op.* 11r²] that a certain proposition must be false since its contrary is true, and then arguing that the contrary in question must be true since its contra-dictory is false. This is surprising for if the last mentioned contradict-ory is indeed false then, on the principle that if a subalternate is false then so also must be its subalternant, it would follow immediately that the contrary of its contradictory must be false. For the contrary of the contradictory of a given proposition, assuming of course that it has a contrary, is simply the subalternant of that proposition.

But it should be said that Lokert was perfectly familiar with the relationships just mentioned, for he argues of two propositions that they must be contraries since each is the subalternant of the contradictory of the other [*De Op.* 14v²]; and he formulates the following principle: 'Given two contrary propositions, the contradictory of one is the subalternate of the other, and given two subcontraries, the contradictory of one will be the subalternant of the other' [*De Op.* 34r²].[7]

Lokert's principle, quoted earlier, that 'A disjunctive affirmative is the subalternate of a conjunctive affirmative composed of the same parts' [*De Op.* 35r¹⁻²], though it certainly accords with the law of subalternation, does not accord with the second of the two conditions laid down, for the principle invokes neither universality nor particularity. And this suggests that from the point of view of identifying a subalternation relation the law, expressed in terms of a one-way implication relation between the propositions, is more important than at any rate the second condition. A second example which is closely related to the one just invoked is this: 'A proposition with a conjunction divisively taken is the subalternant of a proposition with a disjunction divisively taken, other things being equal' [*De Op.* 34r¹].[8] Thus 'Some A is B and C' where the predicate is taken divisively (that is, where the proposition is equivalent to 'Some A is B and the same A is C') is the subalternant of 'Some A is B or C' where, again, the predicate is taken divisively (that is, where the proposition is equivalent to 'Some A is B or some A is C').

Further evidence that Lokert attached little weight to the second of the conditions of subalternation is provided by the statement that: 'There can be two subaltern propositions composed of singular terms and not containing common terms. This is obvious from "Socrates necessarily is Socrates" and "Socrates possibly is Socrates"' [*De Op.* 34r¹]. Here also, as in the case of conjunctive and disjunctive subalterns, there is no question of a subalternate being formed by the replacement of a sign of universality in the subalternant by a sign of particularity. The replacement in this example, evidently, is of one modal adverb by another weaker one.

One last point may be made here about subalternation. Lokert presents the principle: 'If a proposition is the subalternant of a second proposition it is also the subalternant of any proposition subalternate to the second one' [*De Op.* 34v¹].[9] Thus, even if, as Lokert appears to have held, any proposition can have only one contradictory, he allows that a proposition may have several subalternates. It would seem to follow from this that a proposition may also have several contraries, if the contrary of a proposition is identified as the contradictory of a subalternate of that proposition.

Lokert also claims that exclusives and exceptives of the first order are subalternants in relation to the corresponding exclusives and exceptives of the fourth order, and that such exponibles of the second order are subalternants of of the corresponding propositions of the third order [*De Op*. 34r¹].

A further kind of case to which reference is made is that where the proposition contains several quantifiers. For example, Lokert makes the suggestion [*De Op*. 9r¹] that: 'Every ass of every man does not run. Therefore every ass of a man does not run' is valid on the grounds that the antecedent and consequent are related as subalternant to subalternate, for the determinator of the subject in the antecedent is universal and in the consequent it is indefinite, and therefore to be treated as particular. But Lokert subsequently denies that the relationship between the two propositions is after all that of subalternant to its subalternate, for, he argues: 'It is required that every singular be true under the determinator'. In other words 'Every ass of a man does not run' is to be understood as meaning that every ass of *any* man does not run, or that there is no man of whom it is not true that every ass of his does not run. And in that case 'a man' in 'Every ass of a man does not run' has a universality that prevents that proposition being a subalternate.

The situation would have been different had the proposition been instead: 'Of some man every ass does not run' for in this proposition it is not required that every singular be true under the determinator. On the other hand, in view of the logically significant inversion of determinator and determinable, a new argument would be required to justify the claim that 'Of some man every ass does not run' is the subalternate of 'Every ass of every man does not run'. Indeed a likelier candidate for the role of subalternate of the last mentioned proposition is 'Some ass of every man does not run'.

However, Lokert, though not pursuing this particular issue, considers a closely related example which leads him to formulate a position which sits very uneasily indeed with the second of the two conditions of subalternation that he gives. The ass Brunellus, we shall suppose, belongs to some man but not every man, that is he is individually owned, and is not jointly owned by all men. Also, he does not run. Then:

(1) 'Brunellus belonging to some man does not run' is true.

(2) 'Brunellus belonging to every man does not run' is also true. But (2) can be true though (1) is false. For if, in fact, Brunellus, who as before is a non-jointly owned ass, is in fact running then (2), as before, will be true, since the subject is a non-referring expression in a negative proposition. But (1) must be false, since on the model Brunellus does belong to someone and does run. Lokert concludes: 'Consequently it is conceded that a proposition with an undistributed term is a subalternant in relation to a proposition with the same term distributed, other things being equal' [*De Op.* 10v²].[10] The reason this is a 'concession' for Lokert is that the second condition of subalternation requires that the inference be from the universal to the particular, yet in the kind of case just considered it is from the undistributed to the distributed, and hence from the particular to the universal.

But Lokert does not pursue this issue further, and for present purposes neither need we. For as regards the chief employment to which he puts the principle that a subalternant implies its subalternate, namely, the task of proving syllogisms, he is very largely concerned with what we earlier identified as the basic kind of case, which is neither exponible nor modal, but which instead conforms to both of the conditions laid down at the start of this section.

We turn now to further kinds of consequence of which Lokert made extensive use.

### III

Following Aristotle closely, Lokert presents the following rules of conversion (see appendix, no.59): 'First rule: a universal negative is converted into a universal negative. This conversion is called "simple" since in the converse and the convertent there is the same quantity and the same quality. Second rule: a universal affirmative is converted into a particular affirmative. This is called accidental conversion, since the converse and convertent have the same quality but not the same quantity. Third rule: a particular affirmative is converted into a particular affirmative. This also is called a simple conversion, just as is a universal negative' [*De Sill.* 10r¹]. The rules of conversion concern ways of transforming a subject/predicate proposition into another proposition like the first except that the subject and predicate terms are reversed. The first proposition is termed the 'converse' and the second the 'convertent'. The rules of conversion show how to convert a proposition in such a way that if the converse is true so also must be the convertent.

The first rule can be written as follows: $SeP \rightarrow PeS$. This rule is derived from the rule of the commutativity of conjunction, for SeP states that there is nothing for which both S and P supposit, and it follows from that that there is nothing for which both P and S supposit. But to say that is to say what is represented symbolically as PeS. It is clear from this consideration that the implicational relation between SeP and PeS is a two-way relation. And hence the rule can be written as: SeP↔PeS.

The third rule, SiP→PiS, can be justified on the basis of similar considerations. SiP states that there is something for which both S and P supposit, from which it follows that there is something for which both P and S supposit; and this latter point is symbolised as PiS. As with the first rule, the third can be presented as a two-way implication, namely SiP↔PiS. These two rules, the first and the third, are the rules of simple conversion, since in each case the converse and the convertent are the same in both quantity and quality.

The third rule can in fact be presented as a consequence of the first, granted two additional premisses, first, that SiP and PiS are respectively the contradictories of SeP and PeS, and secondly, that the following rule is allowed: 'If some proposition is converted in some way, then the contradictory of that proposition ought to be converted in the contradictory way, that is, through the proposition which contradicts the other convertent' [*De Op.* 4r$^2$].[11] Thus if $p$ converts with $q$ then $\sim p$ converts with $\sim q$. This rule of contradictory conversion can be applied in this way:

(1) SeP→PeS
(2) $\sim$(SeP)→$\sim$(PeS)
   From (1) by rule of contradictory conversion.
(3) $\sim$(SeP)↔SiP
(4) $\sim$(PeS)↔PiS
(5) SiP↔PiS
   From 2, 3 and 4 by replacement of equivalents by equivalents.

The second rule of conversion, SaP→PiS, which is the only rule of accidental conversion given by Lokert, is provable from the third rule, given also the rule, displayed in the square of opposition, that a subalternant implies its subalternate. Lokert writes: 'Every proposition which is converted into a universal proposition can also be converted into a particular, since if a proposition implies a subalternant it must also imply the subalternate of that subalternant' [*De Sill.* 10r$^2$].[12] The proof can be set out as follows:

1. SiP→PiS
   1. = rule 3.

2. SaP→SiP

From subalternant to subalternate is a valid consequence.

3. SaP→PiS

From 1. and 2. since whatever (in this case SaP) implies
an antecedent (SiP) implies that antecedent's consequent
(PiS).

Although he does not state it explicitly, we can add to Lokert's list
of conversion rules the further rule of accidental conversion: SeP→
PoS, which has a proof similar in structure to the preceding one:

1. SeP→PeS

1. = rule 1.

2. PeS→PoS

From subalternant to subalternate is a valid consequence.

3. SeP→PoS

From 1. and 2. since whatever (in this case SeP) implies
an antecedent (PeS) implies that antecedent's consequent
(PoS).

It should be noted that just as the relation between subalternant and
subalternate is a one-way implication, so also the relations between
SaP and PiS, and between SeP and PoS, are one-way implications.
Lokert employs slightly different terminology. He writes: 'Some conversions are mutual, others non-mutual. A conversion is mutual when
the convertent implies the converse, and vice versa. And a conversion
is non-mutual when the converse implies the convertent, and not vice
versa' [*De Sill.* 10r²].

It has to be understood that these rules have a carefully restricted
application. For example, Lokert points out [*De Sill.* 10v¹] that a
universal negative proposition does not have simple conversion if the
predicate term is a singular term; the convertent of 'No man is Socrates' is not a universal negative proposition, since, on Lokert's view
of the matter, the convertent in question is 'Socrates is not a man',
which he would classify as a particular negative, from which it would
follow that the conversion is merely accidental.

Furthermore, there are kinds of universal affirmative proposition
which have simple and mutual conversion, despite the rule that a
universal affirmative converts merely accidentally and non-mutually.
Lokert has in mind here those universal affirmatives which have a
distributed predicate term [*De Sill.* 10v¹], for example, 'Every man is
every animal', which is true if there is just one man and just one animal
and that one man is that one animal. Here the predicate 'animal' is
distributed, since it is possible to descend to a conjunction of singulars
under 'animal' (though the conjunction is degenerate, since there is

only one conjunct in it). Furthermore, 'a particular affirmative with a distributed predicate could be converted into a universal affirmative with mutual conversion' [*De Sill.* 10v¹]. For example, 'Some animal is every man' (which is true if there is just one man and he is an animal) converts mutually with 'Every man is an animal'.

To all such counter-examples, and further kinds also, Lokert replies by saying that: 'The rules [of conversion] are laid down for propositions composed of common terms ordinarily understood, where, in affirmative propositions, the predicates are undistributed, and in negative ones they are distributed' [*De Sill.* 10v²].

Another kind of problem case raised by Lokert concerns an area of medieval logic which has received less attention than it deserves, namely, the area which deals with propositions with complex copulas, particularly those copulas formed by two verbs which do not have the same tense. Granted the simple convertibility of particular affirmative propositions, we should expect Lokert to argue that 'A white [thing] is and was a man' converts simply with 'A man is and was white'. But he argues that the first proposition does not imply the second. 'Let us suppose' he says 'that Socrates in the past was white and in the present exists but is not white, and let us assume further than no other man exists; then the antecedent "A white [thing] is and was a man" would be true, and the consequent ("A man is and was white") would be false' [*De Sill.* 14v¹]. The antecedent is true since 'white' supposits for the past Socrates, for 'That (pointing to Socrates) is or was white' is, on Lokert's model, true. And the consequent is false, since 'That (pointing to Socrates) is white' must be false. Lokert's view is that where the copula is a complex consisting of several verbs not all with the same tense, conversion cannot be carried out mechanically in accordance with rules designed for propositions with a simple copula. In the case under consideration the convertent of 'A white [thing] is and was a man' is 'What is and was a man is or was white' [*De Sill.* 14v²).

Lokert's introduction of the proposition 'No man is Socrates' as a possible counter-example to the rule that a universal negative has a universal negative convertent, while unacceptable from a strictly Aristotelian point of view, since that view did not countenance propositions with singular predicates, is indicative of a lively interest that late medieval logicians had in propositions with singular terms. Since the expository syllogism, discussed by Lokert amongst many others, contained just such extremes, and since the provability of such syllogisms depended upon the convertibility of the premisses, rules for the convertibility of propositions with at least one singular extreme were constructed. The most obvious concern those where each extreme is a singular term. Where there is a simple copula, for example, 'is', the proposition, whether affirmative or negative, is simply and mutually convertible. If Cicero is Tully then Tully is Cicero, and vice versa; and if Cicero is not Caesar then Caesar is not Cicero, and vice versa.

Other rules of mutual convertibility could be specified. A particular affirmative with a common subject term and a singular predicate is mutually convertible with a proposition in which that common term is the predicate and the singular term is subject; and a universal negative with a common subject and a singular predicate is mutually convertible with a proposition in which that common term is the predicate and the singular term is subject. Since Lokert maintains, as we saw, that a singular proposition should be classified as a particular, it follows that 'Socrates is a man' converts mutually and also simply with 'Some man is Socrates'. But on the other hand 'Socrates is not an ass' does not convert simply with 'No ass is Socrates' though the conversion is mutual. For the converse is a particular while the convertent is universal [*De Sill.* $10v^1$].

## IV

However, not every conversion involving a proposition with a singular subject is mutual. (1) 'Socrates is not an ass' implies (2) 'No ass is Socrates'. Since a subalternant implies its subalternate, (2) implies (3) 'Some ass is not Socrates'. Hence (1) implies (3), with (1) the converse and (3) its convertent. But the move from (3) to (1) is not formally valid, since counter-examples exist. For instance, though 'Some man is not Socrates' is true it is converted into 'Socrates is not a man' which is clearly false. It seems, then, that a particular negative proposition with a singular predicate term can be converted only if the subject term also is singular (as in 'Cicero is not Caesar'). What should be said about the convertibility of a particular negative in which both extremes are common? So far we have dealt only with the convertibility of universal affirmatives, particular affirmatives and universal negatives. Particular negatives, however, raise special issues. Lokert quotes Aristotle's view that 'Particular negatives are not convertible' [*De Sill.* $10r^{1-2}$], but adds that in the textbooks particular negatives are said to be convertible by contraposition. The distinctive feature of contrapositive conversion is that the subject and predicate terms of the converse appear infinitised in the convertent, that is, the terms are negated. Thus to take the stock example, (1)

'Every man is an animal' is converted into (2) 'Every non-animal is a non-man', and (3) 'Some man is not a stone' is converted into (4) 'Some non-stone is not a non-man'. Since (2) implies (5) 'Some non-animal is a non-man' (from subalternant to subalternate is a valid consequence), (1) implies (5). Likewise since (6) 'No man is a stone' implies (3) (from subalternant to subalternate is a valid consequence), (6) implies (4). Using the notation ~( ) (a tilde operating on a bracketed term) to symbolise term negation, the foregoing examples can be formalised as follows:

(1) SaP→ ~(P)a~(S)
(2) SoP→ ~(P)o~(S)
(3) SaP→ ~(P)i~(S)
(4) SeP→ ~(P)o~(S)

But these formulae are not plain sailing. The problems arise chiefly in connection with a concept much used, as we have seen, by Lokert, namely, that of *constantia*. As we know, it was held that an affirmative proposition whose subject fails to stand for something is false, and a negative proposition whose subject term fails to stand for something was deemed true. The possibility is thus raised that a true affirmative proposition is converted contrapositively into a proposition whose subject is a negative term which fails to stand for anything, and since a proposition is not any the less affirmative for having negative terms, the convertent will be false though its converse is true. And likewise a negative proposition with a subject term which fails to refer would be true, and yet it may be converted by contraposition into a proposition which is false. Two examples should make the point clear. First, 'Every man is an entity' should be convertible by contraposition into 'Every non-entity is a non-man'. However, the first of these propositions is true; but the second is false since it is an affirmative proposition whose subject term 'non-entity' stands for nothing. Secondly, 'Some chimera is not a man' should be convertible by contraposition into 'Some non-man is not a non-chimera'. But whereas the first proposition is true since it is a negative proposition with a subject term 'chimera' which does not stand for anything, the second proposition is false since its contradictory, namely, 'Every non-man is a non-chimera', is true. For since there are no chimeras, whatever exists is a non-chimera, and hence all non-men also (i.e. as well as all men) are non-chimeras. Lokert does not tell us how these apparent counter-examples to the foregoing rules of contrapositive conversion should be dealt with. But it was commonly held that the counter-examples were more than merely 'apparent', and that a revision of the rules of contraposition was called for.

Lokert's colleague Robert Caubraith presents two proposals in his *Quadripertitum* (Paris 1510, 57v$^{1-2}$) (see appendix, no.60). First, a universal affirmative proposition is contrapositively convertible only if it is assumed that there is something which is signified by the negated predicate of the converse. In effect this amounts to the claim that the contrapositive is derived not from a single premiss but from two, one of which is the converse and the other of which is a statement of existence. Thus, though 'Every S is P' does not imply 'Every non-P is non-S', the latter proposition is implied by 'Every S is P & There exists a non-P'. This proposal enables us to deal with the fact that 'Every man is an entity' is true whereas its contrapositive is not, for Caubraith's proposal requires that the contrapositive 'Every non-entity is a non-man' should derive from the conjunction 'Every man is an entity & There exists a non-entity'. The point about his proposal is now clear. The second conjunct is false, and hence the conjunction is false, and hence a falsehood is not being derived from a truth.

Caubraith's second proposal is that a particular negative proposition is contrapositively convertible only if it is assumed that there is something which is signified by the subject term of the converse. This amounts to the claim that the contrapositive is derived not from a single premiss, but from two, one of which is the converse and the other of which is a statement of existence. Thus, though 'Some S is not P' does not imply 'Some non-P is not non-S', the latter proposition is implied by 'Some S is not P & There exists an S'. This proposal enables us to deal with the fact that 'Some chimera is not a man' is true whereas its contrapositive is not, for Caubraith's proposal requires that the contrapositive should derive from the conjunction 'Some chimera is not a man & There exists a chimera'. But since the second conjunct is false the conjunction is false, and hence it is not possible to argue validly from truth to falsity in arguing from converse to contrapositive convertent.

One further type of relation between individual propositions need here be mentioned in preparation for considering proof procedures for syllogisms. The relation in question is that of equipollence. Two propositions are equipollent if (1) the two have the same subject term, the same predicate term and the same copula, (2) the two are equivalent, (3) at least one contains the word 'not', and (4) they differ with respect to where the word 'not' occurs in them. Equipollent relations, of which there are a basic eight, are derived from the relations exhibited in the square of opposition:

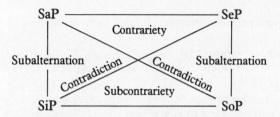

Four equipollences are based on the relation of contradiction, since each proposition in the square is equivalent to the denial of its contradictory:

(1) $SaP \leftrightarrow \sim(SoP)$

(2) $SeP \leftrightarrow \sim(SiP)$

(3) $SiP \leftrightarrow \sim(SeP)$

(4) $SoP \leftrightarrow \sim(SaP)$

Not all of (1) to (4) need appear as axioms in an axiomatised syllogistic, since (1) implies (3), and (2) implies (4). For example:

1. $SaP \leftrightarrow \sim(SoP)$
   $(1. = (1))$

2. $\sim(SaP) \leftrightarrow \sim\sim(SoP)$
   From 1. by the principle that if two propositions are equivalent then their negations also are equivalent.

3. $\sim\sim(SoP) \leftrightarrow SoP$
   Application of the law of double negation.

4. $\sim(SaP) \leftrightarrow SoP$
   From 2. and 3., replacement of equivalent by equivalent.

5. $SoP \leftrightarrow \sim(SaP)$ (= fourth of the foregoing rules of equipollence).
   From 4. by commutativity of equivalents.

Two equipollences are based on the relation of contrariety. First, every S is P if and only if no S is not P, or, in symbols:

(5) $SaP \leftrightarrow (Se\sim P)$

The symbols '$\sim P$' do not represent an infinitising of the term P, but predicate denial. (The relation between these is close. Lokert [*De Op.* $10r^2$] invokes the principle: $Si\sim(P) \rightarrow Si\sim P$).

The second equipollence based on the relation of contrariety is 'No S is P if and only if every S is not P', or, in symbols:

(6) $SeP \leftrightarrow Sa\sim P$.

Two equipollences are based on the relation of subcontrariety, namely: 'Some S is P if and only if some S is not (not P)' and 'Some S is not P if and only if some S is (not P)', or, in symbols:

(7) $SiP \leftrightarrow So\sim P$

(8) SoP↔Si~P.

From these various equipollent relations further ones can be derived, for example:

1. SeP↔~(SiP)   ( =rule(2))
2. SeP↔Sa~P   ( =rule(6))
3. ~(SiP)↔Sa~P

   From 1. and 2. since propositions equivalent to the same proposition are equivalent to each other.

4. ~~(SiP)↔~(Sa~P)

   From 3. since if two propositions are equivalent their negations also are equivalent.

5. SiP↔~~(SiP)

   Application of law of double negation.

6. SiP↔~(Sa~P)

   From 4. and 5., replacement of equivalent by equivalent.

Thus we can add:

(9) SiP↔~(Sa~P)

to the list of rules of equipollence. By a very similar line of reasoning, this time based on rules (1) and (5), the following also can be proved:

(1) SoP↔~(Se~P)

Further rules of equipollence can be proved as follows:

1. SaP↔~(SoP)   ( =rule(1))
2. SoP↔Si~P   ( =rule(8)
3. ~(SoP)↔~(Si~P)

   From 2. since if two propositions are equivalent their negations are equivalent.

4. SaP↔~(Si~P)

   From 1. and 3. since propositions equivalent to the same proposition are equivalent to each other.

Hence we can add an eleventh rule of equipollence:

(11) SaP↔~(Si~P)

A further proof:

1. SiP↔So~P   ( =rule(7))
2. SiP↔~(SeP)   ( =rule(3))
3. ~(SeP)↔So~P

   From 1. and 2. since propositions equivalent to the same proposition are equivalent to each other.

4. ~~(SeP)↔~(So~P)

   From 3. since if two propositions are equivalent their negations are equivalent.

5. ~~(SeP)↔(SeP)

   Application of law of double negation.

6. SeP$\leftrightarrow\sim$(So$\sim$P)

From 4. and 5., replacement of equivalent by equivalent.

Hence we can add a twelfth rule of equipollence:

(12) SeP$\leftrightarrow\sim$(So$\sim$P)

## V

The rules of conversion and equipollence which have just been discussed concern implicational relations between two categorical propositions. We turn now to a consideration of implicational relations where, as before, what is implied is a categorical proposition but where what that proposition follows from is not a categorical proposition but is instead either a pair of propositions or a hypothetical proposition consisting of a conjunction of two propositions. The relation between antecedent and consequent can, however, be described in the same terms in which relations between converse and convertent were described. For where the consequence is good then it is not possible for things to be as they are described by the antecedent yet not be as they are described by the consequent, and a consequence is bad if it is possible for things to be as they are described by the antecedent yet not be as described by the consequent. The difference lies only in the structure of the antecedent.

Arguments of the more complex kind just described can be classified as, in a broad sense, syllogisms. Two kinds of syllogism are distinguished, namely, those which are hypothetical and those which are categorical. A syllogism is hypothetical if at least one premiss is hypothetical: 'Common examples of this' writes Lokert 'are the argument from a disjunction and the denial of a disjunct to the affirmation of the disjunct; and the argument from a conditional and the affirmation of the antecedent to the affirmation of the consequent, and from a conditional and the denial of the consequent to the denial of the antecedent. It is agreed that such consequences are not strictly speaking syllogisms, though in the ordinary way of speaking they are called hypothetical syllogisms. Something is called a categorical syllogism when both premisses are categorical' [*De Sill.* 4r$^2$] (see appendix, no. 55). It is the categorical that is the focus of attention in the *De Sillogismis* and which will concern us for the remainder of this chapter.

In the simplest kind of case discussed by Lokert each premiss contains just two categorematic terms, but in such a case a syllogism is ill-formed if the premisses contain four distinct categorematic terms, for it is a crucial requirement of the categorical syllogism that a term which occurs in the first premiss also occurs in the second. The shared term is called the 'middle term', since it plays a mediating role in

relating the remaining two terms as subject and predicate in the conclusion, though the middle term itself cannot occur in the conclusion.
Lokert devotes considerable space to the investigation of the validity
of syllogisms whose middle term is not in fact the whole of one extreme of each premiss, but is instead a part of one or even a part of
each, as is the case in, say: 'Every ass of every man runs and every
white thing is a man. Therefore of every white thing some ass runs'
[De Sill. 19v[1]]. For in that syllogism the middle term is 'man' which
occurs as part of the subject in the first premiss. For the time being,
however, we shall concentrate on the simpler case of a syllogism
whose middle term forms the entire extreme of each of the two premisses.

In view of the fact that the basic kind of categorical syllogism has
just two premisses sharing a simple extreme, it might seem that the
premisses can display just three shapes or 'figures', for either the
middle term is subject in one premiss and predicate in the other, or it
is subject in both premisses, or it is predicate in both. These three
figures are derived from a consideration of the various kinds of position that the middle term can occupy in the two premisses, and
according to this principle of classification there are indeed just three
figures of the categorical syllogism.

But this was not how Lokert, or most other medieval logicians,
approached the question of the number of figures of the syllogism, for
Lokert made a distinction between the two premisses with respect to
the order in which they appeared. He writes: 'If the antecedent has
two conjoined principal parts then the first is called the "major" and
the second the "minor" . . . This whole argument: "Every man runs
and Socrates is a man. Therefore Socrates runs" is called a consequence . . . The major is "Every man runs" and the minor is
"Socrates is a man"' [De Term. 3v] (see appendix, no.54). The fact
that the premisses were to be regarded as in a certain order meant that
theoretically four figures could be described. Lokert describes just
three of them (see appendix, no.61): 'A due disposition of the premisses consists of a due arrangement of the three terms with respect to
subject and predicate, viz. one of the terms is subject in one premiss
and predicate in the other, according to the disposition of the first
figure; or one of the terms is predicate in each premiss, according to
the disposition of the second figure; or is subject in each premiss,
according to the disposition of the third figure' [De Sill. 4r[2]]. But in
describing the first figure he has in mind a fixed order of the premisses, for the middle term is subject only in the major premiss and is
predicate in the minor. Hence a fourth figure, ignored by Lokert, can

be described, for the middle term can be predicate in the major premiss and subject in the minor. One of the reasons for Lokert's neglect of this fourth possibility might be the ambiguity of his description of the disposition of terms in the first figure, for there he says merely that one of the terms is subject in one premiss and predicate in the other, a description which covers both the first and also the fourth figures. Other possible reasons will be discussed shortly when the syllogism has been more fully described.

Meantime, it is plain, we have to deal with four figures, not three, and the additional figure (figure four) enters the scene because whereas reversing the order of the premisses when the middle term occurs twice as subject, or twice as predicate, does not change the basic shape of the syllogism, reversing the order of the premisses when the middle term occurs as subject in one premiss and predicate in the other does change that shape. The non-middle term in the first premiss can occur as either the subject or the predicate in the conclusion, and so also can the non-middle term in the second premiss. It might then seem that there are in fact eight figures of the categorical syllogism, namely:

| a A B | 1b A B | 2a B A | 2b B A | 3a A B | 3b A B | 4a B A | 4b B A |
|-------|--------|--------|--------|--------|--------|--------|--------|
| C A   | C A    | C A    | C A    | A C    | A C    | A C    | A C    |
| ───   | ───    | ───    | ───    | ───    | ───    | ───    | ───    |
| C B   | B C    | C B    | B C    | C B    | B C    | C B    | B C    |

It should not, however, be said on this account that there are eight figures rather than four, since the number of figures is based on the number of possible dispositions of the middle term within the premisses.

Nevertheless, the foregoing schemata do make a point, for a distinction is made between syllogisms that are 'direct' and those that are 'indirect'. A syllogism is said to be direct if the predicate of the conclusion occurs in the major premiss, and indirect if the predicate of the conclusion occurs in the minor premiss. Two important pieces of terminology can now be introduced. In a direct syllogism the predicate of the conclusion is the 'major term' and the subject of the conclusion is the 'minor term'. Hence, in such a syllogism the major term occurs also in the major premiss and the minor term in the minor premiss. The situation is reversed in the case of the indirect syllogism. There the major term is the subject in the conclusion and the minor term is predicate.

Aristotle, who was the first to give a systematic exposition of syllogistic theory, omitted any reference to a fourth figure in the *Prior*

*Analytics,* and this fact alone may explain why so little attention was subsequently paid to it, though it has to be noted that Aristotle's practice and his theory were not, in this matter, as in others, entirely in step. For in at least one place [*Prior Analytics* 44a, 12–35] he discusses what is in fact a fourth figure syllogism, namely, 'If every A is B and every B is E then some E is A', which is an example of the syllogistic mood termed 'Bramantip' by the medievals.

Another reason for neglect of the fourth figure might be that the order of the premisses in the fourth figure is simply the reverse of the order in the first figure, and since the order of premisses can make no difference to the validity or otherwise of the argument, the fourth figure might seem to be merely the first in disguise, and hence investigation of the first figure would be implicitly also investigation of the fourth. There is force to this point, but it sits uneasily with the account of the major term as that term which occurs both as the predicate of the conclusion and also as an extreme in the first premiss. For reversal of the order of premisses in a first-figure syllogism results in the major term being in the second premiss. If we insist that the major term must occur in the first premiss, and that the first premiss is the major one, then the obvious conclusion to draw is that investigation of the first-figure direct syllogism is not implicitly also of the fourth-figure direct syllogism but of the fourth-figure indirect syllogism. To avoid confusion on this matter we shall hereafter follow Lokert's practice and use 'major term' to refer to the non-middle term in the first premiss, and 'major premiss' to refer to the first premiss. The direct syllogism, which was the only sort studied by Lokert, will be a syllogism in which the major term also occurs as the predicate in the conclusion.

It is clear that the relation between the first and the fourth figures is not an entirely straightforward matter. What is evident, however, is that if the order of premisses in a valid direct first-figure syllogism is reversed the result is a valid indirect fourth-figure syllogism. But reversing the order of the premisses in a valid direct first-figure syllogism and then replacing the subject by the predicate, and the predicate by the subject, in the conclusion is not a reliable way of constructing a valid direct fourth-figure syllogism. In that sense study of the first-figure syllogism is not implicitly study of the fourth figure.

## VI

There is, then, good reason for recognising four syllogistic figures, and in what follows account will be taken of the effect of general principles of syllogistic decision procedures on fourth-figure syllogisms as well as on syllogisms of the other kinds.

Given that each syllogism contains three propositions and that each proposition is universal affirmative, universal negative, particular affirmative or particular negative, i.e. is an *a*, *e*, *i* or *o* proposition, the total number of kinds of direct syllogism is 256, since there are four figures and there are 64 kinds in each figure. Each of these kinds is called a 'mood'. Thus 'Every M is P and every S is M. Therefore every S is P' is one mood in the 256. How many of the 256 are valid?

Let us use the variables *p*, *q* and *r* to represent respectively the major premiss, minor premiss and conclusion of a syllogism. Each of these can be an *a*, *e*, *i* or *o* proposition. There are 64 possible ways of assigning *a*, *e*, *i* and *o* to three variables. Those 64 are set out in table I (p.148). Clearly any categorical syllogism can be accommodated within the framework provided by one or other of these 64 ordered triples. But most of these triples cannot form a basis for a valid syllogism. Beneath two overarching regulative principles, namely, the *dici de omni* principle, that whatever is predicated of all is predicated of each, and the *dici de nullo*, that whatever is predicated of none is denied of each, Lokert presents four ground rules which cannot be infringed by any valid syllogism.

For a valid syllogism, Lokert writes (see appendix, no.61):

There is a due disposition of premisses in a due quantity and a due quality. A due quality of premisses is when one is affirmative. For that reason it is customary to give the following rule: From two negative premisses a conclusion of a syllogism cannot be drawn. A due quantity of premisses is that one is universal. For that reason another rule is presented: From [two] particular premisses no conclusion of a syllogism follows. As regards the first rule, purely negative propositions are what are at issue, since from implicitly negative premisses, or from premisses one of which is implicitly negative, a valid conclusion can follow, as is obvious in the case of exclusives and exceptives . . . Two [further] rules are customarily presented: First rule: If one of the premisses is negative the conclusion ought to be negative. What was said about the meaning of 'negative' with reference to the first of the preceding rules applies here also. Second rule: If one of the premisses is particular the conclusion likewise ought to be particular. This ought to be understood to mean that if in the premisses particularity is placed on the side of one of the extremes that particularity ought to be preserved in the conclusion. [*De Sill.* 4r²–v¹]

Lokert immediately adds what are in effect two further rules, namely, the standardly stated requirements that the middle term must be distributed in at least one premiss, and a term undistributed in a premiss cannot occur distributed in the conclusion.

*Table* I

| | p | q | r | | | p | q | r | | | p | q | r | |
|---|---|---|---|---|---|---|---|---|---|---|---|---|---|---|
| 1 | a | a | a | | 23 | e | e | i | [1,2] | 45 | i | o | a | [2,3,4] |
| 2 | a | a | e | | 24 | e | e | o | [1] | 46 | i | o | e | [3,4] |
| 3 | a | a | i | | 25 | e | i | a | [2,4] | 47 | i | o | i | [2,3] |
| 4 | a | a | o | | 26 | e | i | e | [4] | 48 | i | o | o | [3] |
| 5 | a | e | a | [2] | 27 | e | i | i | [2] | 49 | o | a | a | [2,4] |
| 6 | a | e | e | | 28 | e | i | o | | 50 | o | a | e | [4] |
| 7 | a | e | i | [2] | 29 | e | o | a | [1,2,4] | 51 | o | a | i | [2] |
| 8 | a | e | o | | 30 | e | o | e | [1,4] | 52 | o | a | o | |
| 9 | a | i | a | [4] | 31 | e | o | i | [1,2] | 53 | o | e | a | [1,2,4] |
| 10 | a | i | e | [4] | 32 | e | o | o | [1] | 54 | o | e | e | [1,4] |
| 11 | a | i | i | | 33 | i | a | a | [4] | 55 | o | e | i | [1,2] |
| 12 | a | i | o | | 34 | i | a | e | [4] | 56 | o | e | o | [1] |
| 13 | a | o | a | [2,4] | 35 | i | a | i | | 57 | o | i | a | [2,3,4] |
| 14 | a | o | e | [4] | 36 | i | a | o | | 58 | o | i | e | [3,4] |
| 15 | a | o | i | [2] | 37 | i | e | a | [2,4] | 59 | o | i | i | [2,3] |
| 16 | a | o | o | | 38 | i | e | e | [4] | 60 | o | i | o | [3] |
| 17 | e | a | a | [2] | 39 | i | e | i | [2] | 61 | o | o | a | [1,2,3,4] |
| 18 | e | a | e | | 40 | i | e | o | | 62 | o | o | e | [1,3,4] |
| 19 | e | a | i | [2] | 41 | i | i | a | [3,4] | 63 | o | o | i | [1,2,3] |
| 20 | e | a | o | | 42 | i | i | e | [3,4] | 64 | o | o | o | [1,3] |
| 21 | e | e | a | [1,2] | 43 | i | i | i | [3] | | | | | |
| 22 | e | e | e | [1] | 44 | i | i | o | [3] | | | | | |

The last two requirements play a leading role in establishing the validity of the preceding four rules concerning particular premisses and negative ones. As regards the requirement that the middle term should have distributive supposition in at least one premiss, if neither premiss affirms something about everything signified by the middle term then the things signified by the middle term in the one premiss may not be the same as the things signified by the middle term in the other premiss. But unless something signified by the middle term on one occurrence is identical with something signified by the middle term on the other occurrence the middle term cannot in fact mediate between the two extremes which constitute the subject and predicate in the conclusion. Thus, for example, that every man is an animal and that some animals are mortal does not sanction the conclusion that every man, or even that some man, is mortal, for amongst those animals which are mortal there may not be a single animal which is also a man.

The second of the two requirements laid down, that a term undistributed in a premiss cannot occur distributed in the conclusion, applies not only to syllogisms but also to arguments with a single premiss. Thus, for example, to take the simplest kind of case, that every S is P does not follow from the premiss that some S is P. And, more generally, from premisses which affirm something about only some members of a class it is not possible to draw a conclusion about every member of that class.

In the light of these two requirements let us now consider the foregoing four rules about negative premisses and particular premisses. For the sake of convenience of reference we shall number the rules 1 to 4.

*Rule 1* From two negative premisses no conclusion follows. If both premisses are universally negative then the middle term supposits for nothing for which either of the other extremes supposits. But this leaves entirely undetermined the relation of the other two extremes. Though no ass is risible or rational, every risible is rational. On the other hand, no ass is feathered or immaterial, and neither does anything immaterial have feathers. The relation between the non-middle extremes in the cases where only one premiss is universal and where neither is, can also be seen to be left undetermined.

*Rule 2* If a premiss is negative the conclusion must be negative. This is clearly true where there is just one premiss. From SeP, both SoP and PoS follow, but neither a universal affirmative nor a particular affirmative conclusion can be drawn. But it is also true where there are two premisses, for the fact that members of one class are not members of a second and are members of a third does not sanction the conclusion that some members of the second are members of the third, though it does sanction the conclusion that some members of the second are not members of the third. Thus, for example, that no man is an ass and some biped is a man sanctions the conclusion that some biped is not an ass, but not that some biped *is* an ass.

*Rule 3* From two particular premisses no conclusion follows. The justification for this is as follows: if both premisses are particular and affirmative then all terms are undistributed. Hence the middle term is undistributed, and no conclusion follows if the middle term is undistributed in each premiss. Therefore, at least one premiss is particular and negative. Hence the conclusion must be negative for (by rule 2) an affirmative conclusion cannot be drawn from premisses of which one is negative. But the major term in a negative conclusion must be distributed, and since the major term in the conclusion must be distributed in the conclusion that term must also be distributed in the major premiss. If the major and the middle terms in the major premiss are distributed then the major premiss must be a universal negative, which contradicts the hypothesis of two particular premisses. Therefore, the major premiss must be a universal affirmative or a particular negative. The first assumption contradicts the basic hypothesis, hence the major premiss must be a particular negative, and therefore must have an undistributed middle. The minor premiss must, then, have a distributed middle term. If the premiss is of the form S M, and has a distributed middle it must be negative in which case both premisses would be negative. But a valid conclusion cannot be drawn where both premisses are negative. Therefore the minor premiss must be of the form M S. But if the M is distributed in the minor premiss, that premiss is either a universal affirmative or a universal negative, each of which alternatives contradicts the basic hypothesis of two particular premisses. Therefore the assumption that a syllogism has two particular premisses and a validly drawn conclusion leads to contradiction. Hence any valid syllogism must have at least one universal premiss.

*Rule 4* If a premiss is particular the conclusion must be particular. This rule can be justified by a *reductio ad absurdum* argument. Let us suppose, contrary to what the rule lays down, that some valid syllogism has a particular premiss and a universal conclusion. [A] Let us assume that the conclusion is a universal negative. Both terms are therefore distributed, and hence both must be distributed in the premisses. But a valid syllogism has a distributed middle term in at least one premiss. Hence at least one premiss has two distributed terms. That premiss must be a universal negative (since of *a, e, i* and *o* propositions only the *e* proposition has two distributed terms). Since (by rule 1) a valid syllogism requires an affirmative premiss the other premiss must be affirmative. But our basic hypothesis is that one premiss is particular. Therefore one premiss is a particular affirmative. In that premiss neither term can be distributed. But then the syllogism must be invalid since one of the terms in that premiss ought to be distributed in view of the fact that both terms are distributed in the conclusion. [B] Let us suppose, then, alternatively that the conclusion is a universal affirmative. Then the major term is undistributed. Since the minor term is distributed the minor premiss must be either universal or negative. It cannot be negative if the syllogism has an affirmative conclusion. Hence the minor premiss must be a universal affirmative. Consequently the minor premiss has a distributed minor term and an undistributed middle. The major premiss must be affirmative and particular and hence both its terms are undistributed.

Therefore the middle term is undistributed in each premiss and hence the syllogism must be invalid. So where a premiss is particular the syllogism cannot be valid if the conclusion is universal.

The foregoing rules can now be brought to bear on the 64 ordered triples in table 1. The rules permit us to discount 48 of those triples. Each triple in the table that is not immediately followed by numerals enclosed in square brackets is not excluded by any of the rules. Those which are followed by numerals in square brackets are excluded by one or more of the rules, and the numerals correspond to the effective rule. For example, triple 61, which describes a syllogism whose premisses are both particular negatives and whose conclusion is a universal affirmative is excluded by all four rules. Since it has two negative premisses it is excluded by rule 1, for no conclusion at all follows from such premisses; since at least one premiss is negative its conclusion, by rule 2, also ought to be negative; since it has two particular premisses no conclusion, by rule 3, can follow validly; and since at least one premiss is particular its conclusion, by rule 4, ought also to be particular. This exclusion procedure leaves the sixteen ordered triples shown in table 11.

*Table* 11

| | p | q | r | | p | q | r | | p | q | r | | p | q | r |
|---|---|---|---|---|---|---|---|---|---|---|---|---|---|---|---|
| 1 | a | a | a | 2 | a | a | e | 3 | a | a | i | 4 | a | a | o |
| 6 | a | e | e | 8 | a | e | o | 11 | a | i | i | 12 | a | i | o |
| 16 | a | o | o | 18 | e | a | e | 20 | e | a | o | 28 | e | i | o |
| 35 | i | a | i | 36 | i | a | o | 40 | i | e | o | 52 | o | a | o |

Each of the sixteen strings in table 11 provides the framework of four direct syllogisms, since there are four figures. Hence our exclusion procedure leaves us with sixty-four syllogisms to investigate. For example, the first string yields the following four syllogisms:

1.1  MaP & SaM ∴ SaP (first figure)
1.2  PaM & SaM ∴ SaP (second figure)
1.3  MaP & MaS ∴ SaP (third figure)
1.4  PaM & MaS ∴ SaP (fourth figure).

Of the above four syllogisms only 1.1 is valid. 1.2 is invalid because in neither premiss is the middle term distributed; 1.3 is invalid because S is distributed in the conclusion and not in the premiss; and 1.4 is invalid because S is distributed in the conclusion and not in the premiss. Similar investigation of the remaining fifteen strings in table 11 reveals just twenty-five moods which survive both sets of exclusion procedure. Of these one is, all the same, invalid, namely, 4.4, which can be disproved, however, by invoking a further syllogistic rule, though not one that Lokert explicitly employs. The rule is that a negative conclusion cannot be drawn syllogistically from affirmative premisses.

We are left, then, with twenty-four valid moods of the direct syllogism. These are as follows (the names which the moods were called by medieval logicians are added in parentheses):

| | |
|---|---|
| 1.1   MaP & SaM ∴ SaP (Barbara) | 3.3   MaP & MaS ∴ SiP (Darapti) |
| 18.1   MeP & SaM ∴ SeP (Celarent) | 35.3   MiP & MaS ∴ SiP (Disamis) |
| 11.1   MaP & SiM ∴ SiP (Darii) | 11.3   MaP & MiS ∴ SiP (Datisi) |
| 28.1   MeP & SiM ∴ SoP (Ferio) | 20.3   MeP & MaS ∴ SoP (Felapton) |
| 3.1   MaP & SaM ∴ SiP (Barbari) | 52.3   MoP & MaS ∴ SoP (Bocardo) |
| 20.1   MeP & SaM ∴ SoP (Celaront) | 28.3   MeP & MiS ∴ SoP (Ferison) |
| | |
| 18.2   PeM & SaM ∴ SeP (Cesare) | 3.4   PaM & MaS ∴ SiP (Bramantip) |
| 6.2   PaM & SeM ∴ SeP (Camestres) | 6.4   PaM & MeS ∴ SeP (Camenes) |
| 28.2   PeM & SiM ∴ SoP (Festino) | 35.4   PiM & MaS ∴ SiP (Dimaris) |
| 16.2   PaM & SoM ∴ SoP (Baroco) | 20.4   PeM & MaS ∴ SoP (Fesapo) |
| 20.2   PeM & SaM ∴ SoP (Cesaro) | 28.4   PeM & MiS ∴ SoP (Fresison) |
| 8.2   PaM & SeM ∴ SoP (Camestrop) | 8.4   PaM & MeS ∴ SoP (Camenop) |

The twenty-four valid moods are arranged in groups of six, since there are six valid moods in each figure. Each mood is preceded by a number. The number before the point corresponds to the number of the relevant ordered triple in table I, and the number after the point indicates the figure of the valid mood.

## VII

We are now in a position to deal with the standard syllogistic proof procedure employed by medieval logicians. The procedure was known as 'reduction to the first figure', though the term 'reduction' has misleading implications. In a sense, indeed, the procedure is the opposite to reduction but we shall retain the terminology. In effect the procedure was axiomatic, in that it treated certain of the moods as axioms and derived all the other moods in the list of valid moods as theorems. The moods treated as axioms were all first-figure moods, namely, Barbara, Celarent, Darii and Ferio. The remaining two valid first figure moods did not need to be included in the list of axioms since Barbari was readily derived from Barbara (by the principle that from a subalternant to its subalternate is a valid consequence, for the universal conclusion of Barbara implies the particular conclusion of Barbari, with the premisses the same in the two moods), and Celaront was readily derived from Celarent (on the basis of the same sort of consideration). Lokert writes of these four moods: 'Every argument duly constructed according to the disposition of one of the four moods holds formally and according to the form of acceptance of the terms, and follows immediately from the rules *dici de omni* or *dici de nullo'* [*De Sill.* 18r²]. The first of these rules, that whatever is predicated of all is predicated of each, is used to prove the two affirmative moods, namely Barbara and Darii. For example, to take Darii, since every M is P it follows by *dici de omni* that each thing signified by M is signified by P. But the second premiss of Darii affirms that something, namely, an S, is signified by M. Therefore some S is P – which is what the conclusion of Darii affirms. And the second of the two rules, that whatever is predicated of none is denied of each, is used to prove the two negative moods, *viz.* Celarent and Ferio. For example, to take Ferio, since no M is P it follows by *dici de nullo* that each thing signified by M is not signified by P. But the second premiss of Ferio affirms that something, namely, an S is signified by M. Therefore some S is not P – which is what the conclusion of Ferio states.

Proofs of the valid moods can now be given. Some examples follow:

Proof of Disamis:
1. AaB & CiA→CiB  ( = syllogism in Darii)
2. CiA ↔ AiC
   By mutual simple convertibility of particular affirmatives.
3. AaB & AiC→CiB
   From 1. and 2. by replacement of an equivalent by its equivalent.
4. CiB ↔ BiC
   By mutual simple convertibility of particular affirmatives.
5. AaB & AiC→BiC
   From 3. and 4. by replacement of an equivalent by its equivalent.
6. AaB & AiC ↔ AiC & AaB
   By commutativity of conjunction.
7. AiC & AaB→BiC
   From 5. and 6. by replacement of an equivalent by its equivalent.
8. MiP & MaS→SiP  ( = Disamis) QED
   From 7. replacing A by M, B by S, C by P.

Proof of Camestrop:
1. AeB & CaA→CeB  ( = syllogism in Celarent)
2. AeB & CaA ↔ CaA & AeB
   By commutativity of conjunction.
3. CaA & AeB→CeB

From 1. and 2. by replacement of an equivalent by its equivalent.
4. AeB↔BeA
By mutual simple convertibility of universal negatives.
5. CaA & BeA→CeB
From 3. and 4. by replacement of an equivalent by its equivalent.
6. CeB↔BeC
By mutual simple convertibility of universal negatives.
7. CaA & BeA→BeC
From 5. and 6. by replacement of an equivalent by its equivalent.
8. BeC→BoC
From subalternant to subalternate is a valid consequence.
9. CaA & BeA→BoC
From 7. and 8. since whatever implies an antecedent implies the consequent of that antecedent.
10. PaM & SeM→SoP    ( = Camestrop) QED
From 9., replacing A by M, B by S, C by P.

Proof of Bocardo:
1. AaB & CaA→CaB    ( = syllogism in Barbara)
2. ~(CaB) & CaA→~(AaB)
From 1. From the contradictory of the conclusion plus the second premiss to the contradictory of the first premiss is a valid consequence [*De Sill.* 24v²]; in modern notation:
$$(P \& Q) \to R \therefore (\sim R \& Q) \to \sim P.$$
3. CoB↔~(CaB)
By equipollence rule 4.
4. CoB & CaA→~(AaB)
From 2. and 3. by replacement of an equivalent by its equivalent.
5. AoB↔~(AaB)
By equipollence rule 4.
6. CoB & CaA→AoB
From 4. and 5. by replacement of an equivalent by its equivalent.
7. MoP & MaS→SoP    ( = Bocardo) QED
From 6., replacing A by S, B by P, C by M.

Granted Barbara, Celarent, Darii and Ferio, the remaining twenty moods of the valid direct syllogism can be proved in the ways just illustrated. The axiom which should appear as the first premiss, i.e. the first figure syllogism to which the syllogism which has to be proved should be 'reduced', is indicated by the initial letter of the syllogism's name. Any syllogism whose name begins with a 'B' should be reduced to Barbara, one beginning with 'C' should be reduced to Celarent, one with 'D' to Darii, and one with 'F' to Ferio.

But the names give away more than this, for they also indicate how the reduction is to be accomplished. First, the first three vowels in the name indicate whether the three propositions constituting the syllogism are *a*, *e*, *i* or *o* propositions. Secondly, if the consonant immediately following a vowel is an 's' the premiss containing that vowel should be simply converted. If the consonant immediately following a vowel is a 'p' the premiss containing the vowel should be accidentally converted. If one of the first two vowels is immediately followed by an 'm' the two premisses should be placed in reverse order. And finally, if one of the first two vowels is immediately followed by a 'c' the negation of the premiss containing that vowel should replace the conclusion, and the negation of the conclusion should replace the premiss. Thus for example, Baroco is reduced to Barbara by replacing the second premiss in Barbara with the negation of the conclusion, and replacing the conclusion with the negation of the second premiss. This single move is sufficient to produce a syllogism in Baroco. Camenop is reduced to Celarent by reversing the order of the premisses in Celarent and replacing the conclusion in Celarent by its accidental convertent.

Baroco and Bocardo are distinctive among the twenty-four valid moods in that procedures of conversion and transposition were not considered sufficient to effect a reduction to a first figure syllogism, but reduction *per impossibile* was employed. That is, the conclusion of the syllogism was assumed to be false and it was argued that in that case one of the premisses had to be false also. Hence granted the truth of one of the premisses, the falsity of the conclusion implied the falsity of the other premiss. Baroco and Bocardo differ, first, with respect to which premiss is assumed to be true. And they differ, secondly and relatedly, with respect to their figure, for replacing the second premiss in Barbara by the negated conclusion of Barbara transforms the syllogism to one of the second figure, and replacing the first premiss by the negated conclusion transforms the syllogism to one of the third figure.

The logical feature that makes Baroco and Bocardo distinct among the twenty-four, and which prompted the employment of the *reductio per impossibile* procedure is the presence of an *o* proposition in the premisses, for such a proposition, as we saw, could not be converted either simply or accidentally (from 'Some animals are not men' we can derive neither 'No men are animals' nor 'Some men are not animals'). And conversion of the other premiss is out of the question for the convertent of a universal affirmative is a particular affirmative, and hence by converting in the only premiss in Baroco and Bocardo where conversion is theoretically possible we would construct a syllogism both of whose premisses were particular. And, as we know, such a syllogism cannot be valid.

On the other hand, if it were permitted to employ the rules of obversion,[13] both Baroco and Bocardo could be reduced to a first figure syllogism without reducing *per impossibile*. For example, the following is a formally valid proof of Bocardo, though it should be noted that it is not a proof that Lokert himself sanctioned:

1. AaC & ~(B)iA→~(B)iC
   1. is a form of Darii.
2. AoB & AaC→AoB
   From a conjunction to a conjunct is a valid consequence.
3. AoB↔Ai~(B)
   A rule of obversion, closely related to equipollence rule 8.
4. Ai~(B)↔~(B)iA
   By mutual simple convertibility of particular affirmatives.
5. AoB↔~(B)iA
   From 3. and 4. by replacement of an equivalent by its equivalent.
6. AoB & AaC→~(B)iA
   From 2. and 5. by replacement of an equivalent by its equivalent.
7. AoB & AaC→AaC
   From a conjunction to a conjunct is a valid consequence.
8. AoB & AaC→AaC & ~(B)iA
   From 6. and 7. since from an antecedent to the conjunction of its consequents is a valid consequence (i.e. if $p$ implies $q$ and also implies $r$ then $p$ implies $q$ & $r$).
9. AoB & AaC→~(B)iC
   From 1. and 8. since whatever implies an antecedent implies the consequent of that antecedent.
10. ~(B)iC↔Ci~(B)
    By mutual simple convertibility of particular affirmatives.
11. AoB & AaC→Ci~(B)
    From 9. and 10. by replacement of an equivalent by its equivalent.
12. Ci~(B)→CoB
    By obversion (see justification of line 3.).

13. AoB & AaC→CoB

From 11. and 12. since whatever implies an antecedent also implies the consequent of that antecedent.

14. MoP & MaS→SoP ( =Bocardo) QED

From 13. replacing A by M, B by P, C by S.

In the foregoing proof of Bocardo, the third-figure syllogism is reduced to Darii. Of course, the initial letter of the name 'Bocardo' indicates that the syllogism should be reduced to Barbara. But that assumes that the letter 'c' in 'Bocardo' is acted on and that in consequence the reduction will be carried out by the method of reduction *per impossibile*.

Although only the two moods, Baroco and Bocardo, signal by the letter 'c' that they are to be reduced to a first figure syllogism by way of a *reductio per impossibile* proof, this is not to say that such a procedure can be used effectively on those two moods only. Lokert writes (see appendix, no.62):

> A syllogism of the second figure is reduced *per impossibile* when from the major and the opposite of the conclusion the opposite of the minor is inferred. Nor is Baroco alone reduced *per impossibile* to the first figure, but every syllogism in each figure or in any other mood can be reduced *per impossibile*. A syllogism in Cesare is reduced *per impossibile* to a syllogism in Ferio, and a syllogism in Camestres is likewise reduced to one in Darii, also Festino to Celarent, and Baroco to Barbara. So it is not unsatisfactory for the one syllogism to be reduced to an affirmative syllogism and also to a negative one. This is evident in the case of Camestres which is reduced by conversion and transposition of the premisses to Celarent [a negative mood] and *per impossibile* to Darii [an affirmative mood]. [*De Sill.* 28r²–v¹]

The examples mentioned here are all drawn from syllogisms of the second figure, omitting only the two subalternate moods Cesaro and Camestrop from the list of valid moods in that figure. But the point can be illustrated as well with moods of the third figure. Having shown how Darapti, Disamis, Datisi, Felapton and Ferison are reduced in the normal way, Lokert then adds (see appendix, no.63): 'Disamis is reduced to Celarent, Datisi to Ferio, and Ferison to Darii, all by reduction *per impossibile*, by inferring the contradictory of the major from the minor and the contradictory of the conclusion. And Darapti is reduced to Celarent, and Felapton to Barbara *per impossibile* by inferring the contradictory of the major from the minor and the contradictory of the conclusion' [*De Sill.* 33r²]. Thus, for example,

MiP & MaS→SiP ( = Disamis) is reduced *per impossibile* to SeP & MaS→MeP ( = Celarent, as is clear if S is replaced by M, and M by S), as well as being reduced directly to MaS & PiM→PiS ( = Darii, as is clear if S is replaced by P, and P by S).

In the foregoing quotation from the *De Sillogismis* it is shown that, with respect to reduction *per impossibile*, Disamis and Datisi fall under a principle of classification from which Darapti is excluded. A further relation in which Disamis and Datisi stand to Darapti is mentioned by Lokert. We have met frequently the principle that from subalternant to subalternate is a valid consequence. But it has to be noted that though the validity of an argument is preserved if a universal conclusion is replaced by its subalternate, it is not necessarily preserved if a universal premiss is replaced by its subalternate. Now, the difference between Darapti and Disamis is that the first premiss in Disamis is the subalternate of the first premiss in Darapti and the difference between Darapti and Datisi is that the second premiss of Datisi is the subalternate of the second premiss of Darapti. Lokert writes (see appendix, no.64): 'Something is a good argument in Darapti from whose major and the subalternate of the minor there does not follow a conclusion in Datisi. And something is a good argument in Darapti from whose minor and the subalternate of the major there does not follow a conclusion in Disamis. And the same thing should be said about Felapton in relation to Bocardo and Ferison' [*De Sill.* 34r$^{1-2}$].

This point is puzzling, and unfortunately Lokert's examples do little to shed light on the matter. He asserts for the sake of argument, but then goes on to accept (in 34r$^{1-2}$):

> This argument is good in Darapti, 'Every man is an animal and every man possibly is risible; therefore a risible possibly is an animal'. But under the major premiss, by subsuming the subalternate of the minor, the conclusion does not follow in Datisi. And likewise this argument is valid in Darapti, 'Every man possibly is an animal and every man is risible; therefore a risible possibly is an animal'. Yet from the minor and the subalternate of the major that conclusion does not follow in Disamis. [*De Sill.* 33v$^1$] (see appendix, no.65)

It is possible that, as Lokert claims, the Disamis and Datisi syllogisms he describes here are invalid, though it is not certain for it is unclear just what effect the modal adverb has on their validity. But by the same token neither is it clear that the Darapti syllogism itself is valid. But certainly a separate argument, and one not provided by Lokert, is required if it is to be shown that he is right to ascribe validity to the Darapti syllogism and not to the other two. It is correct to say that a

valid argument, all three of whose propositions are universal, loses its
validity if one of the premisses is replaced by its subalternate and the
conclusion is left universal, though there could be no example of such
a syllogism from the third figure, since it is a feature of that figure (and
a distinctive one) that each of its valid moods has a particular conclusion. But the point is that howsoever a syllogism in Datisi or Disamis comes to be constructed, whether by operating on a syllogism in
Darapti or by some other means, the syllogism duly constructed
must, if it really has the form of Datisi or Disamis, be valid.

There is certainly no significant sense in which Darapti has priority
over Disamis and Datisi in the system. On the contrary none has
priority over the others. All can be proved from a first figure mood in a
single short sweep of argument whose basic structure permits the
proof of the three moods in any order. For example:

1. MeP & SaM→SeP   (=Celarent)
2. SeP→SoP
   From subalternant to subalternate is a valid inference.
3. MeP & SaM→SoP
   From 1. and 2. since whatever implies an antecedent implies
   the consequent of that antecedent.
4. ~(SoP) & SaM→~(MeP)
   From 3. since the contradictory of the conclusion plus the
   minor implies the contradictory of the major.
5. SaP & SaM→MiP
   From 4. by equipollence (~(SoP)↔SaP, and
   ~(MeP)↔MiP).
6. MaP & MaS→SiP   (=Darapti) QED
   From 5. replacing S by M, M by S.
7. ~(SeP) & SaM→~(MeP)
   From 1. since the contradictory of the conclusion plus the
   minor implies the contradictory of the major.
8. SiP & SaM→MiP
   From 7. by equipollence (~(SeP)↔SiP, and
   ~(MeP)↔MiP).
9. MiP & MaS→SiP   (=Disamis) QED
   From 8. replacing S by M, M by S.
10. MiP & MaS↔MaS & MiP
    By commutativity of conjunction.
11. MaS & MiP→SiP
    From 9. and 10. replacing an equivalent by its equivalent.
12. SiP↔PiS
    By mutual simple convertibility of particular affirmatives.

13. MaS & MiP→PiS

From 11. and 12. replacing an equivalent by its equivalent.

14. MaP & MiS→SiP   ( = Datisi) QED

From 13. replacing S by P, P by S.

## VIII

Inspection reveals that as well as the so-called subaltern*ate* moods (Barbari, Celaront, Cesaro, Camestrop and Camenop) whose premisses permit also the subalternant of the conclusion, there are syllogisms which are subaltern*ant* in the sense that the premisses are stronger than they need to be in order to sanction the conclusion, for the premisses contain a universal premiss which could be replaced by its subalternate without invalidating the syllogism. Of course, this move works for only a special class of argument. Most especially the conclusion must already be particular for otherwise a universal conclusion would be drawn from a set of premisses not both of which were universal; and both premisses must, before replacement occurs, be universal for otherwise replacement would result in both premisses being particular, and from such premisses, as we know, no conclusion can validly be drawn.

Two classes of syllogism emerge from this discussion. First are those moods where replacing a universal premiss by its subalternate results, without further change, in a valid mood. Four valid moods are within this class, namely, Darapti, which is transformed into Disamis and also into Datisi; Felapton, which becomes Bocardo and also Ferison; Bramantip, which becomes Dimaris; and Fesapo, which becomes Fresison.

In the second class are those syllogisms whose validity is preserved if a universal premiss is replaced by its subalternate but only if its conclusion is likewise replaced – the conclusion is forced into particularity along with the premiss. The four transformations in this class are from Barbara to Darii, Celarent to Ferio, Cesare to Festino, and Camestres to Baroco.

It has to be noted, however, that it is not the case that wherever a valid mood has two universal premisses, validity is preserved if either of those premisses is replaced by its subalternate, even if the conclusion is replaced by its subalternate. For example, in the first figure every valid mood has a universal major premiss, and replacing that premiss by its subalternate is bound to result in an invalid syllogism whether the conclusion is already particular or not. For if we assume that the major of a first figure syllogism is particular it will follow that the subject (the middle term) must be undistributed. But the minor premiss must be affirmative since there can be no negative minor in a first-figure syllogism (the reason for this will be given shortly). Therefore the middle term of the minor (i.e. the predicate) must be undistributed. Hence the syllogism commits the fallacy of the undistributed middle. (The reason why the minor premiss in a first-figure syllogism must be affirmative is as follows: if it is negative, the major premiss must be affirmative and hence the major term must be undistributed. But if a premiss is negative the conclusion must be negative. And where a conclusion is negative its major term must be distributed. Hence the major term would be undistributed in the premiss and distributed in the conclusion.)

All valid second-figure syllogisms, just like all valid first-figure ones, have a universal major premiss, and replacing that premiss by its subalternate is bound to result in an invalid syllogism, whether the conclusion is already particular or not. If the major in a second-figure syllogism were particular it would be either affirmative or negative. If it were affirmative the major term would be undistributed as would be the middle term. Hence the middle term must be distributed in the minor premiss. Hence the minor premiss must be negative, and so the conclusion also must be negative. Consequently the major term in the conclusion must be distributed. Yet that term is undistributed in the major premiss. Let us then suppose that the major premiss is negative. Then the major term must be undistributed. But the conclusion must be negative, since *ex hypothesi* a premiss is negative, and in that conclusion the major term must be distributed. Hence a basic rule of validity is broken if we suppose the major premiss in the second figure to be particular. Therefore the first premiss cannot *salva validitate* be replaced by its subalternate.

The third figure has already been considered in some detail. As regards the fourth figure, one rule relevant to our present concern is that no universal negative premiss can be replaced *salva validitate* by its subalternate. For let us suppose that the major premiss is a particular negative. Its major term must, therefore, be undistributed. But if the premiss is negative so also is the conclusion, and the major term in a negative conclusion must be distributed. If, on the other hand, the minor premiss is a particular negative then its middle term is undistributed. Hence, to avoid the fallacy of the undistributed middle, the middle term must be distributed in the major premiss. But since the minor premiss is negative the major must be affirmative, in which case its middle term is undistributed. Hence, in a valid fourth figure syllogism with a universal negative premiss validity is lost if that premiss is replaced by its subalternate.

Before leaving the topic of the basic forms of the syllogism, one
point may be added concerning the kind of figure we have just been
considering, namely, the fourth. We quoted earlier a judgment by
Lokert that: 'Nor is Baroco alone reduced *per impossibile* to the first
figure, but every syllogism in each figure or in any other mood can
be reduced *per impossibile*' [*De Sill.* 28r²–v¹]. Lokert discussed this
point, as we saw, in connection with valid moods of the second figure,
and we considered its implications for the third figure also, and found
that there too his principle held good. Nothing was then said about
the fourth figure, the one whose valid direct moods Lokert ignored
throughout the *De Sillogismis*. But it should be noted that had he
turned his attention to that figure he would have had to revise his
principle, for it fails in application to the fourth figure. The trouble
arises from the fact that altering a fourth figure syllogism by replacing
either premiss by the contradictory of the conclusion and replacing
the conclusion by the contradictory of the replaced premiss results in a
syllogism which is still in the fourth figure. That is, in the case of
figures two and three, any valid syllogism can be reduced in a single
step to a valid mood of the first figure by replacing a premiss (the
minor premiss if the figure is second, and the major premiss if the
figure is third) by the negated conclusion, and the conclusion by the
negation of the replaced premiss. But in the case of the fourth figure
switching the minor and the conclusion in this way results in a fourth
figure syllogism, as also does switching the major premiss and the
conclusion. Thus the fourth figure A*B & B*C→C*A results, when
the major and the conclusion are switched, in C*A & B*C→A*B
(using '*' as a variable ranging over *a, e, i* and *o*). Since B is, after the
switch, the major term (since it is the predicate in the conclusion) it
must figure in the major premiss. The premiss just reached must
therefore be commuted. The result is B*C & C*A→A*B, which is of
the fourth figure. The same result is reached by switching the minor
premiss and the conclusion. In this sense, at any rate, the fourth figure
is further removed from the first than is either the second or the third.

## IX

Before leaving the topic of the syllogism a few words should, for the
sake of completeness, be said about Lokert's brief account of the
so-called 'expository syllogism'.

In various places in the *De Sillogismis* Lokert attends to the role
played in syllogistic reasoning by the relative pronoun of identity, that
is, 'the same'. Thus, for example, the rule that a conclusion cannot
follow syllogistically from two particular premisses might be ques-

tioned on the ground that valid syllogisms with just such premisses
can be constructed if the relative pronoun of identity is employed in
one of the premisses. One example Lokert gives is 'Some man runs
and Socrates is the same man. Therefore Socrates runs' [*De Sill.* 6r¹].
The minor premiss is particular, given his classification of singulars,
and the argument may be a valid first-figure syllogism. But the argument has an odd ring in English. Whether it is valid depends on
whether a certain interpretation is correct; and about that there is
room for dispute. However, one need have no qualms about the following closely related third-figure syllogism: 'Some man runs and the
same man is white. Therefore some white thing runs'. If the minor
premiss is indeed particular, and at any rate it seems more appropriate
to classify it as particular than as universal, then such an argument
does in fact appear to constitute a counter-example to the principle
that from two particular premisses no conclusion follows syllogistically.

However, it might be said, and Lokert would certainly say, that it is
not a counter-example, for the description of the 'due disposition' of
terms in a syllogism made no reference to relative pronouns of identity, and hence that it has to be understood that the rules of validity
apply only to syllogisms lacking such pronominal devices.

But it has to be noted that the same effect can be secured without
explicit employment of the relative of identity. For if a proper name is
employed in the first premiss, then recurrence of that name in the
second premiss carries with it the implication that it is the *same* thing
that is being signified in the two propositions. Thus, for example, in
'Socrates is a man and Socrates is white. Therefore a white thing is a
man' it is assumed that the one man is referred to by the two occurrences of the name. Two things should be noted about this syllogism.
The first is that, given that singular propositions are to be classified as
particulars, then both premisses in the syllogism are particular. The
second is that the syllogism is clearly valid, and hence that there seem
after all to be counter-examples to the principle that no conclusion
follows validly from a pair of particulars. Even so, Lokert can reply
that the rules of syllogistic validity were designed only for cases where
the middle term is a common term and not a singular one. Of course,
had he followed the Ockhamist line and argued that singular propositions should be classified as universals, for in an affirmative singular
proposition the predicate term is said to supposit for *everything* for
which the subject term supposits, this problem would not have arisen.

Nevertheless, that syllogisms of the sort described can be valid is an
interesting logical fact that can hardly be disregarded, and Lokert

does not disregard it. He deals with such syllogisms under the heading 'expository syllogism'. Its definition is given as follows: 'An expository syllogism is one whose middle term is held singularly' [*De Sill.* 42r¹] (see appendix, no.66). Thus it is not sufficient that a singular term occurs as an extreme – 'Every man is mortal and Socrates is a man. Therefore Socrates is mortal' is not an expository syllogism. For a syllogism requires to have the same singular term in two extremes if it is to be expository.

Granting the possibility of syllogisms structured in this way, Lokert writes: 'In arguing expositorily it should be observed that there are similar conditions as regards mood and figure on the side of the extremes and of the middle just as in arguing with a common middle term, except for the distribution of the middle for which, in arguing expositorily, the singularity of the middle term is posited' [*De Sill.* 42r¹⁻²] (see appendix, no.66). Thus the requirement that a term distributed in the conclusion must also be distributed in the premiss is valid for the expository syllogism no less than for the ordinary kind. But the requirement that the middle term must be distributed in at least one premiss has no application in the expository syllogism, for there the middle term is already singular on each occurrence and hence descent to a conjunction of singulars is not possible; it is, so to say, too late.

The rule, that from a set of premisses one of which is negative only a negative conclusion follows syllogistically, holds for the expository syllogism also. From 'Socrates is not white and Socrates is a man' the only proposition that follows syllogistically is 'Some man is not white'; the two middle terms cannot be combined in an affirmative conclusion. It should be noted here that had it been the minor premiss rather than the major that was negative in the foregoing example no conclusion would have followed. For from 'Socrates is a man and Socrates is not white' we cannot validly conclude 'Some white thing is not a man', for it could be that every white thing is a man even though the class of men who are white does not include Socrates.

Why the syllogism works if the first premiss is negative and fails if the second premiss is negative, is an interesting question which we shall not pursue here. Lokert had, unfortunately, nothing to say on this topic and little on the expository syllogism, his very brief discussion being added as an appendage to his long and densely packed discussion of syllogisms composed of common, rather than singular, terms. We shall turn instead, in the following chapter, to a consideration of salient features of his account of contradiction, and of other forms of opposition between propositions.

# CHAPTER FIVE
## Opposed Propositions

### I

The square of opposition displays the relations of contradiction, contrariety, subcontrariety and subalternation. Lokert asserts [*De Opp*. 11[1]] that 'taken widely' all four relations can be classed as relations of 'opposition', but 'taken strictly' only the first three can be so classed. The last of the four relations is the odd man out with respect to an important principle of classification, for two propositions can be related as subalternant to subalternate only if they are of the same quality, whereas two propositions can be contradictories, contraries or subcontraries only if they are opposed in quality.

An important area of late medieval logic involved investigation of propositions opposed in this last way. These investigations contributed to the theory of 'opposition'. Lokert wrote a long treatise (178 columns of text) entitled *De Oppositionibus*, packed with ideas and arguments about the various kinds of relation of opposition. Much of the extremely difficult discussion is concerned with close analysis of highly technical matters which are perhaps best left for exposition and criticism in a separate work. Here I shall focus on certain aspects of that discussion which shed further light on Lokert's views on a topic we have already investigated, namely, supposition. His discussion of oppositions sheds light on many aspects of his system of logic, and is particularly interesting for the light that it casts on the last mentioned topic.

It is important here to be clear that two propositions are opposed,[1] if at all, in virtue of a syntactic relation in which they stand to each other, rather than in virtue of any semantic considerations. Thus, it might be argued that subcontrary propositions should not be described as opposed, for it is possible for both to be true, and when they are both true they are surely not opposed to each other. But this misses the point of classifying them as opposed, which is not to highlight a semantic fact about the relations between their truth values, but to highlight the syntactic fact that what distinguishes a pair of subcontrary propositions is that one of them has a negation sign where the other does not. Of course, we should expect certain semantic relations between the propositions to be attendant upon such a major syntactic relation. But the point is that the semantic considerations are secondary when it is a matter of deciding whether two propositions are or are not opposed.

Once the syntactic distinction between opposed propositions is noted something can then be said about their semantic relation. In particular Lokert couches a series of 'laws of opposites' in semantic terms. 'A law of opposites' he writes 'is said to be a proposition clarifying the agreement and disagreement of such propositions with regard to truth and falsity' [*De Opp.* 2v[1]]. The laws are as follows:

> The law of contraries is this: if one of a pair of contrary propositions is true the other is false, and not vice versa, so that contrary propositions cannot be true together but can well be false together . . . The law of contradictories is this: if one contradictory is true the other is false, so that contradictories cannot be true together or false together.[2] And the law of subcontraries is this: if one of the subcontraries is false the other is true, and not vice versa. Subcontrary propositions cannot be false together but they can be true together. [*De Opp.* 2r[2]–v[1]] (see appendix, no.69)

However, cases can arise where the usual relation between syntactic and semantic criteria is put under strain, where, that is to say, attention to the semantics of the situation leads to classifying a pair of propositions as opposites of one sort, and attention to the syntactic facts, for example that the two propositions are universals differing only in that in one of them a negation sign is placed immediately before the predicate, leads to classifying the pair of propositions as opposites of a different kind. With this in mind Lokert makes a distinction between opposites 'in the manner of expression only' and opposites 'as regards the law only' [*De Opp.* 2v[1-2]]. Propositions are opposites of a certain kind 'in the manner of expression only' if they are opposites of that kind with respect to purely syntactic features only, for example, whether they are universal or particular and how, if at all, they are negated; and they are opposites of a certain kind 'as regards the law only' if they are opposites of that kind with respect to the kind of semantic features that are expressed in the various laws of opposition.

Lokert illustrates this distinction with the pair of propositions 'Every man is himself' and 'Every man is not himself', of which he says: 'They are contraries as regards the mode of expression only, and contradictories as regards the law only' [*De Opp.* 2v[2]]. The point he is making is that if the decision concerning the kind of opposites in question here is made on the basis of purely syntactic considerations then what has to be noted is that one of the propositions is a universal affirmative and the other is a universal negative, and the sole difference is the occurrence of a negation sign in one of them; and this is the distinction between propositions occupying the top left and top right hand corners in the square of opposition. In other words, as regards mode of expression the propositions are contraries. But as regards the truth values of these two propositions the situation is quite otherwise. Granted the existence of men, the universal affirmative proposition is necessarily true, and the universal negative necessarily false. And since, according to the law of contradictory opposites, two propositions are contradictories if they cannot be true together or false together, the two propositions must after all be contradictories. In particular, despite the syntactic considerations, they cannot be contraries since it is impossible for them to be false together, since it is impossible for one of them to be false at all. The point still stands if questions of *constantia* are brought to bear, for if no man exists, then the universal affirmative proposition is bound to be false, since the subject term does not signify anything that is, and the universal negative is bound to be true for precisely the same reason.[3]

## II

Lokert presents a number of rules for the construction of opposites of given types of proposition. In this section we shall work our way through some of the simpler rules that he presents. The problem that he sets himself can be simply stated. It is this: given any proposition, what transformations should be carried out on it in order to construct a proposition which is the contrary, contradictory or subcontrary opposite of the original proposition? It is not assumed that every proposition has a contrary, contradictory and subcontrary; indeed Lokert is quite explicit that some propositions cannot be opposed in all three ways. But he does say what marks a proposition must have if it is to have an opposite of a given kind. We shall follow certain of these transformation rules.

Lokert asserts: 'In two contradictory propositions there ought not to remain the same universality nor the same particularity; but any universality in the one contradictory proposition ought to be changed into particularity in the other, and vice versa' [*De Opp.* 5r[1]]. The simplest application of this rule, that is, the one which invokes propositions of the kind employed in the basic square of opposition, is spelled out in these terms: 'A term in one of a pair of contradictories distributed in respect of a term with merely confused disjunctive supposition, in the other contradictory ought to have determinate supposition in relation to the distributed term which in the other proposition has merely confused disjunctive supposition. For example, "A man is not white" will have a contradictory in which the "white" will have merely confused disjunctive supposition' [*De Opp.* $5r^2$] (see appendix, no.70).

The simplest kind of case of a proposition in which a term has distributive supposition in relation to a term with merely confused disjunctive supposition is the universal affirmative 'Every A is B'. What Lokert is saying is that the contradictory of this proposition is constructed by transforming 'Every A is B' into a negative proposition (since it must be opposed in quality) in which the term with distributive supposition (*viz.* A) has determinate supposition, and the term with merely confused supposition (B) has distributive supposition. The proposition thus constructed is the particular negative 'Some A is not B'. This clearly accords with the requirement that 'any universality in the one contradictory proposition ought to be changed into particularity in the other, and vice versa', for 'A' is distributed in the first proposition and not in the second, and 'B' is distributed in the second proposition and not in the first.

Attention to the formal expression of this rule reveals a fact about merely confused disjunctivee supposition that has not previously emerged in our examination of Lokert's logic. Since in 'Every A is B' 'A' has distributive supposition and 'B' has merely confused disjunctive supposition, it follows that descent must first be made to a conjunction of singular propositions under 'A' and then to a disjunction of singular terms under 'B'. The moves can be represented as follows:

1. Every A is B
2. $A^1$ is B & $A^2$ is B
3. $(A^1$ is $B^1 \vee B^2) \& (A^2$ is $B^1 \vee B^2)$

(I assume here, as elsewhere, that each domain has just two members. The assumption keeps the formulae down to a manageable size). Likewise descent from 'Some A is not B' should be made first to a disjunction of singular propositions under A and then to a conjunction of singular propositions under 'B'. Thus:

4. Some A is not B
5. $A^1$ is not B $\vee A^2$ is not B
6. $(A^1$ is not $B^1 \& A^1$ is not $B^2) \vee (A^2$ is not $B^1 \& A^2$ is not $B^2)$

Since 1 and 4 are contradictories, 3 is equivalent to the negation of 6. The negation of 6 is equivalent to:

7. $\sim(A^1$ is not $B^1 \& A^1$ is not $B^2) \& \sim(A^2$ is not $B^1 \& A^2$ is not $B^2)$

which in its turn is equivalent to:

8. $(A^1 \text{ is } B^1 \vee A^1 \text{ is } B^2) \& (A^2 \text{ is } B^1 \vee A^2 \text{ is } B^2)$.

It follows from this that $A^1$ is $B^1 \vee B^2$ (i.e. the first conjunct in 3) is equivalent to $A^1$ is $B^1 \vee A^1$ is $B^2$ (i.e. the first conjunct in 8). The implication of this is that two singular propositions are equivalent if they have the same subject, the same copula and the same predicate save that in one proposition the predicate has determinate supposition and in the other the predicate has merely confused disjunctive supposition.

To display the relation formally it is necessary to introduce into one of the propositions a special quantifier whose function was noted in chapter two. The quantifier is '$a$' and its effect is to impose merely confused supposition on the immediately following term. Thus, one implication of the contradictoriness of 'Every A is B' and 'Some A is not B' is that the following equivalence is valid:

9. $A^1 \text{ is } B \longleftrightarrow A^1 \text{ is } a \text{ B}$.

This is one of the very few kinds of case where a proposition's truth value is unaffected by the transformation of a term in it from one with determinate supposition to one with merely confused supposition.[4]

It has to be noted here that the situation just described can arise in its present form only because of Lokert's requirement that a singular proposition should be classified as a particular. For it is in virtue of that requirement that 'B' in '$A^1$ is B' would naturally be treated as having determinate supposition, and hence has to be operated on by the $a$ quantifier in order to ensure that it has merely confused supposition. Had Lokert taken the more frequently followed Ockhamist line that singular propositions are universal then the 'B' would naturally have merely confused supposition and there would be no need to introduce the $a$ quantifier.

In describing the syntactic properties of the contrary of the universal affirmative 'Every A is B' Lokert writes: 'A term distributed in one of a pair of contrary propositions in respect of a term with merely confused disjunctive supposition, in the other proposition has distributive supposition . . . in respect of such a term [*sic* the term distributed in the first proposition] provided that the same universality remains in both propositions' [*De Opp.* 5v¹] (see appendix, no.71). (Where I have placed dots in the foregoing quotation Lokert adds 'or even determinate supposition'. This is clearly an error. And it is to be noted that in furnishing examples of contrary propositions he ignores the remark about determinateness.) Hence the proposition being described as the contrary of 'Every A is B' is:

10. No A is B.

In 10 both 'A' and 'B' have distributive supposition. Hence it is immaterial whether descent is made first under 'A' or first under 'B'. Whichever is given precedence the outcome will be a conjunction of negative singular propositions, *viz.*

11. $A^1$ is not $B^1$ & $A^1$ is not $B^2$ & $A^2$ is not $B^1$ & $A^2$ is not $B^2$.

3, which is the symbolic spelling out of 'Every A is B', is equivalent to 8, and it is easy to show that 8 and 11 are contraries. For the truth of either implies the falsity of the other, and both can be false, as, for example, where $A^1$ is $B^1$ and no other A is identical to any B.

Lokert further points out that universal propositions can be opposed not only by contraries and contradictories but also by subcontraries. For 'Every A is B' has a subcontrary, described as follows: 'A term which is distributable in one of a pair of subcontrary propositions in respect of a term with merely confused disjunctive supposition, in the other subcontrary will be able to have confused disjunctive supposition in relation to the other distributed term which had confused disjunctive supposition in the other proposition' [*De Opp.* 5v²] (see appendix, no.72). What is being said here is that 'Every A is B' has a subcontrary in which the 'A' has merely confused supposition and the 'B' has distributive supposition. Without the use of special quantifiers such a proposition cannot be constructed, and indeed much of the impetus in early sixteenth-century logic for developing the theory of special quantifiers derived specifically from the need to describe the transformation rules by which, given any proposition, its contrary, contradictory or subcontrary opposite could be described. Using the special quantifier '*a*' the subcontrary proposition described by Lokert can readily be constructed. It is

12. *a* A is not B.

By virtue of the *a* the subject term has merely confused disjunctive supposition and by virtue of being governed directly by the negation operator the predicate term has distributive supposition.

That 'Every A is B' and '*a* A is not B' are subcontraries can easily be shown once the two are spelled out. We know that 'Every A is B' should be expressed as 3 above, and that 3 is equivalent to 8. And in spelling out 12 descent should be made first to a disjunction of singular terms under A (since a term within the scope of a special quantifier has priority over other terms in determining the order in which descent should be made under the terms of a proposition), and then to a conjunction of singular propositions under B. Thus we reach:

13. $(A^1 \vee A^2$ is not $B^1)$ & $(A^1 \vee A^2$ is not $B^2)$.

Bearing in mind that the 'is' in these singular propositions which couple two singular extremes is the 'is' of identity, and that therefore the relation observed to hold between 3 and 8 must hold between 13 and another proposition, that other proposition must be:

14. $(A^1$ is not $B^1 \vee A^2$ is not $B^1) \& (A^1$ is not $B^2 \vee A^2$ is not $B^2)$.

8 and 14 are subcontraries because the falsity of either implies the truth of the other and the two can be true together. For example, if 14 is false then its negation is true. Its negation is equivalent to:

15. $\sim(A^1$ is not $B^1 \vee A^2$ is not $B^1) \vee \sim(A^1$ is not $B^2 \vee A^2$ is not $B^2)$

which in turn is equivalent to:

16. $(A^1$ is $B^1 \& A^2$ is $B^1) \vee (A^1$ is $B^2 \& A^2$ is $B^2)$.

That 16 implies 8 can readily be shown, for whichever disjunct in 16 is true both of that disjunct's conjuncts will be true in which case at least one disjunct in each conjunct of 8 will be true, and hence 8 will be true. By a similar line of reasoning it can be shown that if 8 is false then 16 is true. Furthermore 8 and 16 can be true together, for example, in the situation symbolised by:

17. $A^1$ is $B^1 \& A^1$ is not $B^2 \& A^2$ is not $B^1 \& A^2$ is $B^2$.

Hence 'Every A is B' and '*a* A is not B' satisfy the conditions laid down for a pair of propositions to be subcontrary opposites.

In the course of his discussion Lokert presents just one proposition as a contrary of the universal 'Every A is B'. But he does not in general hold that every proposition with a contrary opposite has only one such opposite; and indeed he furnishes examples of two propositions that are each a contrary of the one proposition. One example worth consideration employs the special operator '*b*', which functions by giving the term upon which it operates determinate supposition. Lokert writes: 'A term which is distributed in one of a pair of contrary propositions in relation to a term which has determinate supposition, in the other proposition in the pair can have either distributive or determinate supposition in relation to that same term' [*De Opp.* 5v[1]] (see appendix, no.71). What he has in mind here is that the proposition:

18. Every A is *b* B

(where the 'A' is distributed and the 'B' determinate) has the two contraries 'Every A is not B' and 'An A is not B'. For in the latter two propositions 'A' has, respectively, distributive and determinate supposition in relation to the term ('B') in relation to which 'A', in 'Every A is *b* B', has distributive supposition. Since in 18 the 'B' has determinate supposition and the 'A' distributive supposition, descent is made first to a disjunction of singular propositions under B and then to a conjunction of singular propositions under A. Thus descent under 18 takes us first to:

19. Every A is $B^1 \vee$ Every A is $B^2$

and then to:

20. $(A^1$ is $B^1$ & $A^2$ is $B^1) \vee (A^1$ is $B^2$ & $A^2$ is $B^2)$.

Descent under 'Every A is not B' and under 'An A is not B', the propositions described as contraries of 18, take us respectively to 11 and 6. It can readily be shown that Lokert is correct in saying that 11 and 6 are both contraries of 18, for it can be shown that the truth of 20 implies the falsity of both 11 and 6, and the truth of either of the latter implies the falsity of 6, and also that all three formulae can be false together. For example, to consider the relation between 20 and 6, if 20 is true then one or other of its disjuncts is true. If the first is true then $A^1$ is $B^1$ and $A^2$ is $B^1$. But if $A^1$ is $B^1$ then the first conjunct in the first disjunct of 6 is false, and if $A^2$ is $B^1$ then the first conjunct in the second disjunct of 6 is false. Hence each conjunction in 6 would be false and in consequence so also would be the entire disjunction. Likewise if 6 is true 20 must be false. Also 6 and 20 are both false in certain situations, for example, where:

21. $A^1$ is not $B^1$ & $A^2$ is $B^1$ & $A^1$ is $B^2$ & $A^2$ is not $B^2$.

The second and third conjuncts in 21 imply that 6 is false, while the first and fourth imply that 20 is false.

Precisely the same sort of consideration can be brought to bear to show that 11 and 18 are contraries. Hence 18 does after all have two contraries. In the previous chapter we considered the idea that the notion of a contrary can be defined in terms of the notions of subalternation and contradiction. In particular it was suggested that the contrary of a given proposition could be identified as the contradictory of that proposition's subalternate. Put in more modern terms what this proposal amounts to is the claim that the contrary of a given proposition $p$ is equivalent to the negation of any proposition weaker than $p$ (to say that $q$ is weaker than $p$ is to say that $p$ implies $q$ but not vice versa). But it was also shown that a proposition could have more than one subalternate, for the relation of subalternation turned out to be transitive (the subalternate of a given proposition is also the subalternate of that proposition's subalternant). In the light of this consideration, that 18 should have at least two contraries would come as no surprise if it could be shown that 18 has at least two subalternates. Now 20 implies:

22. $(A^1$ is $B^1 \vee A^1$ is $B^2)$ & $(A^2$ is $B^1 \vee A^2$ is $B^2)$,

which states that every A is B. Furthermore 22 does not itself imply 20, since, given this model:

23. $A^1$ is $B^1$ & $A^1$ is not $B^2$ & $A^2$ is not $B^1$ & $A^2$ is $B^2$,

22 is true and 20 false. Thus 22 can be classified as a subalternate of 20. Hence any formula equivalent to the negation of 22 will be a contrary of 20. By negating 22 we reach first:

24. $\sim(A^1$ is $B^1 \vee A^1$ is $B^2) \vee \sim(A^2$ is $B^1 \vee A^2$ is $B^2)$,
from which there follows:

25. $(A^1$ is not $B^1 \& A^1$ is not $B^2) \vee (A^2$ is not $B^1 \& A^2$ is not $B^2)$,
which is our original 6, which symbolises 'Some A is not B'.

Also, if 20 is true then since at least two of the singular propositions from which it is formed must be true, so also must at least one of the singular propositions be true. Hence 20 implies the proposition composed out of all of those singulars disjoined with each other. Hence 20 implies the following:

26. $A^1$ is $B^1 \vee A^1$ is $B^2 \vee A^2$ is $B^1 \vee A^2$ is $B^2$,
which states that some A is B. But the implication does not work in the reverse direction. For on a model in which just one of the disjuncts of 26 is true, 26 itself will be true but 20 will be false. Consequently 26 is a subalternate of 20. Hence any formula equivalent to the negation of 26 will be a contrary of 18. One formula equivalent to the negation of 26 is 11. 11 is then a contrary of 18.

Now the two subalternates, 22 and 26, of 20, are themselves related as subalternant to subalternate, with 22 the stronger of the two propositions. Since the relation of subalternation is, as was noted, transitive, it comes as no surprise to discover that 26, which is the subalternate of a subalternate (22) of 20 is itself a subalternate of 20. But more importantly, we now have a neat way of characterising the two formulae which Lokert presented as contraries of 18, for they are simply the negations of a pair of propositions related as subalternant to subalternate. But two propositions related in this way must themselves be related as subalternant to subalternate, for if there is a one way implication between two propositions there must likewise be a one way implication between the negations of those propositions, with the implication going in the opposite direction. That is, if $p$ is a subalternant of $q$ then $\sim q$ is a subalternant of $\sim p$. Granted, then, that 26 is the subalternant of 22, it follows that 11, which is equivalent to the negation of 26, is the subalternant of 6, which is equivalent to the negation of 22. Since 11 and 6 are symbolic representations of, respectively, 'No A is B' and 'Some A is not B', this claim is clearly correct.

Lokert discusses the $b$ quantifier not only in the course of identifying propositions which are contrary to a proposition containing that operator, but also in the course of identifying contradictory and sub-contrary propositions of propositions containing it. Let us start with what he says about the $b$ quantifier by asking what the contradictory of 18 is. That proposition is expressed symbolically as 20. Its contradictory is its negation:

27. $\sim(A^1$ is $B^1$ & $A^2$ is $B^1)$ & $\sim(A^1$ is $B^2$ & $A^2$ is $B^2)$,

which is equivalent to:

28. $(A^1$ is not $B^1 \vee A^2$ is not $B^1)$ & $(A^1$ is not $B^2 \vee A^2$ is not $B^2)$.

In line with our discussions following formulae 8 and 9 above, 28 is equivalent to:

29. $(A^1 \vee A^2$ is not $B^1)$ & $(A^1 \vee A^2$ is not $B^2)$.

Thus the contradictory of 'Every A is *b* B' must be a negative proposition in which the subject term has merely confused disjunctive supposition and the predicate term has distributive supposition. The contradictory in question must therefore be:

30. *a* A is not B.[5]

This is precisely Lokert's own conclusion. He writes (see appendix, no.73): 'A term distributed in one of a pair of contradictories in relation to the other term which has determinate supposition [i.e. 18] ought in the other contradictory to have merely confused disjunctive supposition in relation to the term which had determinate supposition in the other . . . "*a* man is not white" has a contradictory whose predicate has determinate supposition' [*De Opp.* 5r²].

This highlights one reason why, granted the employment of the *a* operator, the *b* operator had to be introduced, for without the *b* operator there is no way, short of using a formula with a number of singular propositions, of saying what the contradictory of 30 is.

We turn now to the question of the identity of the (or at least a) subcontrary of 18. What we require is a proposition which must be true if 18 is false and which may be true even if 18 is. 18 is false if neither of the conjunctions in 20 is true, and that occurs if at least one conjunct in each conjunction is false. But if at least one conjunct in each conjunction is false then at least one of the singular propositions out of which 20 is composed is false. Hence given the falsity of 20, the following is true:

31. $A^1$ is not $B^1 \vee A^2$ is not $B^1 \vee A^1$ is not $B^2 \vee A^2$ is not $B^2$,

i.e. there is some A or other that B is not, or, more briefly (and following closely the Latin mode of expression):

32. Some A B is not.

Also if 31 is false then every singular proposition in 20 is true, from which it follows that 20 itself is true. Furthermore 20 and 31 may be true together, as for example in the following situation:

33. $A^1$ is $B^1$ & $A^2$ is $B^1$ & $A^1$ is $B^2$ & $A^2$ is not $B^2$.

Hence 20 and 31 are subcontraries, for the negation of each implies the other and they are true together in certain situations. And consequently the subcontrary of 18 is 32. This is the position that Lokert takes. He writes: 'A term distributed in one of a pair of subcontraries in relation to a term with determinate supposition, in the other sub-contrary could have determinate supposition with no universality posited . . . Of this proposition: "Every man is *b* animal" there could be given no other subcontrary than this: "A man an animal is not" or its equivalent' [*De Opp.* 5v²] (see appendix, no.74).

Having identified a subcontrary of 18, the way is open to making a further identification which, though not explicitly made by Lokert, follows directly from positions which he held. We have so far picked out formulae 22 and 26 as subalternates of 18, and the question is naturally prompted as to the identity of the proposition of which 18 itself is a subalternate. Now the subalternant of a given proposition is the contradictory of that proposition's subcontrary (just as the sub-alternate of a given proposition is the contradictory of that propos-ition's contrary). Hence one subalternant of 18 is the contradictory of 31. That contradictory, most simply expressed, is:

34. $A^1$ is $B^1$ & $A^2$ is $B^1$ & $A^1$ is $B^2$ and $A^2$ is $B^2$,

which may be expressed, paralleling 32, as:

35. Every A every B is.

35, conceived as expressing the point made by 34, is true just if there is only one B and it is A.

34 clearly implies 20, for if 34 is true then so also is every singular proposition of which 20 is composed. And the implication is only one way, for 20 is true even if only the first two conjuncts in 34 are true. Hence 34 is a subalternate of 20 and hence of 18. Consequently 34, 18, 22 and 26 form a single chain of subalternation, with 34 the strongest point in the chain and 26 the weakest.

Nor is it being suggested, and it is certainly not implied by Lokert, that 18 and 22 are the only two possible propositions in the chain between those terminal points. Other propositions can be identified, on the basis of considerations already employed in this section, as fitted for insertion in the chain.

From consideration of relations such as those just discussed Lokert formulates a number of transformation rules by which a pair of pro-positions related in one way can be transformed into a pair of propos-itions related in a quite different way. Thus, for example, he writes: 'Given two propositions in which are preserved the conditions requis-ite for a contradiction save that the term which ought to have deter-minate supposition in relation to a distribution, has merely confused disjunctive supposition in relation to that distribution, then those two propositions are subcontraries, at any rate as regards the law' [*De Opp.* 15r²–v¹] (see appendix, no. 75). Thus (1) 'Every A is B' and (2) 'Some A is not B' satisfy the conditions for contradictoriness. In (2)

'A' has determinate supposition in relation to 'B' which is distributed. What Lokert's rule asserts is that (2) can be transformed from a contradictory, to a subcontrary, of (1) by transforming 'A' in (2) from a term with determinate supposition to one with merely confused supposition. This is done, as we know, by bringing it within the scope of the $a$ quantifier. Thus given that (2) is the contradictory of (1), the subcontrary of (1) must be (3) '$a$ A is not B'. That (1) and (3) are subcontraries has been established earlier in this chapter.

A second rule presented by Lokert is: 'Given two propositions in which are preserved all the requirements for contradiction save that the term which ought to have merely confused supposition in relation to a distributed term has determinate supposition in relation to that distributed term, then those two propositions are contraries' [De Opp. 15v[1]] (see appendix, no.76). Thus, granted once again that (1) and (2) in the preceding paragraph are contradictories, and also that in (1) 'B' has merely confused supposition in relation to 'A' which is distributed, then (1) and (2) can be transformed into a pair of contraries by transforming 'B' in (1) from a term with merely confused supposition to one with determinate supposition. This is done by bringing it within the scope of the $b$ quantifier. Hence the contrary of (2) is (4) 'Every A is $b$ B'. The contrariety of (2) and (4) was established earlier in this chapter.

## III

We shall not here pursue further Lokert's discussion of these and similar rules, but shall turn instead to a brief account of aspects of his complex and subtle discussion of propositions of a kind which we considered in chapter two, namely, those containing three categorematic terms of which one stands in a genitival relation to another. In chapter two a list of eight such propositions was given (p.48). The list is incomplete in so far as it omits schemata with negations. But Lokert makes extensive use in the De Oppositionibus of such negated schemata. Since in chapter two we attended solely to affirmative examples of such propositions we shall concentrate here on negative examples. One negative form of no. 5 in the original list is:

    36. Of some B some A is not C.

In this particular negative proposition both 'A' and 'B' have determinate supposition and 'C' has distributive supposition. Since in the analysis of a proposition descent is made under a term with determinate supposition before it is made under one with distributive supposition, the predicate term in 36 must be dealt with last. There is a further rule, which we saw in operation in chapter two, that where two terms stand in the relation of determinable to determinator, descent is made under the latter first. Hence in the analysis of 36 descent is made under the categorematic terms, coincidentally, in the order in which they appear in the proposition. The three stages of analysis are as follows (where the 'is' or 'is not' occur relating only singular terms I shall, for the sake of brevity, write '=' and '≠' respectively. These are not misleading devices here since in such contexts the 'is' is a genuine 'is' of identity):

37. $(Of B^1 \text{ some } A \text{ is not } C) \vee (Of B^2 \text{ some } A \text{ is not } C)$

38. $(Of B^1 A^1 \text{ is not } C \vee Of B^1 A^2 \text{ is not } C) \vee$
    $(Of B^2 A^1 \text{ is not } C \vee Of B^2 A^2 \text{ is not } C)$

39. $[(Of B^1 A^1 \neq C^1 \ \& \ Of B^1 A^1 \neq C^2) \vee (Of B^1 A^2 \neq C^1 \ \&$
    $Of B^1 A^2 \neq C^2)] \vee$
    $[(Of B^2 A^1 \neq C^1 \ \& \ Of B^2 A^1 \neq C^2) \vee (Of B^2 A^2 \neq C^1 \ \&$
    $Of B^2 A^2 \neq C^2)].$

Having established that 39 sets out the truth conditions for 36, we can now raise the question of what the contrary opposite of 36 is. For we now know that what we are looking for is a proposition $p$ such that $p$ and 36 each imply the negation of the other, and both may be false on the same assignment of values to the component singular propositions.

Lokert in fact gives two contraries. He writes: 'This proposition: "Of some man some ass is not an animal" is contrary to both of these: "Of every man every ass is $c$ animal" and "Of every man every ass is $d$ animal"' [*De Opp.* 15r²]. Replacing 'man' by 'B', 'ass' by 'A' and 'animal' by 'C', what this amounts to is the claim that 36 has the two contraries:

40. Of every B every A is $c$ C

41. Of every B every A is $d$ C.

The two quantifiers $c$ and $d$ confer, we saw in chapter two, mixed supposition on the immediately following term, since $c$ confers confused supposition in relation to the first term in the proposition and determinate supposition in relation to the second term, whereas $d$ confers determinate supposition in relation to the first term and merely confused supposition in relation to the second. Hence, to take 40 first, 'C' has merely confused supposition in relation to 'B' and has determinate supposition in relation to 'A'. Consequently descent must be made first under 'B', then under 'C' and finally under 'A'. The three stages in the analysis are therefore as follows:

42. Of $B^1$ every A is $c$ C & Of $B^2$ every A is $c$ C

43. $(Of B^1 \text{ every } A \text{ is } C^1 \vee Of B^1 \text{ every } A \text{ is } C^2) \ \&$
    $(Of B^2 \text{ every } A \text{ is } C^1 \vee Of B^2 \text{ every } A \text{ is } C^2)$

44. $[($Of $B^1$ $A^1 = C^1$ & Of $B^1$ $A^2 = C^1) \vee ($Of $B^1$ $A^1 = C^2$ &
    Of $B^1$ $A^2 = C^2)] \,$&
    $[($Of $B^2$ $A^1 = C^1$ & Of $B^2$ $A^2 = C^1) \vee ($Of $B^2$ $A^1 = C^2$ &
    Of $B^2$ $A^2 = C^2)].$

If Lokert is correct 39 and 44 must each imply the negation of the other, and it must be possible for both to be false on the same truth conditions. Inspection shows him to be correct on both these points. We need not here work our way through all the permutations by which the first of the two points is established. But consideration of one permutation will be sufficient to show how the various permutations are constructed and worked through. If 44 is true then each conjunct in the overall conjunction must be true, and hence each disjunction must be true. The two disjunctions are themselves each composed of a pair of conjunctions, and consequently at least one conjunction in each disjunction must be true. Let us suppose that the first conjunction in each disjunction is true and the second false. On this model 39 must be false. The truth of either conjunction in the first disjunction of 44 conjoined with either conjunction in the second disjunction will likewise imply both the truth of 44 and the falsity of 39. By making a precisely parallel set of moves it can be shown that any set of conditions sufficient for the truth of 39 will be sufficient for the falsity of 44. This shows that not both of 39 and 44 can be true.

Lokert also claims that they can be false together. He is correct in this. There is indeed more than one model on which both formulae are false, for example, the following:

45. Of $B^1$ $A^1 \neq C^1$ & Of $B^1$ $A^2 = C^1$ & Of $B^1$ $A^1 = C^2$ &
    Of $B^1$ $A^2 \neq C^2$ &
    Of $B^2$ $A^1 \neq C^1$ & Of $B^2$ $A^2 = C^1$ & Of $B^2$ $A^1 = C^2$ &
    Of $B^2$ $A^2 \neq C^2$

Hence Lokert's assertion that 36 and 40 are contraries is justified. He also claimed that 36 is a contrary of 41. Dealing with this claim will at least provide an opportunity to see how the $d$ quantifier works.

Since in 41 'C' has determinate supposition in relation to 'B' and merely confused supposition in relation to 'A', it follows that descent must be made under 'C' before being made under 'B', and under 'A' before it is made under 'C'. Hence in the analysis we deal first with 'A', then with 'C' and finally with 'B'. The three stages of analysis are as follows:

46. Of every B $A^1$ is $d$ C & Of every B $A^2$ is $d$ C
47. (Of every B $A^1$ is $C^1$ $\vee$ Of every B $A^1$ is $C^2$) &
    (Of every B $A^2$ is $C^1$ $\vee$ Of every B $A^2$ is $C^2$)

48. $[(\text{Of } B^1 A^1 = C^1 \ \& \ \text{Of } B^2 A^1 = C^1) \lor (\text{Of } B^1 A^1 = C^2 \ \& \ \text{Of } B^2 A^1 = C^2)] \ \&$
$[(\text{Of } B^1 A^2 = C^1 \ \& \ \text{Of } B^2 A^2 = C^1) \lor (\text{Of } B^1 A^2 = C^2 \ \& \ \text{Of } B^2 A^2 = C^2)].$

If Lokert is correct then 39 and 48 must each imply the negation of the other, and it must be possible for both to be false on the one set of truth conditions. He is correct on both these matters. To take the first one first: we shall not develop the entire argument, but shall indicate how the argument runs by taking just one of the steps. If 48 is true then each of the conjuncts in the overall conjunction is true. Each conjunct is a disjunction, and hence at least one disjunct in each conjunct must be true. Suppose that it is the first in each. We are, that is, assuming:

49. $\text{Of } B^1 A^1 = C^1 \ \& \ \text{Of } B^2 A^1 = C^1 \ \& \ \text{Of } B^1 A^2 = C^1 \ \& \ \text{Of } B^2 A^2 = C^1.$

Granted the truth of the first and third conjuncts in 49, the first half of 39 is false, since each conjunction making up the disjunction has a false conjunct. And likewise, granted the truth of the second and fourth conjuncts in 49, the second half of 39 is false. Similarly, whichever disjunct in the first half of 48 and whichever disjunct in the second half are assumed true (and one from each half must be true if 48 is true), 39 will be false.

By similar reasoning it can be shown that any set of conditions sufficient for the truth of 39 will be sufficient for the falsity of 48. Hence not both of 39 and 48 can be true. But additionally there is more than one model on which both are false, for example, the following:

50. $\text{Of } B^1 A^1 = C^1 \ \& \ \text{Of } B^2 A^1 \neq C^1 \ \& \ \text{Of } B^1 A^1 \neq C^2 \ \&$
$\text{Of } B^2 A^1 = C^2 \ \&$
$\text{Of } B^1 A^2 = C^1 \ \& \ \text{Of } B^2 A^2 \neq C^1 \ \& \ \text{Of } B^1 A^2 \neq C^2 \ \&$
$\text{Of } B^2 A^2 = C^2.$

Hence 41 is, as Lokert asserted, a contrary of 36. His claim that both 40 and 41 are contraries of 36 is thus established.

It should be added that just as 36 has at least two contraries, so also do both 40 and 41. Lokert tells us [*De Opp.* 15v¹] that as well as 36, another contrary of 40 is:

51. Of every B every A is not C

and that as well as 36, another contrary of 41 is:

52. Of *a* B every A is not C.

The correctness of these claims can readily be established by employment of the procedures just used on 40 and 41.

## IV

'Not every proposition can have a contrary but only one in which there is universality; and so not every proposition can have a subcontrary but only one in which there is particularity' [*De Opp.* 6r[1]]. The propositions we have discussed so far in our account of oppositional relations have not come into conflict with this statement. But towards the end of the *De Oppositionibus* Lokert presents a series of rules which do come into conflict with it. What he does in effect is describe a square of opposition for hypothetical propositions where the propositions which occur in the hypotheticals are themselves unanalysed and which therefore cannot be said to contain either universality or particularity. Thus he writes (see appendix, no.77): 'A disjunctive affirmative is the subalternate of a conjunctive affirmative composed of the same parts . . . The reason for this is that all that is required for the truth of a disjunction is required for the truth of a conjunction . . . and not vice versa' [*De Opp.* 35r[1-2]]. He adds: 'Affirmative conjunctive propositions composed of contradictory or contrary parts are opposed as contraries. And disjunctive affirmatives composed of contradictory or subcontrary parts are opposed as subcontraries'. And finally, 'An affirmative conjunction and an affirmative disjunction composed of contradictory parts are contradictory. But a conjunction and a disjunction composed of contrary parts are contraries. And if they are composed of subcontrary parts they are subcontraries' [35r[2]–v[1]].

Packed into this passage are descriptions of three squares of opposition. They can be schematised as follows:

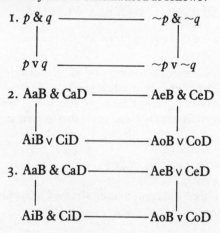

1. $p \& q$ —————— $\sim p \& \sim q$

   $p \vee q$ —————— $\sim p \vee \sim q$

2. AaB & CaD ——— AeB & CeD

   AiB ∨ CiD ——— AoB ∨ CoD

3. AaB & CaD——— AeB ∨ CeD

   AiB & CiD ——— AoB ∨ CoD

It is evident that the first of the above three squares of opposition does not accord in the least with the quotation at the start of this section,[6] and perhaps the safest assumption that we can make in assigning an interpretation is that what Lokert was saying was intended there to apply only to categorical propositions and not to hypothetical ones.

An important point is suggested by squares 2 and 3. We have already seen in this chapter that a single proposition can have several subalternates and also several contraries, and in view of that it can come as no surprise to notice that in squares 2 and 3 the schema AaB & CaD has two contraries and two subalternates. But in contrast with those two kinds of opposition, there can be only one contradictory of a given proposition.[7] It follows from this that the content of a square of opposition is not fixed once the termini of one of the diagonals are fixed, but the content is fixed if we know the termini of either of the subalternation relations or know the termini of the contrariety or the subcontrariety relations. For in order to complete the square we need only construct the contradictories of the two propositions standing in the relation of subalternant to subalternate, of contrary to contrary, or of subcontrary to subcontrary.

Clearly the possibility of a single proposition having several contraries is closely related to the possibility of its having several subalternates, for the subalternate of a proposition can be constructed by contradicting a contrary of that proposition. Hence if the first proposition has a given number of contraries, say three, it can have no fewer subalternates. Thus, for example, instead of writing out three squares of opposition, we could instead write out a single one in which the diagonal lines indicate which proposition is the contradictory of which, as follows:

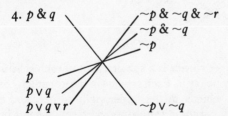

4. $p$ & $q$      $\sim p$ & $\sim q$ & $\sim r$
             $\sim p$ & $\sim q$
             $\sim p$

$p$
$p \lor q$
$p \lor q \lor r$      $\sim p \lor \sim q$

Thus, if a given proposition has $n$ contraries the contradictory of that proposition must have $n$ subcontraries. That the three subcontraries on the left hand side of square 4 are all genuine subcontraries of $\sim p \lor \sim q$ is plain from the fact that if $\sim p \lor \sim q$ is false then its contradictory must be true and the set of three subcontraries are all implied by $p$ & $q$; and likewise if any of those three subcontraries is false its contradictory must be true, and $\sim p \vee \sim q$ is implied by each of the three contraries on the right hand side of the square. Also, where $p \,\& \sim q$, all four subcontraries are true.

Lokert does not himself set out precisely the complex square of opposition we have just constructed. But the squares 2 and 3 set out earlier, which were described by him in detail, can be set out in a similar way to the one just constructed:

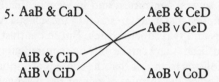

5.  AaB & CaD            AeB & CeD
                                AeB ∨ CeD

     AiB & CiD
     AiB ∨ CiD                 AoB ∨ CoD

The upper of the two affirmative subalternates is itself the subalternant of the lower one. It is tempting to supplement 5 with a second subalternant, above the pair of subalternates, where the additional subalternant is itself a subalternate of AaB & CaD. The obvious candidate at first sight is AaB ∨ CaD, which would have the corresponding contradictory AoB & CoD. But this proposal fails, first, because AaB ∨ CaD is not a subalternant of AiB & CiD (as is clear if we assume AaB and CeD), and secondly, and relatedly, AoB & CoD is not a subalternate of AeB ∨ CeD (as is clear if we assume AeB and CaD). But two further schemata would each serve satisfactorily as a second subalternant under AaB & CaD. They are AaB & CiD and AiB & CaD. For example, by adding the first of these formulae and its contradictory to square 5, we reach the following:

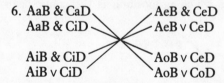

6.  AaB & CaD           AeB & CeD
     AaB & CiD           AeB ∨ CeD

     AiB & CiD           AoB ∨ CeD
     AiB ∨ CiD           AoB ∨ CoD

Each schema in an upper corner is a subalternant of each schema in the corner immediately below it. Each schema in the upper left corner is a contrary of each schema in the upper right corner, and each schema in the lower left corner is a subcontrary of each schema in the lower right corner.

In the absence of explicit discussion by Lokert of this topic we shall pursue it no further.

In this chapter we have considered only a very small part of Lokert's extensive discussion on rules for constructing squares of opposition, and in particular have not commented on his difficult remarks on the opposites of propositions which have copulas which are not present tensed, or have complex copulas in which the verb 'to be' has a different tense on each occurrence. But I hope that enough has been said to give some idea of the kinds of problem raised by Lokert in his investigation of oppositions, and of the kinds of solution that he gave.

CHAPTER SIX

# Lokert's Place in Medieval Logic

George Lokert and the other logicians working in the first few decades of the sixteenth century made the last significant contribution to the single great sweep of logical enquiry that had been under way in Europe since the time of Abelard. That tradition was to be replaced by one with a different conception of the place of logic in the arts and sciences and hence with a different conception of logic itself. For one feature of the encroaching humanism, of which there had already been clear signs in the previous century with the works of Lorenzo Valla and Rudolph Agricola, and which was to overwhelm the arts faculties of the great universities, was the return to a classical conception of logic as a branch of rhetoric, and the consequent notion that the chief value of a training in logic lay in its improving the diligent student's powers of persuasion.

Thus for example in his *De Inventione Dialectica* Agricola makes it clear that rhetoric is to be seen as the master science and that logic, the discovery and deployment of telling arguments, was an essential part of the orator's craft. Establishing that the arguments to be deployed were in fact formally valid was only a small part of what was required.

Now if what this amounted to were merely that the goal of persuasion could only be helped, never hindered, by the employment of valid arguments it would be almost too trite to be worth saying. The interesting thing, however, is that the *De Inventione*, which is an orator's handbook if ever there were one, was in fact accepted in some quarters (humanist quarters) as a textbook of logic. It was not so accepted by the inveterate logicians of early sixteenth-century Paris, and in particular Agricola's account of the place of logic could not have been more unlike Lokert's.

The total absence from Lokert's writings of any suggestion that logic is merely a branch of the art of persuasion derives from his acceptance of logic as being supreme rather than subsidiary, as being, in Peter of Spain's telling phrase, 'the art of arts and the science of sciences, containing the route to the principles of all methods',[1] for even if theology or even metaphysics is said to be the queen of sciences discussion within those sciences has to be conducted in accordance with canons of valid inference which it is the task of logic to lay down. For essential to the terminist conception of logic was the notion of a science of valid inference.

It will be clear from the foregoing chapters that the notion of inference employed was purely formal. In particular it was neither metaphysical nor epistemological, and most especially the terminists' logic is entirely unsullied by psychologism. It is true that terminists paid close attention to the cognitive act by which the signification of a proposition or a term could be grasped, and that such cognitive acts were themselves conceived of as items of a mental language which could itself be subjected to a syntactic and semantic study. And it is also the case that it was thought that the semantic study of spoken and written language could not be made without regard to the mental linguistic correlate. In all this the terminists could be seen as taking up and developing the Platonic conception of thought as the soul discoursing with itself. But all this does not amount to, or even, when properly grasped, approach the fundamental psychologistic notion that logic is to be understood as 'the laws of thought', where this notion is understood descriptively as the laws governing the way people actually do think. Mental language, which, directly or indirectly, is signified by spoken and written language, is no less subject than spoken and written language to the one set of laws of thought, prescriptively understood, which prescribe how we are to reason if conclusions are to be validly drawn from their premisses. Whether such rules were always, often or seldom obeyed was considered irrelevant to the logician's enterprise.

The theory of inference conditions, or 'theory of consequences', treated in this purely formal, un-psychologistic way, was supplemented by the theory of truth conditions, the 'theory of supposition', for of course the terminists were not interested in constructing uninterpreted systems – the purpose of their formalist approach was to achieve rigour, and the purpose of the rigour was to ensure that no intuitive leaps were made in inference in an attempt to reach a true conclusion from true premisses. It was thus necessary to lay down the truth conditions of different kinds of proposition, most obviously propositions, whether affirmative or negative, with quantifier expressions; but also exponible propositions; for it was such types of proposition which figured as premisses in the area of the theory of inference conditions with which the terminists were most concerned, namely, syllogistic. But here again there was no hint of psychologism in their approach. The problem was the formal one of identifying the transformation rules by which a given proposition, perhaps quantified and perhaps exponible and perhaps also hypothetical, could be transformed into an appropriately structured equivalent proposition which could itself be investigated for truth and falsity.

These investigations were carried out in a natural language, Latin, but this fact should not be allowed to conceal the point that the logical investigations were every bit as formal as are modern logical investigations pursued in the Peano-Russell or the Polish notation of modern logic textbooks. The crucial point is not whether a natural language is used, but how the logical terminology in that language is employed. If a term is borrowed from a natural language and precise rules for its employment are laid down and rigorously followed, then that term, whether it is 'all', 'no', 'and' etc., serves just as effectively as a logical symbol as would any new symbol created to do the same job. The outcome is that the logic textbooks such as those of Lokert's that we have been studying are written in a scientific style entirely lacking in literary flourishes, and as far as could be from the polished elegant Ciceronian style adopted by the humanists as the ideal vehicle for persuasion. On the other hand the Latin of the late-scholastic logicians was perfectly suited for the job it was required to do. Several centuries of writing about truth conditions and valid inference had led to the fashioning of a language with the appropriate syntactic forms and the appropriate terminology for saying the kinds of thing that the terminists thought had to be said if the notion of validity was to be properly defined. Lack of elegance was a small price to pay, hardly a price at all, for being brought to such a destination.

Nevertheless the terminist logicians did not lose sight of the intimate links between logic and ordinary, non-scientific natural language, and in particular saw themselves as providing the canons of valid inference which those employing natural language had to obey if their arguments, expressed in natural language, were to be valid. For whatever the canons of valid inference laid down in the scientific language of the terminists those canons had to be so expressed that it was possible on the basis of them to determine for any given argument in ordinary language whether that argument was or was not valid. In order that this requirement be fulfilled there had to be clear procedures by which ordinary sentences could be mapped onto the valid forms presented by the logicians.

This need to keep an eye on the behaviour of ordinary language was no less great for the study of truth conditions than for the study of inference conditions. Thus, for example, we noted in our discussion of Lokert's treatment of the application of supposition theory to non-present tensed propositions, that it was required that for the truth condition of the proposition to be clearly formulated the non-present tensed proposition had to be written in the present tense and the tensed part of the original proposition had to be represented in the metalinguistic predicate within which the present tensed proposition was embedded. And rules were laid down describing precisely how the non-present tensed proposition was to be transformed into one in the present tense, and precisely how the metalinguistic predicate was to be formulated. The result of such transformations was a proposition which contained a present tensed proposition of the object language occurring as an argument in the single argument place of a metalinguistic predicate. The overall effect was of a hideously unliterary sentence at the opposite pole from the humanistic ideal of literary elegance. But all the same the metalinguistic proposition expressed the truth conditions of the proposition of ordinary language as clearly as it possibly could be done, given the need to operate within the theory of supposition.

Within the terminists' overall approach, the notion of a proposition played a pivotal role, acting as a kind of intermediary between terms on the one hand and arguments on the other. In particular the rules of valid immediate, and mediate inference cannot be established without a prior consideration of terms, for conversive, equipollential, contrapositional and syllogistic inferences are inexplicable without an understanding of the role played in propositions by syncategorematic terms. But though propositions are composed of terms, it should be noted that 'term' was standardly defined in terms of 'proposition' and not vice versa. A term is 'a sign placeable in a proposition', but a proposition is not 'a collection of terms'. In the tradition within which Lokert worked a proposition was treated as a unit of speech (an *oratio*) signifying something true or false. Nevertheless though the basic linguistic unit was in this sense the proposition rather than the term, the logicians with whom we are here concerned are fairly classed as terminists rather than 'propositionalists'. For their most striking contribution to logic, and the area in which they advanced most spectacularly beyond the logic of Aristotle, lay in the investigation of the properties, especially signification and supposition, of terms.

In a sense the contrast here being drawn is a false one for the properties of terms were themselves expounded in terms of the contribution they made to the truth of the propositions containing them, and in particular the supposition of a term was described in terms of the syntactic relation between subject and predicate terms within a proposition. Also, as we have seen, exponible terms were clarified in terms of the exposition of exponible propositions. The term 'begin', for example, was explained by reference to the disjunction of conjunctions forming the exponents of an exponible proposition of inception.

But whether or not the title 'terminist' is judged to overemphasise the concern with terms as opposed to propositions, the logicians themselves saw themselves as terminist logicians and the title makes a point even if it is thought to make it a little too firmly in the light of the priority officially seen as due to propositions.

It is, then, beyond dispute that the terminists' conception of logic was of a science of language, and though their discussions were conducted in an increasingly formalised and scientific Latin they remained to the end faithful to the forms of natural language. As further evidence for this, it may be noted that without the real desire to stay as close as possible to natural language the deep interest in exponible terms could hardly have developed. Modern logicians are interested in a far narrower range of syncategoremata than were their medieval counterparts, and part of the reason for this is the much greater distance from natural language at which modern logicians operate.

It is in the area of exponibles as much as in any other that the terminists had something to say that is worth saying and from which we can now learn. And it is to Lokert as much as to any other of the terminists that we should turn in order to gain new insights into the notions of exclusion, exception, immediateness, inception, cessation and so on. This is not to deny the obvious point that in many areas modern logic has vastly outdistanced medieval logic. Most especially the basic syllogistic is now seen to be a small fragment of the lower predicate calculus. But by no means all of the late medieval syllogistic is so easily dealt with. Syllogisms whose syncategorematic terms include exponibles are an obvious case in point. Where the premisses include past or future tensed propositions of immediateness, inception and cessation the normal machinery of syllogistic has to be augmented by a highly sophisticated tense logic if the modern notation is not to present a travesty of the arguments which the late terminists handled with such assurance. Similarly the terminists were interested in arguments involving subjunctive conditionals (in particular in connection with the theory of propositional complexes) and there is little agreement amongst present-day logicians about how such expressions should be handled.

Also the special quantifiers which, as we have seen, Lokert employed extensively and which are a distinctive feature of the logic treatises composed in the second and third decades of the sixteenth century, have no modern counterpart. But we have observed that a great many interesting logical points, particularly concerning contradiction and contrariety, but concerning other types of relation also, can be made with the aid of them. Those quantifiers certainly merit close investigation, though it is by no means clear what the most appropriate notation for their study would be in the context of the modern notation for the expression of subject-predicate propositions.

In all this it has to be recognised that Lokert was no trail blazer. Historically, though not conceptually, speaking he stood at the end of a trail rather than at the beginning. In the early decades of the sixteenth century numerous treatises on the properties of terms, on exponibles, consequences and oppositions were published. Professors and regents lectured on these topics and then had the lectures printed. And the treatises in any one of these fields present at least on first reading a very similar appearance. There was a fairly well established order in which individual topics were raised and there were a number of standard theses, proofs, counter-arguments and defences that were worked through. Sometimes points are made that had not been made (in extant treatises) up till that time, though whether the point was original to the author of the treatise in which it is thought first to have appeared is in general impossible to say. For we are dealing here with a close-knit community of scholars living, as it were, very much in each other's intellectual pockets. Ideas could travel quickly because on the whole they did not need to travel very far. For a number of years, for example, Major and Lokert occupied the same house in Paris, and it is beyond belief that two such friends in such proximity did not spend a very great deal of time discussing logical matters.

It has also to be remembered in this context that there was a tradition of mobility among scholars. In the first chapter something was said about the travels of Major and Lokert; and their experiences in contributing to the teaching and administration in several universities was the norm. Thus the question of whether a given point made by a given logician was or was not original to him is not settled simply by reference to the fact that amongst extant treatises the point occurs in his writings at an earlier date than it occurs in anyone else's. Nor even can we safely assume that if the point was made by him in print at a later date than by another then he had not been the first to teach it. In some cases we might be able to give an answer that is fairly free of speculation, but those cases would be exceptional.

For these reasons I have not attempted in these pages to pursue an investigation into the originality of Lokert. Nor do I think that such an investigation would in any case be worthwhile. The important question for logic is not that of who said what first, but of what was said that was important and that we can learn from. Thus in this book

Lokert has been treated primarily as a fine representative of a school of logicians whose doctrines are significant and worth developing today. The very names of the members of the school, not to mention their distinctive doctrines, are known now by very few indeed. Hence though much of what Lokert taught was standard within his circle it is new to us, and its newness for us is my justification for focusing attention on Lokert. At numerous points in these pages reference is made to other logicians, most especially to Major himself, either to clarify points made by Lokert or to indicate that the doctrines in question were indeed part of the common intellectual currency of the time, and were not peculiar to him; though it has to be said that Lokert wrote with great clarity and incisiveness, and his writings could hardly be bettered from that point of view as a starting point for an investigation of the early sixteenth-century terminists. This is not to say that a great deal is not to be learned by the study of other logicians of that period, and indeed we have considered in the fore-going pages only a very small part of Lokert's own teachings. There is a very large story to be told about late terminist logic and thus far, despite the great contributions of such researchers in the field as Nuchelmans, Kretzmann and Ashworth, only a very small part has been told. It is only from the close scrutiny of many such texts as the treatises of Lokert that a basis will be provided for an adequate esti-mate of the achievement of late-scholastic logic in general, and of the circle of John Major in particular. Once our understanding of their logical ideas is sufficiently developed the task of relating those ideas to the terminists' metaphysical and epistemological concerns comes within reach.

A further, different kind of benefit from such studies should here be mentioned. Among the top flight of late-scholastic logicians was a quite disproportionate number of Scots. How Scotland came to pro-duce so many men of such calibre is a question which cannot be answered, or even profitably discussed, here. But it should at least be said that, by whatever means it came about that the grammar schools of Scotland produced so many men destined to enjoy international high esteem as logicians, philosophers and theologians, to fail to note the nature and magnitude of their achievement is to ignore an extra-ordinary accomplishment of Scottish culture.

As was remarked in the first chapter, Scotland has a long tradition of producing men of great philosophical stature. Histories of philo-sophy which have something to say about the Scottish contribution, and all do, generally have most to say about the eighteenth century, which can hardly be ignored given the presence of such figures as

Thomas Reid, Adam Smith and David Hume, and have very little if anything to say about any other period, except the early fourteenth century when Duns Scotus lived. It is no part of the purpose of this book to argue that the sixteenth century does after all vie with the eighteenth for the title of *saeculum mirabile* of Scottish philosophy. Whether the earlier century can issue an effective challenge to the later in this respect is a matter which could not be settled without much more extensive study of the writings of the circle of John Major. But I would hope at least to have made out an effective case for the claim that the writings at issue are full of interesting ideas which are deserving of the closest scrutiny, with a view both to enabling us to enrich our understanding of sixteenth-century Scottish culture and to making a contribution to debates now in progress in logic and the philosophy of language.

# APPENDIX
# Latin Texts

**1.** (Major *Liber Terminorum* 1r[1])
Terminus accipitur dupliciter uno modo phisice ut convenit rebus ad extra quemadmodum dicimus de termino a quo et de termino ad quem. Secundo modo ut convenit dicibilibus et hoc quintupliter. Primo modo capitur extenso termino large (vulgo dicimus) pro omni signo ponibili in propositione. Secundo modo capitur minus large pro omni signo significative sumpto ponibili in propositione sive fuerit complexum sive non. Tertio modo capitur proprie pro omni signo incomplexo significative sumpto in propositione ponibili. Quarto modo propriissime pro omni illo quod significative sumptum potest esse extremum propositionis respectu verbi personalis modi finiti. Quinto modo strictissime pro incomplexo quod potest esse extremum significative sumptum etc. Ista equivocatio potest probari ex communi modo loquendi in artibus. Quinta acceptio est trita et quarta patet ex primo priorum. Terminum voco in quem resolvitur propositio ut in predicatum et illud de quo dicitur apposito vel diviso esse vel non esse. Et Petrus Hyspanus dicit aliquas propositiones nullo termino participare esto quod copulis participent quae ibidem non reputantur termini. Tres prime acceptiones sunt satis famose.

**2.** (Lokert *De Terminis* 3v)
Diffinitio est oratio convertibilis cum diffinito alicuius rei importate per diffinitum naturam explicans. Nec in dicta descriptione capitur natura solum pro causa intrinseca ut in ii Physicorum, sed pro quacunque causa conditione vel proprietate ipsius rei. Ratione explicare naturam rei est ipsam declarare naturam non declaratam per ipsum diffinitum vel magis declarare talem naturam minus declaratam per ipsius diffinitum. Diffinitum est terminus convertibilis cum diffinitione aliquid significans cuius naturam declarat ipsa diffinitio. Patet ex dictis nullum purum sincathegoreuma potest esse diffinibile secundum quod huiusmodi. Patent secundo conditiones requisite ad bonam diffinitionem scilicet quod convertatur cum diffinito et quod rei importate per diffinitum naturam explicet. Solet superaddi tertia scilicet quod bona diffinitio nihil contineat superfluum. Ista declarantur exemplo. Talis oratio signum ponibile in propositione est bona diffinitio

huius dictionis terminus. Primo dicta oratio convertitur cum illa dictione terminus quod pro presenti non est aliud nisi quacunque re data pro qua verificatur illa dictio terminus mediante quacunque copula pro eadem mediante simili copula verificatur illa oratio signum ponibile in propositione et econtra. Et dicta oratio signum ponibile in propositione declarat aliquam conditionem rei importate per illam dictionem terminus. Nec in dicta diffinitione aliquid ponitur superfluum. Dicitur aliquid superflue poni in aliqua diffinitione quando remote illo residuum manet bona diffinitio equaliter declarans naturam rei respectu eiusdem diffiniti.

**3.** (Lokert *De Terminis* 3v)

Ulterius adverte respectu cuiuscunque diffinitionis est aliquod diffinitum propinquum et est illud de quo prius mentionem fecimus. Est etiam aliquod diffinitum remotum et est illud quod significatur per diffinitum propinquum eiusdem diffinitionis secundum quod huiusmodi. Hoc declaratur. Illius diffinitionis signum ponibile in propositione illa dictio terminus est diffinitum propinquum et quelibet res significata per illam dictionem terminus secundum talem significationem est diffinitum remotum respectu eiusdem diffinitionis. Ex quo sequitur quod quilibet terminus est diffinitum remotum respectu dicte diffinitionis. Et ita idem terminus est diffinitum propinquum et diffinitum remotum respectu eiusdem diffinitionis. Sequitur ulterius licet respectu eiusdem diffinitionis secundum eandem significationem non sunt plura diffinita propinqua non convertibilia eiusdem tamen diffinitionis sunt plura diffinita remota non convertibilia secundum eandem eius diffinitionem. Similiter licet sequatur hoc est diffinitum propinquum ergo hoc est eodem utrobique demonstrato, non tamen sequitur hoc est diffinitum remotum ergo hoc est etiam pronomine univoce capto in antecedente et consequente.

**4.** (Lokert *De Terminis* 5v)

Primo ut dictum est arguendo quando diximus terminos syncathegoreumaticos non posse diffiniri debet intelligi secundum significationes syncathegoreumaticas. Et quando ulterius arguitur de illa diffinitione terminus significans aliqualiter dicitur illa est diffinitio illius termini terminus syncathegoreumaticus. Modo ille terminus terminus syncathegoreumaticus non est terminus syncathegoreumaticus sed cathegoreumaticus.

**5.** (Lokert *De Terminis* 4r)

Alia est propositio ypothetica et est illa in qua formaliter vel equivalenter coniunguntur plures propositiones vel plura complexa propositionalia per aliquod coniungibile. Et tales propositiones ypothetice sumunt denominationes ab illis coniungibilibus sic scilicet quod si coniungibile sit copulativum denominatur propositio copulativa, si disiunctum disiunctiva et si rationale denominatur propositio rationalis et ita de aliis. Exempla faciliter dari possunt. (Complexum propositionale est complexum quod non est propositio potens esse antecedens vel consequens in aliqua consequentia, et dantur communiter talia signata propositione cathegorica mutando verbum eius principale in verbum optativi modi).

**6.** (Lokert *De Terminis* 4v)

Dividitur significare in significare naturaliter et in significare ad placitum. Unde naturaliter significare est apud omnes significare vel seclusa quacumque impositione formali aut virtuali significare. Et quando terminus naturaliter significans seipso et nullo alio mediante significat dicitur naturaliter proprie significare et taliter soli termini mentales significant loquendo de terminis proprie dictis. Quando vero terminus naturaliter mediante alio significat secundum quod huiusmodi dicitur naturaliter communiter vel naturaliter improprie significare, et taliter dicitur quelibet res mundi significare seipsam. Patet ex istis quemlibet terminum mentalem utroque dictorum modorum significare. Declaratur de uno termino mentali et eodem modo de quolibet. Naturalis similitudo Sortis naturaliter proprie significat Sortem postquam quelibet naturalis similitudo significat naturaliter proprie illud cuius est naturalis similitudo. Et eadem naturalis similitudo Sortis significat naturaliter communiter ipsummet per regulam communem quelibet res mundi seipsam naturaliter communiter significat. Significare ad placitum est significare non apud omnes vel significare ex impositione formali aut virtuali. Dicitur impositio formalis voluntaria institutio facta per actum formalem voluntatis alicuius habentis auctoritatem vel per plures actus tales plurium habentium auctoritatem. Et terminus dicitur significare ex impositione virtuali quando ex sola consuetudine vel consecutive ad impositionem formalem significat. Unde terminus dupliciter potest significare consecutive ad impositionem formalem, uno modo quando aliquis terminus formaliter imponitur ad significandum aliquid talis terminus consecutive significat res convenientes cum illo ad quod formaliter imponebatur ad significandum. Isto modo iste terminus homo formaliter impositus ad significandum homines consecutive significat homines pictos. Alio modo terminus dicitur significare aliquid consecutive ad impositionem formalem propter convenientiam quam habet talis terminus cum termino formaliter imposito ad illud idem significandum. Quomodo naturaliter similitudo illius termini homo significat omnes homines. Eodem modo dupliciter potest dici terminus significare consecutive ad significationem naturalem propriam et similiter ad significationem naturalem communem.

7. (Lokert *De Terminis* 12r–13r)

Respondeo ad primum dubium [utrum bene dividatur significare in significare naturaliter et in significare ad placitum et ita de aliis subdivisionibus]. Presupponuntur conditiones requisite ad bonam divisionem logicaliter loquendo de divisione. Prima conditio divisum non debet excedere disiunctum ex membris dividentibus nec tale disiunctum debet excedere ipsum divisum quod non est aliud quam disiunctum ex membris dividentibus converti cum diviso. Et hoc intelligatur secundum significationes secundum quas sunt divisum et membra dividentia.

Secunda conditio membra dividentia eiusdem divisionis non debent coincidere secundum rationes formales hoc est membra dividentia bone divisionis non debent verificari pro eodem eadem ratione. Tunc dicitur ad dubium quod sufficienter dividitur significare in significare naturaliter et in significare ad placitum et ita alie subdivisiones sunt sufficientes . . .

Confirmatur contra illam divisionem qua dividitur significare in significare naturaliter et in significare ad placitum idem terminus significat naturaliter et etiam significat ad placitum. Igitur divisio insufficiens. Antecedens patet de illa voce homo que naturaliter seipsam significat et etiam significat ad placitum omnes homines. Igitur. Si forte dicatur non inconvenit eundem terminum unam rem significare naturaliter et ad placitum aliam sed esset inconveniens quod aliquis terminus eandem rem significaret naturaliter et ad placitum. Contra illud arguitur iste terminus vocalis vel scriptus ens significat seipsum naturaliter et etiam significat ipsum ad placitum postquam omnia entia ad placitum significat et ipsummet est unum ens. Igitur. Si forte dicatur iterum non inconvenit aliquem terminum significare naturaliter et ad placitum aliquod idem significatum sed non potest aliquis terminus quodlibet eius significatum quod ad placitum significat naturaliter significare et econverso. . . .

Ad confirmationem ubi queritur de illa divisione qua dividitur significare in significare naturaliter et in significare ad placitum pono propositiones. Prima idem terminus significat naturaliter et ad placitum. Ista propositio patet de quolibet termino significante ad placitum. Secunda propositio idem terminus eandem rem significat naturaliter et ad placitum. Hoc patet de quolibet transcendente et pluribus aliis terminis. Tertia propositio non inconvenit aliquem terminum etiam idem naturaliter et ad placitum significare. Hoc probat argumentum per novam impositionem. Nec ex illo sequitur talem terminum illud non apud omnes significare sed solum quod talis terminus illud non apud omnes significat illa ratione quia ad placitum illud significat. Ex isto patet quarta propositio quod non potest aliquis terminus idem naturaliter et ad placitum significare eadem ratione quod sufficit ad membra dividentia bone divisionis non coincidere sicut declarabatur in secunda conditione.

**8.** (Lokert *De Terminis* 14v)

Ad confirmationem ubi queritur utrum terminus naturaliter aliquid significans cuilibet potentie cognitive illud aptitudinaliter representat et dico primo quilibet talis terminus quantum est ex suo modo significandi cuilibet potentie cognitive aptitudinaliter representat. Et si non potest cuilibet representare erit deffectus et impedimentum ex parte potentie cognitive et non ex parte significationis termini. Dicitur secundo sufficit ad terminum significare naturaliter quod aptitudinaliter apud omnes res habentes potentias eiusdem speciei representat sic scilicet quod si aliqua noticia alicui potentie cognitive naturaliter significet sufficit quod cuilibet alteri potentie eiusdem rationis aptitudinaliter representat. Modo dico quod potentia cognitiva hominis et potentia cognitiva asini vel alterius bruti non sunt eiusdem rationis.

**9.** (Lokert *De Terminis* 14v)

Ad secundam dubitationem ubi querebatur utrum terminus possit cadere a sua significatione respondetur per duas propositiones. Prima terminus naturaliter significans non potest cadere a tali significatione sic scilicet quod potest esse talis terminus in rerum natura et non taliter significare. Ista propositio probari potest postquam terminus non habet ab aliquo extrinseco ut taliter significet sed ex sua propria natura. Secunda propositio terminus ad placitum significans potest cadere a tali significatione qua ad placitum significat. Volo dicere quod aliqua res nunc significans ad placitum potest manere in rerum natura et non taliter ad placitum significare. Hoc etiam probari potest postquam terminus habet ab extrinseco scilicet a voluntaria institutione alicuius vel plurium ut ad placitum significet vel a tali dispositione suarum partium. Modo talis terminus potest aliter disponi secundum suas partes vel voluntarie deponi a tali significatione ab eodem vel alio habente auctoritatem.

**10.** (Lokert *De Terminis* 15r–v)

Confirmatur capta illa propositione homo non est animal illa negatio in tali propositione naturaliter significat negative scilicet negando copulam propositionis et tamen potest cadere ab illa significatione quod sic probatur. Superveniente alia negatione in principio propositionis impedietur prior negatio a negatione copule alias propositio post adventum secunde negationis maneret negativa quod non est dicendum. Igitur prior negatio que negabat copulam ante adventum

secunde negationis et post eius adventum non ultra negat illam copulam cadit a priori significatione qua naturaliter significabat. Igitur . . .
Ad confirmationem negatur quod talis negatio [que] est in illa mentali homo non est animal possit cadere a sua significatione. Et licet negative significet non sequitur quod propter adventum secunde negationis cadat ab illa priore significatione vel negatione quia superveniente secunda negatione licet non negatur copula in ordine ad illam totam non homo non est animal negatur tamen a prima negatione in ordine ad illam homo non est animal quod sufficit ad hoc quod prima negatio non cadat a priore significatione. Et per primam negationem semper intelligo illam que immediate fertur supra copulam verbalem.

11. ( Lokert *De Terminis* 16r–v)
Ad tertiam dubitationem [utrum ad terminum significare ad placitum proprie sufficit et requiritur ipsum esse impositum ad significandum] respondeo presumptive quod multiplex potest fieri impositio termini ad significandum. Una est impositio sufficiens et est talis impositio ex qua terminus potest esse significativus. Et aliquando terminus imponitur impositione sufficiente simpliciter et absolute ad aliquid vel aliqualiter determinate significandum ut si aliquis habens auctornitatem imponat aliquam rem ad significandum Sortem qualitercunque talis res disponatur et hoc pro quocunque loco vel tempore. Aliquando terminus imponitur impositione sufficiente dependente vel conditionata quando scilicet imponitur ab aliquo habente auctoritatem non simpliciter et absolute qualitercunque talis res imposita se habeat quod significet sed sub certa dispositione vel certa conditione adimpleta sicut impositi sunt termini scripti et forte vocales. Istud etiam declarari potest exemplo. Si aliquis habens auctoritatem imponeret ly a ad aliquid significandum si Sortes tangeret pilare et non aliter non significaret ly a ex tali impositione nisi adimpleta conditione inclusa in impositione. . . .
Respondetur ad dubium per aliquas propositiones [dubium utrum ad terminum significare ad placitum proprie sufficit et requiritur ipsum esse impositum ad significandum]. Prima ad terminum significare ad placitum proprie requiritur quod sit impositus talis terminus ad significandum. Secunda propositio ad terminum significare ad placitum proprie non sufficit quod talis terminus sit impositus ad significandum. Patet primo de impositione facta ab aliquo non habente auctoritatem. Etiam licet fuisset facta impositio ab aliquo habente auctoritatem poterat deponi ab illa significatione ab eodem vel alio habente auctoritatem. Etiam nulla facta depositione poterat imponi impositione insufficiente et quando fuisset terminus sufficiente impositione

impositus dummodo fuisset impositio dependens vel conditionata non oportet terminum significare ex tali impositione nisi adimpleta conditione vel posito illo a quo dependet significatio habenda ex tali impositione.

**12.** (Lokert *De Terminis* 17r)

Ad aliud punctum argumenti ubi queritur utrum terminus impositus ad significandum imponebatur per alios terminos vel aliquo alio modo dicitur aliqui termini imponebantur per alios terminos sed non quilibet terminus imponebatur per alios et ita non oportet procedere in infinitum in impositis. Sed deveniendum ad primum terminum impositum qui non imponebatur per alios terminos prius impositos sed per signa exteriora imponebatur talis terminus. Et ita oportet concedere quod primo non imponebantur termini sincathegoreumatici sed prius termini cathegoreumatici et consequenter sincathegoreumatici.

**13.** (Lokert *De Terminis* 20r)

Et si queratur qualiter talia syncathegoreumata [sc. necessario possibiliter contingenter etc.] significant dicitur difficile est immo forte impossibile explicare per terminos simplices modum significandi quorumcunque terminorum syncathegoreumaticorum. Sed poterunt explicari significationes talium terminorum per circumlocutionem partim per terminos cathegoreumaticos et partim per terminos syncathegoreumaticos ut si petatur qualiter significat ly improprie dicendum est quod habet talem modum significandi quod quando additur tali termino significat denotat ipsum accipi pro aliquo termino secundum aliquam significationem significante non ex impositione nec seipso nullo alio mediante. Et ita ly naturaliter proprie sive in mente sive in voce sive in scripto habet propriam modum significandi taliter scilicet quod quando additur tali termino significat denotatur ratione talis determinationis accipi pro termino habente significationem qua seipso et nullo alio mediante significat. Et ita alia syncathegoreumata habent suos proprios modos significandi qui possunt explicari aliquo modo per circumlocutionem et non per terminos simplices ut est dictum.

**14.** (Lokert *De Terminis* 10v)

Ulterius presupponitur quid sit suppositio. Unde suppositio est acceptio termini in propositione pro suo significato pro quo talis terminus est verificabilis in potentia propinqua eodem modo acceptus sicut accipitur in tali propositione quoad proprietates logicales maxime ampliationem restrictionem et appellationem sicut in propositione in qua dictus terminus accipitur. Et in predicta descriptione ly suo significato absolvatur a numero. Unde terminum pro aliquo verificari est ipsum predicari in propositione cathegorica affirmativa que red-

ditur vera pro illo eodem pro quo dicitur terminus verificari ut in ista
propositione homo est animal ly animal pro quolibet homine qui est
verificatur et in illa Sortes est animal solum verificatur ly animal pro
Sorte supposito etiam quod sit Sortes et proportionaliter in aliis propositionibus affirmativis veris est dicendum. De singulis speciebus
suppositionis proprio loco videbitur.

15. (Lokert *De Terminis* 10v–11r)
Prima [regula] ad veritatem propositionis cathegorice affirmative non
modalis nec exponibilis nec se falsificantis in qua nullum ponitur
signum distributivum nec alia universalitas sufficit et requiritur quod
subiectum et predicatum eius pro aliquo eodem supponant. Secludo
propositiones compositas ex terminis significantibus res divinas. Ista
regula declaratur exemplo. Talis propositio homo est animal est cathegorica affirmativa etc. sicut dicebatur in regula ad cuius veritatem
sufficit et requiritur quod pro aliquo eodem supponat ly homo pro quo
supponit ly animal secundum acceptiones quas tales termini habent in
dicta propositione et propter deffectum illius ista est falsa homo est
asinus. Dicebatur in regula propositionis cathegorice affirmative quia
illud nec sufficit nec requiritur ad veritatem cathegorice negative sed
veritates negativarum opposito modo cognoscuntur ut inferius declar-
abitur. Dicebatur in dicta regula non modalis quia ad veritatem cathegorice affirmative modalis illud non sufficit maxime in modalibus de ly
impossibiliter vel ly necessario vel ly contingenter ut specialiter capitur immo nec forte in modalibus affirmativis de ly possibiliter.
Sed hic queritur qualiter attenditur veritas in talibus propositionibus
modalibus. Respondetur breviter pro presenti veritates propositionum modalium attenduntur penes propositiones illarum de inesse sic
scilicet quod ad veritatem propositionis modalis immediate probande
ratione modi si sit de ly possibiliter affirmato sufficit et requiritur
possibilitas eius de inesse. Et si talis propositio fuerit de ly impossibiliter affirmato et immediate probanda ratione modi impossibiliter im-
possibilitas eius de inesse sufficit et requiritur. Et si talis propositio
fuerit de ly necessario sufficit et requiritur necessitas sue de inesse. Si
vero sit talis propositio de ly contingenter generaliter capto eodem
modo dicatur sicut esset de ly possibiliter quia ly possibiliter et ly
contingenter ut capitur generaliter equivalent.
Eodem modo dicatur quod veritates propositionum de preterito et de
futuro cognoscuntur penes propositiones de presenti illis respond-
entes sic scilicet quod ad veritatem propositionis cathegorice affirmative de preterito immediate probande ratione copule de preterito sufficit et requiritur quod aliquando sua de presenti fuisset vera vel quod
ita fuisset sicut per suam de presenti significaretur. Et ita ad veritatem

propositionis talis de futuro requiritur et sufficit quod sua de presenti aliquando erit vera vel quod aliquando erit ita sicut per suam de presenti significaretur. Et istud precipue intelligatur de propositionibus quarum aliqua extrema vel partes extremorum sequuntur tales copulas de preterito vel futuro.

Dicebatur in regula propositionis non exponibilis quia veritates talium propositionum cognoscuntur per exponentes. Qualiter tales exponuntur suo loco videbitur. Similiter dicebatur in regula non se falsificantis quia quod dicitur de aliis cathegoricis non sufficit ad veritatem alicuius talis propositionis.

Secunda regula ad veritatem propositionis cathegorice negative non modalis non exponibilis nec insolubilis in qua non ponitur aliqua particularitas sufficit et requiritur quod subiectum et predicatum non supponant pro eodem. Quare ponentur ille particule non modalis non exponibilis nec insolubilis patet ex priore regula. Alia particula scilicet in qua non ponitur particularitas ponitur consimili ratione qua ponebatur in regula precedente in qua non ponitur universalitas quia ad veritatem negative in qua ponitur particularitas non requiritur subiectum et predicatum non supponere pro eodem sicut ad veritatem affirmative in qua ponitur universalitas non sufficit subiectum et predicatum pro aliquo eodem supponere. Qualiter tales propositiones sint probande probabitur in tractatu suppositionum. Secluduntur etiam ab ista regula sicut a priore propositiones composite ex terminis significantibus res divinas.

**16.** (Lokert *De Terminis* 3v–4r)

Consequenter declarandi sunt aliqui termini pertinentes ad argumentationem. Unde antecedens est oratio ex qua denotatur inferri consequens. Consequens vero est oratio que denotatur sequi ex antecedente et si antecedens habeat duas partes principales copulative ad invicem unitas prima dicitur maior et secunda minor. Nota illationis est coniungibile ratione cuius consequens denotatur inferri ex antecedente et tota consequentia resultat ex antecedente consequente et nota illationis. Istud declaratur. Ista tota oratio omnis homo currit et Sortes est homo ergo Sortes currit dicitur consequentia cuius antecedens est hoc totum omnis homo currit et Sortes est homo. Consequens vero est illa propositio Sortes currit. Maior [est] illa omnis homo currit. Minor est illa Sortes est homo. Et nota illationis est ly ergo . . .

Consequentia aliqua dicitur bona et est illa consequentia que sic se habet quod non potest ita esse sicut significatur per eius antecedens quin ita sit sicut significatur per eius consequens secundum talem significationem. Consequentia mala opposito modo diffinitur quando

scilicet potest ita esse sicut significatur per eius antecedens non existente ita sicut significatur per eius consequens. Ista declaratur exemplo. Talis consequentia est bona si Sortes currit Sortes movetur
postquam non potest esse quod Sortes currit quin sit ita quod Sortes
movetur. Et opposito modo probari potest quod ista consequentia est
mala si Sortes movetur Sortes currit.

**17.** (Lokert *De Terminis* 21v)
Presupposito ex superius dictis quod sit divisio logicaliter loquendo
de divisione cum conditionibus ad bonam divisionem requiritur sit
ista prima divisio terminorum alius mentalis alius vocalis et alius
scriptus. Qualiter dandus sit sensus cathegoricus vel ypotheticus talis
divisionis patet ex superioribus dictis. In dicta divisione ly terminus
est divisum et illi tres termini scilicet terminus mentalis terminus
vocalis et terminus scriptus sunt membra dividentia. Dicitur terminus
scriptus qui oculo corporali percipi potest. Terminus vocalis est terminus qui auditu corporali percipi potest. Et terminus mentalis est
terminus significans seipso et nullo alio mediante.

**18.** (Lokert *De Terminis* 23v)
Ad confirmationem dicitur non oportet quamlibet qualitatem existen-
tem in potentia cognitiva esse noticiam aut terminum mentalem. Hoc
patet primo ut supra dicebatur terminus scriptus vel alia qualitas
materialis potest poni in potentia cognitiva per potentiam divinam.
Similiter ut dicebatur arguendo in potentia cognitiva sunt passiones et
habitus tamen tales non sunt noticie nec termini mentales. Non enim
possunt actualiter representare potentie cognitive seipsis et non medi-
antibus aliis. De actibus voluntatis diverse sunt opiniones doctorum
utrum dicantur noticie. Sed sive dicantur noticie sive non non videtur
quod aliquis talis actus sit terminus postquam ut dicebatur arguendo
non potest talis actus poni in propositione tanquam pars propinqua
etc. Et ita videtur dicendum de noticia indicativa licet sit noticia non
tamen est terminus mentalis nec terminus simpliciter secundum talem
significationem.

**19.** (Lokert *De Terminis* 22r)
Item divisum [sc. terminus] verificaretur pro aliquo pro quo nullum
membrorum dividentium [sc. mentalis vocalis aut scriptus] verificaretur quia si angelus vel anima imponeretur ad significandum ab
aliquo habente auctoritatem impositione sufficiente esset terminus et
nec esset mentalis nec vocalis nec scriptus ut patet ex diffinitionibus
datis illorum membrorum. Nec valet dicere ut divisio sit simpliciter
bona addendum est aliud membrum scilicet terminus qui a solo intellectu percipi potest quia ponendo illud membrum superflue poner-
etur in eadem divisione illud membrum scilicet terminus mentalis.

Similiter qualitates perceptibiles aliis sensibus ab auditu et visu sicut sunt qualitates prime sapores et odores possunt esse termini ex impositione sicut angelus vel anima. Et tamen nulla talis qualitas esset terminus mentalis vocalis vel scriptus aut a solo intellectu perceptibilis nec etiam terminus mixtus ex talibus partibus. Igitur.

**20.** (Lokert *De Terminis* 24r)

Respondetur ad argumentum ut dictum est arguendo ad terminum vocalem requiritur quod sit immediate perceptibilis ab auditu corporali. Et quando replicatur de termino scripto dicitur non requiritur ad terminum scriptum quod sit immediate perceptibilis visu corporali. Et dissimilitudo de termino vocali et scripto dari potest ex diffinitionibus illorum terminorum et ex communi modo loquendi.

**21.** (Lokert *De Terminis* 24v)

Dicitur terminus cathegoreumaticus terminus aliquid vel aliqua significans et terminus sincathegoreumaticus est terminus significans aliqualiter. Dividitur terminus cathegoreumaticus in terminum cathegoreumaticum significatione tantum et in terminum cathegoreumaticum officio tantum et in terminum cathegoreumaticum significatione et officio simul. Proportionabiliter dividitur terminus sincathegoreumaticus. Dicitur terminus cathegoreumaticus significatione tantum terminus secundum aliquam eius significationem aliquid vel aliqua significans non potens habere officium in propositione secundum talem significationem. Communiter datur exemplum de obliquo secundum significationem secundum quam est obliquus et de adiectivo secundum quod pure adiective tenetur. Terminus dicitur habere officium in propositione secundum aliquam eius significationem quando secundum talem significationem potest esse pars principalis alicuius propositionis. Dicetur terminus cathegoreumaticus officio tantum terminus secundum aliquam eius significationem nichil nec aliqua significans potens tamen habere officium in propositione secundum talem significationem ut est terminus potens esse copula propositionis cathegorice vel ypothetice. Et terminus dicitur cathegoreumaticus significatione et officio simul quando secundum aliquam eius significationem aliquid vel aliqua significat et potest habere officium in propositione secundum talem significationem sicut sunt termini potentes esse subiectum et predicatum cathegorice propositionis.

**22.** (Lokert *De Terminis* 25v–26v)

Confirmatur nullus est terminus sincathegoreumaticus. Igitur. Assumptum probatur. Si esset aliquis maxime esset ly omnis. Sed illud probatur falsum. Ly omnis non significat aliqualiter. Igitur non est terminus sincathegoreumaticus. Consequentia est bona et antecedens probatur querendo quid sit terminum significare aliqualiter. Si forte dicatur sicut communiter dicitur terminum significare aliqualiter est ipsum habere talem modum significandi quod ratione talis modi significandi aliter accipitur quam acciperetur sine tali termino habente illum modum significandi.

Contra illud arguitur sequeretur istum terminum omnis in ista propositione omnis homo qui est Sortes currit non significare aliqualiter postquam illud complexum homo qui est Sortes non aliter accipitur propter adventum illius significationis quam acciperetur sine tali signo ex quo illud complexum est terminus singularis. Eodem modo ly aliquis in ista propositione aliquis homo currit non esset terminus sincathegoreumaticus non enim facit quod ly homo aliter accipiatur quam acciperetur sine tali signo.

Item ly homo significaret aliqualiter et esset terminus sincathegoreumaticus postquam ex eius additione alicui termino talis terminus aliter accipitur quam acciperetur sine tali termino homo. Hoc patet in illa propositione animal quod est homo currit ubi illud complexum aliter accipitur quam in ista animal quod est currit. Et ita ly hominis facit quod ly asinus aliter accipiatur in ista propositione hominis asinus currit quam acciperetur sine illa determinatione hominis. Tamen nec ly homo nec ly hominis est terminus sincathegoreumaticus. Igitur. . . .

Ad confirmationem communiter dicitur ut arguendo est dictum. Illud tamen sufficienter est improbatum per illos terminos cathegoreumaticos homo hominis et ita poterit improbari per alios. Idcirco dicitur ad terminum significare aliqualiter sicut in proposito intelligimus requiritur quod habeat aliquam significationem qua nichil nec aliqua significet sed ratione talis significationis possit terminum cui additur facere aliter accipi etc. ut dicebatur in arguendo. Et quando dicitur ly omnis in illa propositione omnis homo qui est Sortes currit non est terminus sincathegoreumaticus nec etiam ly aliquis in illa aliquis homo currit illud negatur. Et ad probationem quando dicitur terminus cui additur ly omnis in prima non aliter accipitur quam acciperetur sine tali signo et ita terminus cui additur ly aliquis in secunda illud negatur. Terminus qui est subiectum prime sumitur universaliter propter ly omnis et subiectum secunde sumitur particulariter ratione signi particularis licet propositio talis equivaleat preiacenti in qua non ponitur tale signum.

### 23. (Lokert *De Terminis* 26v–27r)

Circa predicta potest dubitari de obliquo tento et de adiectivo tento qualiter sunt termini cathegoreumatici significatione tantum. Videtur primo quod obliquus potest habere officium in propositione etiam secundum significationem eius obliquam. Patet respectu verbi impersonalis vel verbi infinitivi modi. Similiter rectus et eius obliquus dicuntur termini sinonimi. Alias verificatio obliqui supponentis non fieret per suum rectum. Ergo si rectus potest habere officium in propositione similiter et eius obliquus. . . .

Ad ista per ordine respondetur. Primo de obliquo secundum eius significationem obliquam probabile est dicere quod talis obliquus potens reddere suppositum verbo impersonali aut infinitivi modi sit terminus cathegoreumaticus officio et non significatione tantum. Nec propterea illud esset concedendum de quocunque obliquo. Quia tamen communiter dicitur quod quilibet obliquus sit terminus cathegoreumaticus significatione tantum secundum quod oblique tenetur dicendum est licet possit esse extremum alicuius propositionis cathegorice non propterea est terminus cathegoreumaticus officio. Sed requiritur quod possit esse copula vel extremum in propositione cathegorica respectu verbi personalis et modi finiti.

Et ad aliud quod dicitur de obliquo et eius recto scilicet quod sunt termini sinonimi est advertendum quod dupliciter aliqui dicuntur termini sinonimi scilicet de significatione essentiali tantum quando scilicet aliqui termini eandem rem precise significant et eodem modo quoad significare absolute vel connotative. Isto modo rectus et eius obliquus dicuntur termini sinonimi. Nec propterea oportet quod quicquid convenit uni illorum terminorum taliter synonimorum quod conveniat alteri. Alio modo dicuntur termini synonimi de significatione essentiali et etiam accidentali sive grammaticali quando noticia respondens uni etiam respondet alteri. Isto modo rectus et eius obliquus non dicuntur termini sinonimi et quicquid convenit uni terminorum taliter synonimorum etiam convenit alteri. Rectus habet aliquem modum significandi accidentalem ratione cuius potest reddere suppositum verbo personali finiti modi et non obliquus.

**24.** (Lokert *De Terminis* 27r–v )

Sequitur tertia divisio terminorum. Mentalium quidem est terminus mentalis ultimatus et alius est terminus mentalis non ultimatus. Unde terminus mentalis ultimatus est terminus respondens alicui alteri termino secundum significationem ultimatam talis termini. Et terminus mentalis non ultimatus est terminus mentalis respondens alicui alteri termino secundum eius significationem non ultimatam. Dicitur significatio ultimata alicuius termini illa significatio qua talis terminus proprie significat. Et significatio non ultimata alicuius termini est illa significatio secundum quam talis terminus improprie significat. Et ita illud significatum termini quod talis terminus proprie significat dicitur significatum eius ultimatum. Et illud quod terminus improprie significat dicitur eius significatum non ultimatum. Istud declaratur de isto termino homo. Quilibet homo est significatum ultimatum talis termini postquam quemlibet hominem ultimate significat quia ad placitum proprie. Et ipsemet terminus est eius significatum non ultimatum quia improprie significat ipsummet scilicet naturaliter communiter vel ad placitum improprie. Et ideo naturalis similitudo omnium hominum dicitur conceptus ultimatus vel terminus mentalis ultimatus illius termini homo. Et naturalis similitudo ipsiusmet est eius conceptus non ultimatus vel terminus mentalis non ultimatus. Et proportionabiliter declarari potest de quolibet alio termino significativo vocali vel scripto. Sequitur correlarie quod nullus terminus non significativus habet terminum mentalem ultimatum sed quilibet terminus mentalis respondens tali termino non significativo est terminus mentalis non ultimatus respectu talis termini non significativi. Hoc patet postquam nullus talis terminus habet significationem qua proprie et ultimate significat.

Sequitur secundo sicut terminus vocalis vel scriptus habet terminum mentalem non ultimatum secundum quod significat seipsum improprie sive naturaliter communiter sic quilibet terminus mentalis habet terminum mentalem non ultimatum in significando ipsummet naturaliter communiter. Et cuiuslibet termini mentalis conceptus reflexus est terminus mentalis non ultimatus illius cuius est conceptus reflexus. Dicitur conceptus reflexus terminus mentalis naturaliter proprie distincte representans noticiam. Alii termini mentales dicuntur noticie directe.

Sequitur tertio non quilibet terminus proprie significans habet terminum mentalem ultimatum secundum talem significationem propriam. Et intelligo pro ly habet habere potest. Hoc patet de terminis mentalibus naturaliter proprie significantibus et non ad placitum proprie. Tales termini non subordinantur terminis mentalibus ultimatis respectu illorum postquam nullis subordinantur secundum tales significationes proprias. Quilibet tamen terminus vocalis vel scriptus proprie significans habet terminum mentalem ultimatum similiter terminum mentalem non ultimatum. Sequitur finaliter quod dicte divisionis divisum non est precise hoc complexum terminus mentalis sed hoc totum terminus mentalis alicuius alterius termini vel hoc totum terminus mentalis respondens alicui alteri termino. Volo dicere quod nullus terminus mentalis dicitur ultimatus vel non ultimatus nisi respective hoc est in ordine ad aliquem alium terminum.

**25.** ( Lokert *De Terminis* 29r–v)
Circa predicta moventur alique dubitationes. Primum dubium utrum sicut termino simplici respondet aliquis terminus mentalis ultimatus

et aliquis terminus mentalis non ultimatus ita termino complexo et similiter totali propositioni respondeat una propositio mentalis ultimata et etiam una propositio mentalis non ultimata.

Secundo dubitatur utrum sicut sunt aliqui termini cathegoreumatici mentales ultimati et aliqui tales termini mentales non ultimati ita similiter sunt aliqui termini sincathegoreumatici mentales ultimati et etiam aliqui termini sincathegoreumatici mentales non ultimati. . . .

Ad primum dubium respondetur affirmative sive detur terminus complexus sive incomplexus subordinatus alicui mentali termino ultimati secundum significationem eius propriam. Talis terminus mentalis dicitur terminus mentalis ultimatus respectu alterius. Et si subordinetur termino mentali secundum significationem impropriam dicitur talis terminus mentalis non ultimatus respectu illius. Et ita propositio vocalis vel scripta sicut ista homo est animal secundum quod significat ad placitum proprie propositionaliter subordinatur propositioni mentali ultimate. Et secundum quod improprie significat dicitur subordinari noticie que dicitur propositio mentalis non ultimata. Et ita naturalis similitudo alicuius propositionis dicitur propositio mentalis non ultimata. . . .

Ad secundum dubium respondetur affirmative. Hoc patet. Sicut dabiles sunt aliqui termini proprie et improprie significantes aliquid vel aliqua etiam sunt dabiles aliqui termini ad placitum proprie et similiter improprie significantes aliqualiter. Et per consequens sunt dabiles termini mentales sincathegoreumatici qui sunt termini mentales non ultimati respectu aliorum terminorum ut actus sincathegoreumaticus qui est terminus mentalis huius vocis omnis est terminus mentalis non ultimatus naturalis similitudinis illius vocis omnis postquam naturalis similitudo talis vocis taliter significat ad placitum improprie qualiter significat illa vox ad placitum proprie. Et ita patet quod non oportet quemlibet terminum mentalem non ultimatum esse naturalem similitudinem distinctam alicuius termini. Immo non oportet quod quilibet talis sit terminus cathegoreumaticus saltem secundum talem significationem.

**26.** (Lokert *De Terminis* 29v–30v)

Terminorum alius est terminus absolutus et alius est terminus cognotativus cuius divisionis divisum solum dicitur de termino cathegoreumatico. Et pro intellectu huius divisionis presupponitur alia divisio qua dividitur terminus in terminum complexum et in terminum incomplexum in qua divisione divisum accipi potest secundum quemcunque acceptionem termini et semper valebit divisio proportionabiliter loquendo de termino in membris dividentibus.

Terminus complexus est terminus cuius significatio formaliter vel equivalenter consurgit ex significationibus plurium terminorum debitam connectionem ad invicem habentium. Terminus incomplexus est terminus cuius significatio non taliter consurgit ex significationibus plurium terminorum etc. et per ly equivalenter intelligimus in proposito quod mentalis termini respondentis significatio taliter consurgat ut est dictum. Dicuntur termini habere debitam connectionem ad invicem quando se habent sicut determinatio et eius determinabile vel quando uniuntur termini ad invicem per aliquod coniungibile. Primo modo fit complexio indistans et secundo modo complexio distans. Facile est exemplificare de quolibet illorum membrorum.

Isto supposito dicitur quod terminus cognotativus est terminus cathegoreumaticus de materiali significato aliquid vel aliqua importans et de formali aliquid aliud vel illud idem aut illa eadem aliqualiter se habere denotans. Et terminus absolutus dicitur terminus cathegoreumaticus nichil ultra eius significatum materiale importans nec eius significatum materiale aliqualiter se habere denotans ubi ly significatum absolvitur a numero. Dicitur significatum materiale alicuius termini illud pro quo talis terminus natus est accipi ex suo modo significandi.

Istud declaratur. Ly homo est terminus absolutus cuius significata materialia sunt homines. Dictus terminus ultra illa significata nichil aliud importat nec illa significata aliqualiter se habere denotat. Et ly album est terminus cognotativus cuius significatum materiale est res alba et ultra illud quod significat res albas cognotat albedinem adiacere illi significato materiali. Ideo albedo est eius significatum formale. Ly sedens similiter est terminus cognotativus de materiali significato significans rem sedentem et ultra illud nichil aliud importat sed bene cognotat eandem rem aliqualiter se habere scilicet tali et tali modo.

Sequunter aliqua correlaria. Primum correlarium si aliquis rectus sit terminus absolutus quilibet obliquus talis recti similiter est terminus absolutus. Et ita si terminus singularis numeri sit terminus absolutus etiam terminus pluralis numeri respondens illi est terminus absolutus. Et proportionaliter est dicendum de termino cognotativo. Ex isto subsequitur ad terminum absolutum non requiritur quod aliquid significet in recto. Patet de obliquo qui est terminus absolutus nichil in recto significans.

Secundum correlarium sicut aliquis terminus cognotativus est complexus ita aliquis terminus cognotativus est incomplexus et talis terminus cognotativus incomplexus eadem significatione et mediante eadem noticia significat eius significata materialia et etiam eius significata formalia ut ly album rem albam et albedinem univoce et incom-

plexe significat. Nec videtur inconveniens concedere quemlibet terminum complexum natum pro aliquo accipi esse terminum cognota-
tivum sive talis terminus constituatur solum ex pluribus terminis
cathegoreumaticis sive includat aliquod sincathegoreuma. Et ex isto
consequenter infertur quod quilibet terminus absolutus est incomplexus et nullus talis est complexus secundum quod huiusmodi. . . .
Sequuntur consequenter due regule pro terminis absolutis et cogno-
tativis. Prima terminus absolutus positus in propositione mediante
copula de presenti non aliunde restrictus supponit pro quolibet eius
significato correspondenti tempori importato per talem copulam ut si
Sortes sit in rerum natura tunc iste terminus Sortes positus in propositione respectu copule presentis temporis supponit pro ipso. Et ita non
stat aliquem hominem esse quin ille terminus homo positus in propositione mediante copula de presenti non aliunde restrictus pro quolibet
homine supponat et proportionabiliter dicatur de aliis terminis absolutis. Secunda regula nunquam terminus cognotativus pro aliquo supponit respectu alicuius copule nisi eius cognotatio illi conveniat in
ordine ad tempus importatum per talem copulam ut si ly album pro
aliquo supponat respectu copule presentis temporis oportet illud
habere albedinem in tempore presenti et proportionabiliter respectu
aliarum differentiarum temporis.

27. (Lokert *De Terminis* 31r–32r)
Terminorum alius est terminus communis et alius est terminus singularis cuius divisionis divisum est hoc totum terminus natus pro
aliquo vel aliquibus accipi ex suo modo significandi ut ly terminus ut
equivalet tali complexo ratione cuius nullus terminus syncathegoreumaticus est terminus singularis vel communis secundum significationem syncathegoreumaticam et ita nec integra propositio nec complexum propositionale secundum quod huiusmodi et ita nec aliquis
alius terminus qui non est natus pro aliquo vel aliquibus accipi ex suo
modo significandi. Unde terminus communis est terminus cui non
repugnat pro pluribus accipi ex suo modo significandi univoce et
divisim ut sunt tales termini homo animal et similes.
Terminus singularis est terminus natus accipi pro aliquo ex suo modo
significandi et non pro pluribus univoce et divisim ut est iste terminus
Sortes et similes. Capitur in proposito ly accipi pro supponere vel
verificari. Et dicitur in diffinitionibus predictis ex suo modo significandi quia non oportet quod quilibet terminus communis vel singularis simpliciter natus sit pro aliquo accipi. Ly chimera est terminus
communis et ly ista chimera terminus singularis. Tamen nullus illorum potest pro aliquo accipi. Intelligo mediante copula non ampliante
ad quinque differentias temporum. Nulli tamen dictorum termin-

orum repugnat ex suo modo significandi pro aliquo accipi. Defectus non est ex parte modi significandi termini sed ex parte rei significate vel cognotationis que nulli potest convenire. Dicebatur in diffinitionibus univoce quia terminus singularis equivoce pro pluribus accipitur. Dicitur terminus univoce accipi pro pluribus quando est terminus mentalis acceptus pro illis secundum quod naturaliter proprie significat vel quando est terminus qui pro illis accipitur mediante eodem termino mentali. Dicebatur divisim in diffinitionibus quia non inconvenit aliquem terminum singularem pro pluribus coniunctim accipi univoce ut ly Sortes pro materia et forma Sortis coniunctim et divisim accipitur.

Contra dicta arguitur si esset aliquis terminus singularis maxime esset ly Sortes. Sed illud probatur falsum quia vel talis terminus secundum quemlibet eius significationem esset terminus singularis vel secundum aliquam eius significationem esset terminus singularis et secundum aliam esset terminus communis. Nullum illorum est dicendum. Igitur. Minor probatur. Si detur secundum eandem rationem quilibet terminus secundum significationem esset terminus communis. Illud non videtur concedendum quia si quilibet terminus esset terminus communis nullus esset terminus singularis. Primum etiam maioris principalis non est dicendum quod multipliciter probatur. Primo ly Sortes aliqua eius significatione significat omnes terminos sibi similes secundum quam significationem non poterit esse terminus singularis. Similiter ly Sortes significat omnes qui vocantur illo nomine Sortes univoce secundum aliquam eius significationem. Et non potest dici terminus singularis secundum talem significationem. Eodem modo si Sortes aliqua significatione significat omnes ymagines Sortis in qua significatione etiam est terminus communis.

Igitur non secundum quamlibet eius significationem est terminus singularis. Pro solutione huius argumenti est notandum quod quilibet terminus habet unam significationem qua ipsummet naturaliter communiter significat et nihil aliud. Similiter habet aliquam significationem qua ipsummet et omnes similes vel synonimos terminos ad placitum improprie significat. Et quilibet secundum primam significationem est terminus singularis et communis secundum aliam significationem et hoc extendendo divisum et membra dividentia dicte divisionis ad terminos non significativos. Nec illud est inconveniens quod quilibet terminus sit singularis et etiam communis secundum diversas significationes improprias.

Adverte ulterius quod iste terminus Sortes dupliciter accipi potest significative uno modo ut equivalet huic complexo vocatum hoc nomine Sortes sic scilicet quod de materiali significato significabit aliquid cognotando quod vocetur Sortes. Et isto modo ly Sortes est terminus communis et cognotativus. Aliter communiter accipitur ly Sortes ut est terminus absolutus singularis non significans plures res univoce et divisim in qua significatione solet concedi quod Sortes erat Sortes antequam vocaretur Sortes et taliter significat aliquem nihil cognotando nec etiam aliqualiter.

**28.** (Major *Liber Terminorum* 10v¹–11r¹)

Terminus communis est terminus cui non repugnat accipi pro pluribus quantum est ex impositione termini secundum significationem secundum quam capitur quia licet sit defectus ex parte rei significate ut patet in istis terminis sol mundus phenix. Tamen non est defectus ex parte modi significandi termini significantis quia si per possibile vel impossibile pure phisice loquendo producatur unus alius sol iste terminus sine nova impositione [illum] significaret. Forte dicis eodem modo si per possibile vel impossibile esset unus alius Sortes ab isto iste terminus Sortes sine nova impositione illum representaret . . .

Respondetur quod ultimate standum est in impositione termini quod Sol communiter imponebatur ad significandum Sortes vero discrete et in terminis mentalibus hoc provenit ex natura rei . . .

Nomina superlativi gradus affirmative exponenda sunt termini communes quia licet eis repugnat accipi pro pluribus in eodem tempore ut dicitur quinto phisicorum tamen per successionem temporis accipiuntur vel accipi non repugnat pro pluribus.

**29.** (Major *Liber Terminorum* 12r¹)

Dubitatur an Sortes fuit Sortes antequam vocabatur Sortes. Et pro intellectu illius ponatur casus quod Sortes nascatur hodie hora quarta et imponatur ei nomen Sortes hora duodecima. Iam arguitur hora duodecima hec est vera hoc fuit Sortes hora octava quia hoc fuit hora octava. Ergo hoc fuit Sortes hora octava. Consequentia tenet a convertibilibus quia postquam Sortes est terminus absolutus de predicamento substantie non refert proponere istum terminum Sortes copule vel postponere. Respondetur quod hoc fuit Sortes in utero matris ut arguit ratio.

Et confirmatur quando dico hoc fuit Sortes predicatum stat significative supponens pro hac re absolute. Preterea nisi sic Sortes potest esse Plato quod non est dicendum quia quemadmodum species predicamenti substantie sunt disparate ita et individua.

Contra hoc arguitur illa de preterito nunquam habuit unam de presenti veram nec habere poterat. Ergo non est vera. Assumptum patet quia ista vocalis non erat vera hoc est Sortes hora octava quia Sortes tunc non significat Sortem ex casu.

Respondetur quod habuit unam de presenti veram hanc scilicet hoc est Sortes in mente quia aliquis vidisset Sortem hora octava poterat formare conceptum singularem et absolutum (si quis nobis possibilis sit) qui representasset Sortem. Et sic illa mentalis esset vera. Sed illa vocalis tunc non fuisset vera.

30. (Lokert *De Terminis* 32v–33r)

Respondetur ad argumentum concedendo ly non Sortes esse terminum communem et non singularem. Intelligo secundum significationem qua proprie significat. Et quando dicitur talis terminus solum significat Sortem illud negatur. Et pro probatione ubi dicitur terminus complexus habens significationem consurgentem ex significationibus suarum partium nichil significat quod non significetur per aliquam eius partem pro quo pono propositiones.

Prima dabilis est aliquis terminus complexus habens significationem formaliter consurgentem ex significationibus suarum partium significans aliquam rem que non significatur per aliquam partem illius complexi. Hoc patet de isto copulato ista materia et ista forma demonstrando materiam et formam Sortis. Totum copulatum significat Sortem et nulla pars eius ipsum significat. Intelligo de illa parte que partialiter significat ad totalem significationem totius copulati.

Secunda propositio est aliquod complexum cuius significatio formaliter consurgit ex significationibus suarum partium significans aliquid quod non significatur per aliquam partem talis complexi. Nec etiam aliqua pars illius significatur per aliquam partem dicti complexi. Hoc patet de termino infinito ly non Sortes ut probat argumentum. Pro quolibet alio a Sorte natum est accipi et supponere et per consequens quodlibet tale significat. Tamen nulla pars eius significat aliquod tale ens nec aliquam partem illius. . . .

Pono similiter propositiones. Prima terminus infinitus cuius terminus infinitatus pro quolibet alio a Sorte natus est accipi solum pro Sorte accipitur et poterit talis terminus infinitus dici singularis. Quanto enim terminus finitus pro pluribus accipitur tanto suus terminus infinitus pro paucioribus accipitur et econverso. Et per istud patet quando aliquis terminus infinitus est terminus singularis vel communis.

Secundo propositio si terminus finitus pro aliquo supponat mediante aliqua copula [eius] terminus infinitus non supponit pro eodem mediante simili copula et in ordine ad eandem differentiam temporis precise. Hoc patet ex hoc quod terminus finitus et eius terminus infinitus sunt termini contradictorii et tales nunquam pro eodem supponunt respectu consimilis copule et in ordine ad easdem differentias temporum precise. Licet datis quibuscunque terminis contradictoriis pro quolibet ente alter illorum sit verificabilis sicut pro quocunque verificatur transcendens mediante quacunque copula pro eodem mediante simili copula verificatur quodcunque disiunctum ex terminis contradictoriis. Et illud vult dicere regula communis terminorum contradictoriorum scilicet de quolibet alterum contradictoriorum de nullo simili ambo.

**31.** (Lokert *De Terminis* 34v–35r)

Terminorum alius est terminus prime intentionis et alius est terminus secunde intentionis cuius divisionis divisum solum dicitur de terminis cathegoreumaticis. Et in proposito sub termino prime intentionis comprehendimus terminum prime impositionis et ita sub termino secunde intentionis terminum secunde impositionis taliter quod membra dividentia dicantur tam de mentalibus terminis quam de vocalibus aut scriptis. Unde terminus secunde intentionis est terminus significans aliquid ea ratione qua illud est signum vel significatum. Et terminus prime intentionis est terminus significans aliquid non ea ratione qua illud est signum vel significatum in quibus diffinitionibus termini absolvuntur a numero. Et intelligatur per signum signum proprie captum. Et ita per ly significatum intelligatur significatum proprie per aliquem terminum. Patet ex dictis diffinitionibus dupliciter terminus potest esse terminus secunde intentionis uno modo quando significat aliquid ea ratione qua est signum ut ly nomen ly propositio ly signum proprie capiendo. Alio modo terminus dicitur secunde intentionis quia significat aliquid ea ratione qua illud est significatum ut tales termini diffinitum remotum equivocum equivocatum ly significatum loquendo de significato proprie. Unde dupliciter intelligi potest quod aliquis terminus significet aliquid ea ratione qua illud est signum uno modo quod terminus taliter significet illud quod si ipsum non sit signum talis terminus secundum talem significationem non supponet pro ipso. Intellige mediante copula de presenti seclusa quacunque ampliatione ut iste terminus nomen significat istam vocem vel scripturam homo taliter quod si ipsa non esset signum ly nomen non supponeret pro illa mediante tali copula.

Aliter intelligi potest terminum significare aliquid ea ratione qua illud est signum similiter quod talis terminus significet illud cognotando formaliter vel equivalenter sicut cognotat ly signum ut ly nomen equivalenter cognotat sicut ly signum. Propterea quod in eius diffinitione ponitur talis terminus signum significans vel significativum aut aliquis alius terminus includens in eius cognotatione cognotationem illius termini signum. Et proportionabiliter dupliciter intelligi potest terminum significare aliquid ea ratione qua est significatum uno modo quia talis terminus non supponeret pro illo mediante copula de presenti nisi significaretur proprie per aliquem terminum. Aliter intelligi potest quod terminus significat aliquid ea ratione qua est significatum quia significat illud cognotando formaliter vel equivalenter sicut cognotat ly significatum. Et in proposito melius est capere ly significare aliquid ea ratione qua est signum vel significatum secundum ultimas acceptiones.

Sequuntur correlaria. Primum quilibet terminus secunde intentionis est terminus cognotativus secundum quod huiusmodi. Hoc patet ex declaratione diffinitionis.

Secundum correlarium quilibet terminus absolutus est terminus prime intentionis. Istud sequitur ex priore. Cum isto tamen stat plures terminos cognotativos esse terminos prime intentionis ut sunt tales album nigrum rationale risibile et similes.

Tertium correlarium utrumque membrum dividens dicte divisionis est terminus secunde intentionis ex quo patet aliquem terminum secunde intentionis solum esse verificabilem pro terminis prime intentionis intelligo mediante copula de presenti. Illud patet de isto complexo terminus prime intentionis.

**32.** ( Lokert *De Terminis* 10r)
Tertia divisio propositionum aliqua dicitur exponibilis illa scilicet in qua ponitur signum exponibile sicut est signum exclusivum exceptivum reduplicativum collectivum terminus comparativus vel superlativus ly incipit ly desinit ly mediate ly differt et ita de quocunque alio termino faciente obscurum sensum propositionis. Alie propositiones in quibus non ponuntur talia signa dicuntur non exponibiles.

**33.** ( Major *De Exponibilibus* 3v²)
Propositio exponibilis est propositio obscurum sensum habens ratione signi in ea positi. Due differentie ponuntur in hac diffinitione. Primo dicitur obscurum sensum habens defectu cuius hec non est exponibilis ignis est calidus. Dicitur ratione signi in ea positi defectu cuius hec et similes hominis *a* asinus quodlibet rudibile est non non est exponibilis secundum eos qui dicunt universales non debere exponi inquantum huiusmodi quia licet propositio data habeat obscurum sensum veritatis quia dubium est ad contradicendum propositioni date.

**34.** (Major *De Exponibilibus* 4r¹⁻²)
Propositio universalis affirmativa exponitur per suam preiacentem et universalem negativam ei respondentem ut omnis homo currit sic exponitur homo currit et nichil est homo quin ipsum currit. Omnis populus est rotondus sic exponitur populus est rotondus et nichil nec aliqua sunt populus quin ipsum vel ipsa sunt populus rotondus vel sic populus est populus rotondus et nullus populus est non rotondus populus.

**35.** ( Major *De Exponibilibus* 1r¹)
Circa initium exponibilium queritur an arguendo ab exponibili ad

eius exponentes et contra sit bona consequentia. Et arguitur quod nonnulla est exponibilis. Ergo titulus questionis presupponit falsum. Consequentia tenet quia titulus presupponit oppositum assumpti. Antecedens patet quia dat oppositum. Tunc vel talis esset cathegorica vel ypothetica sed nec hoc nec illud. Igitur. Non illud probatur et quia idem est iudicium quoad omnes capio hanc exponibilem tantum animal est homo et arguitur sic mentalis huius vocalis est ypothetica. Ergo hec vocalis non est cathegorica. Consequentia tenet. Et antecedens probatur quia omnia sunt explicita in mente saltem ultimata quod non contingeret si foret aliqua mentalis ultimata exponibilis. Et sic oportet dicere quod hec vocalis subordinatur eidem mentali cum suis exponentibus.

36. ( Major *De Exponibilibus* 4v$^2$ )
Hoc arguitur ille equivalent ypotheticis. Ergo sunt ypothetice. Consequentia patet . . .
Ad primum argumentum trita est distinctio. Dupliciter propositiones dicuntur equivalere uno modo in consequendo vel in inferendo ( hoc est quando utraque est illativa alterius) alio modo in significando eo quod subordinantur eidem mentali vel una est mentalis et altera vel plures si sint ei subordinate. Vel brevius potest dici equivalere in significando est quando propositiones sunt synonime. Tunc quando dicitur de equivalentibus idem est iudicium si intelligatur de equivalentibus in consequendo hoc debet intelligi quoad esse verum et quoad esse falsum et non hoc universaliter quia in se fallentibus non oportet quia ista de quolibet est vel non est equivalet isti formaliter papa dormit vel nullus papa dormit. Et tamen opinantes reciperent primam cathegoricam de disiuncta copula et secunda nemini cadit in dubium est ypothetica. Si intelligatur de equivalentibus significando nego assumptum.

37. ( Lokert *De Exponibilibus* 1r$^1$–1v$^2$ )
Quattuor communiter ponuntur ordines vel genera exclusivarum. In primo ordine sunt propositiones in quibus nec negatur signum exclusivum nec copula principalis. Et in secundo ordine sunt propositiones in quibus signum exclusivum affirmatur et copula principalis negatur. Propositiones tertii ordinis sunt contradictorie propositionum primi ordinis et ita propositiones quarti ordinis sunt contradictorie propositionum secundi ordinis. Facile est exemplificari. De talibus propositionibus tantum homo et non tantum asinus sunt animalia dici potest quod sunt secundi ordinis et hoc ratione primi signi affirmati. Unde pro expositione talium propositionum ponuntur due propositiones. Prima propositiones exclusive primi et secundi ordinis exponibiles gratia alietatis exponende sunt copulative per duas exponentes ubi

prima exponens erit preiacens in forma et secunda opposite qualitatis et quantitatis ut in pluribus ad primam de subiecto contradictorio si denotetur fieri exclusio ab opposito tocius subiecti. Et si denotetur exclusio fieri ab opposito partis extremi precise debet infinitari illa pars a cuius opposito denotatur fieri exclusio. . . . Propositio declaratur. Ista exclusiva tantum homo est animal exponitur per talem copulativam homo est animal et nullum non homo est animal, et ista tantum homo non est animal per talem copulativam homo non est animal et omne non homo est animal, eodem modo ista tantum homo animal non est per istam homo animal non est et omne non homo quodlibet animal est. Proportionabiliter exponantur propositiones in quibus fit exclusio ab opposito partis extremi illo dempto quod in secunda exponente infinitetur solum illud a cuius opposito denotatur fieri exclusio. Et si talis terminus in exclusiva ponatur in obliquo similem obliquitatem debet habere terminus eius contradictorius in secunda exponente.

Secunda propositio exclusive tertii et quarti ordinis exponuntur per duas exponentes disiunctive contradictorio modo ad exclusivas primi et secundi ordinis que illis contradicunt ut ista non tantum homo est animal exponitur per talem disiunctivam non homo est animal vel non homo est animal una parte capiendo negationem neganter et in alia infinitanter, et ista non tantum homo non est animal per talem disiunctivam exponitur non homo non est animal vel non homo non est animal negatione posita in principio capta in una neganter et in alia infinitanter utrobique capta alia negatione que cadit immediate in copulam neganter vel exponatur dicta exclusiva quarti ordinis per istam disiunctivam que priori equivalet omnis homo est animal vel aliquid non homo non est animal et ita de aliis dicatur.

Ex istis propositionibus sequuntur correlaria. Primum correlarium signum exclusivum affirmatum est universalitas et tale signum negatum est particularitas. Ideo in propositionibus subcontrariis vel contradictoriis non debet manere tale signum affirmatum nec in contrariis vel contradictoriis negatum. Ex quo subsequitur quod oppositio contraria accipienda est inter exclusivas primi ordinis et exclusivas secundi ordinis et oppositio subcontraria inter exclusivas tertii et quarti ordinis et oppositio subalternativa inter exclusivas primi et quarti ordinis similiter inter exclusivas secundi et tertii ordinis. De oppositione contradictoria non est difficultas in talibus propositionibus. Patet ex dictis quod sumenda est talis oppositio inter exclusivas primi et tertii ordinis et inter exclusivas secundi et quarti ordinis.

Secundum correlarium exclusiva in qua preponitur signo exclusivo affirmato terminus communiter tentus non distributus prius est resolvenda ex parte talis termini communiter accepti quam exponatur copulative ratione talis signi affirmati. Si tamen preponatur terminus communiter tentus distributus tali signo affirmato poterit sufficienter exponi talis propositio copulative in propria forma sive resolutione talis termini distributi et intelligatur in prima parte nisi tali termino non distributo in secuna exponente addatur relativum ydemptitatis. Istud correlarium patet de istis duabus propositionibus alicuius hominis tantum asinus currit et cuiuslibet hominis tantum asinus currit quarum secunda in propria forma est exponibilis et non prima nisi determinationi adderetur relativum ydemptitatis in secunda exponente. Sequitur ex isto quod exclusiva exponibilis disiunctive in qua preponitur signo terminus distributus non est immediate exponenda sed prius resolvendus est talis terminus distributus in singulares nisi addatur relativum ydemptitatis tali termino in secunda exponente proportionabiliter sicut dictum est in principali correlario de exclusiva exponibili copulative ubi preponitur signo terminus communiter tentus non distributus. Si tamen exclusiva exponibili disiunctive preponatur terminus communiter tentus non distributus poterit talis propositio in propria forma exponi sive resolutione talis termini. Istud declaratur in contradictoriis propositionum positarum in principali correlario et proportionabiliter dicendum est in aliis propositionibus exponibilibus copulative et disiunctive. Sequitur finaliter quod propositio in qua signum exclusivum preponitur immediate copulato vel disiuncto complexive capto vel aggregato ex determinatione et determinabili est distinguenda penes hoc quod tale signum potest denotare exclusionem debere fieri ab opposito tocius complexi vel ab opposito partis eius et aliquando fit exclusio singulariter tantum quando scilicet terminus infinitus in secunda exponente includit transcendens singularis numeri precise. Et proportionabiliter dicitur fieri exclusio pluraliter tantum quando terminus infinitus includit transcendens pluralis numeri precise. Sed quando talis terminus infinitus includit transcendens singulare et plurale indifferenter dicitur esse exclusio simpliciter. Secundum istud distinguenda est talis propositio tantum ens est entia et similiter talis tantum entia sunt ens.

**38.** ( Lokert *De Exponibilibus* $1v^2-2v^1$ )

Ulterius presupponitur pro conversionibus propositionum exclusivarum quod exclusiva primi ordinis exponibilis gratia alietatis in qua fit exclusio ab opposito totius subiecti convertitur conversione mutua in universalem affirmativam in terminis transpositis cuius ratione est quia sicut signum universale affirmativum distribuit terminum immediatum et distribuit terminum mediatum. Et istud de conversione dicta intelligatur quando predicatum talis exclusive est terminus communiter tentus non impeditus a distributione. Dicebatur ubi fit exclusio ab opposito totius subiecti quia propositiones tales in quibus excluditur ab oppositis partium subiectorum non habent universales convertibiles cum illis de eisdem extremis transpositis licet ut in pluribus assignantur universales convertibiles cum illis composite ex similibus terminis ut patebit ex processu argumentorum.

Sequitur ex isto quod exclusiva tertii ordinis que contradicit tali exclusive primi ordinis convertitur in particulare vel in defuntam negativam in terminis transpositis quia si alique propositiones sint convertibiles oportet contradictorias illarum esse convertibiles. Ista faciliter declarari possunt exemplo. Exclusiva etiam primi ordinis saltem cum constantia contradictorii subiecti infert exclusivam eiusdem ordinis in terminis transpositis mutatis terminis finitis in terminos infinitos. Hoc patet ratione secunde eius exponentis sicut etiam quilibet talis exclusiva primi ordinis infert exclusivam quarti ordinis in terminis transpositis. De exclusiva secundi ordinis dicitur supposita constantia extremorum convertitur in exclusivam eiusdem ordinis in terminis transpositis non tamen simpliciter. Et proportionabiliter exclusiva quarti ordinis supposita constantia extremorum convertitur in exclusivam eiusdem ordinis in terminis transpositis sed non simpliciter. Quelibet tamen exclusiva cuiuscunque ordinis poterit converti in exclusivam eiusdem ordinis in terminis transpositis dummodo servetur proportionabilis probatio illarum scilicet quod una exponatur per convertentes exponentium alterius. Istis omnibus presuppositis ponitur talis conclusio. Quelibet exclusiva exponibilis copulative quamlibet eius exponentem infert in bona consequentia. Sed non ex qualibet infertur licet inferatur ex totali copulativa composita ex exponentibus et etiam inferat illam. Eodem modo exclusiva exponibilis disiunctive infertur ex qualibet eius exponente sicut ex totali disiunctiva. Non tamen infert aliquam eius exponentem sed bene totalem disiunctivam. Intelligatur semper in consequentia tenente de forma acceptionis terminorum.

**39.** (Caubraith *Quadrupertitum* 62r[1])

Quelibet talis exclusiva secundi ordinis potest in unam exclusivam eiusdem ordinis posita constantia subiecti converti. Patet propositio quoniam hec consequentia est formalis tantum homo non est animal et homo est ergo tantum animal non est homo. Immo econtra formaliter sequitur similiter posita constantia subiecti. Contra hanc enim consequentiam tantum animal non est homo et animal est ergo tantum homo non est animal et homo estnon potest dari instantia de forma vel de forma acceptionis terminorum ut claret. De primo ad ultimum ostendi potest. Nam ex prima exponente huius tantum animal non est homo cum constantia subiecti sequitur ista animal est non homo et ex illa hec non homo est animal ex qua cum secunda exponente illius exclusive sequitur ista omne non homo est animal per contrapositionem que est secunda exponens consequentis. Et simili modo potest inferri prima sic arguendo tantum animal non est homo ergo omne non animal est homo. Et ultra sequitur non animal est homo quam convertendo habebis hanc homo est non animal ex qua evidenter sequitur hec homo non est animal. Et similiter hec homo est. Et sic patet quid de conversione istarum dicendum sit et per consequens quid de illarum contradictoriis postquam in talibus opposito modo procedendum est.

**40.** ( Lokert *De Exponibilibus* 16v²–17r¹ )

Sequitur secundus articulus in quo determinandum est de exclusivis exponibilibus gratia pluralitatis pro quarum expositione presupponitur quod quattuor sunt ordines illarum exclusivarum proportionabiliter ut dictum est de exclusivis exponibilibus gratia alietatis. Et tales propositiones eodem modo exponuntur illo dempto quod pro negatione infinitante que ponitur in secunda exponente exclusive exponibilis gratia alietatis ponitur in secunda exponente exclusive exponibilis gratia pluralitatis ly plura quam vel ly plures quam. Et signum exclusivum non denotat exclusionem gratia pluralitatis nisi addatur termino numerali vel collectivo formaliter vel equivalenter sicut termino pluralis numeri vel copulato complexive capto. In talibus propositionibus potest denotari exclusio gratia pluralitatis suppositorum termini cui additur signum exclusivum et tunc ly plura vel ly plures in secunda exponente includit talem terminum. Potest etiam denotari exclusio gratia pluralitatis quoruncunque entium et tunc ly plura in secunda exponente includit transcendens ut ista propositio tantum duo homines currunt. Si signum denotat exclusionem gratia pluralitatis suppositorum termini cui additur tale signum habebit istam secundam exponentem non plures homines quam duo homines currunt. Sed si excludatur gratia pluralitatis quoruncunque entium habebit istam secundam exponentem non plura entia quam duo homines currunt et proportionaliter in aliis propositionibus dicatur.

Ulterius est advertendum quod exclusiva primi ordinis gratia pluralitatis convertitur cum propositione affirmativa in extremis transpositis cuius subiectum sumitur cum signo collectivo cuius ratio poterit assignari. Sicut signum collectivum facit stare terminum cui immediate additur confuse tantum copulatim et nullam virtutem habet respectu termini mediate sequentis tale signum sic signum exclusivum exponibile gratia pluralitatis nullam virtutem habet respectu termini immediati sed terminum mediate sequentem ipsum facit stare confuse tantum copulatim ut ista propositio tantum duodecim sunt apostoli dei capiendo signum ut excludat gratia pluralitatis convertitur cum ista omnes apostoli dei sunt duodecim capiendo ly omnes collective et ita de aliis dicatur.

**41.** ( Lokert *De Exponibilibus* 21r¹–v² )

Consequenter determinandum est de propositionibus exponibilibus ratione signorum exceptivorum. Qualia sunt ista preter preterque et nisi. Ly nisi aliquando capitur conditionaliter sicut communiter in illo sophismate nullus homo legit parisius nisi ipse sit asinus. Accipi solet ly preter etiam capitur aliquando subtractive ut in prima propositione decem preter quinque sunt quinque et aliquando additative sicut conceditur ista decem sunt duo preter octo. Sed de istis acceptionibus non est ad propositum pro expositione propositionum exceptivarum.

Presupponendum est quattuor esse ordines propositionum exceptivarum sicut exclusivarum. In primo ordine sunt tales propositiones omnis homo preter Sortem currit non omnis homo non preter Sortem currit et contradictorie illarum in tertio ordine. In secundo sunt tales omnis homo preter Sortem non currit non omnis homo non preter Sortem non currit et in quarto contradictorie illarum. In qualibet propositione exceptiva sunt quattuor consideranda primo signum exceptivum secundo terminus extra captus et est ille qui sequitur immediate signum exceptivum tertio terminus a quo fit exceptio et est terminus qui precedit immediate dictionem exceptivam saltem cathegoreumaticus et quarto predicatum principale vel aliud extremum ab illo in quo ponitur signum exceptivum. Solet communiter dici ad proprietatem exceptive requiritur quod terminus a quo fit exceptio sumatur cum signo universali affirmativo vel negativo impedito vel non impedito et quod terminus extra captus non sit superior nec disparatus respectu termini a quo fit exceptio sed illud stat ad nomen et in significatione termini. Isto presupposito dicitur quod exceptiva secundi vel primi ordinis exponenda est copulative per tres exponentes quarum prima erit preiacens in forma illo dempto quod pro signo exceptivo ponenda est negatio infinitans et terminus extra captus si ponatur in obliquo debet mutari in rectum dummodo terminus a quo fit exceptio ponatur in recto. Secunda exponens erit affirmativa in qua predicabitur terminus a quo fit exceptio de termino extra capto. Et tertia exponens debet esse opposite qualitatis ad primam exponentem in qua predicabitur predicatum principale de termino extra capto vel in tertia exponente terminus extra captus ponatur pro uno extremo et aliud extremum exponibilis ab primo in quo ponitur signum exceptivum pro alio. Et contradictorio modo exponantur exceptive tertii et quarti ordinis per tres exponentes sub disiunctione quarum una est preiacens accepta modo dicto alia negativa in qua predicatur terminus a quo fit exceptio de termino extra capto et tertia opposite qualitatis ad primam cuius uno extremo ponendus est terminus extra captus et pro alio aliud extremum exceptive ab illo in quo ponitur signum exceptivum.

Ista declarantur. Talis propositio omnis homo preter Sortem currit sic exponitur omnis homo non Sortes currit et Sortes est homo et Sortes non currit. Et ista omnis homo preter Sortem non currit exponitur per istam copulativam omnis homo non Sortes non currit et Sortes est homo et Sortes currit. Opposito modo exponantur disiunctive contradictorie illarum propositionum. Et est observandum in expositione exceptivarum illud quod diximus circa expositionem exclusivarum scilicet si propositio sit exponibilis copulative et preponitur terminus distributus poterit manere in propria forma et immediate exponi et terminus stans determinate precedens signum exceptivum resolvendus est etc nisi talis terminus fuerit terminus a quo fit exceptio.

Solet poni in ista materia talis regula scilicet universalis in parte vera et in parte falsa potest reddi vera per exceptionem illorum pro quibus talis propositio falsificatur ut ista propositio omne animal est homo est in parte vera et in parte falsa postquam sub subiecto distributo aliqua singularis est vera et aliqua falsa. Ideo redditur vera per exceptionem isto modo omne animal preter brutum est homo ad istum sensum quod termino distributo addendo signum exceptivum et terminum extra captum qui solum accipitur pro illis pro quibus falsificabitur universalis data resultat exceptiva vera.

Et ista secunda infertur correlarie quod due propositiones subcontrarie hoc est copulativa ex talibus composita infert propositionem exceptivam primi ordinis et ut in pluribus exceptivam etiam secundi ordinis, in exceptiva primi ordinis excipiendo illa pro quibus denotatur verificari subcontraria negativa et in exceptiva secundi ordinis excipiendo illa pro quibus denotatur verificari subcontraria affirmativa, quod convenientius fieri potest pro termino extra capto exceptive primi ordinis ponendo complexum resultans ex extremis subcontrariarum et pro termino extra capto exceptive secundi ordinis ponendo complexum ex talibus extremis cum negatione infinitante media sicut complexum ex subiecto et contradictorio predicati. Et proportionabiliter accipiendus est terminus extra captus reddendo universalem in parte veram et in parte falsam veram per exceptionem.

Istud declaratur. Ista consequentia est bona aliquod animal est homo et aliquod animal non est homo ergo omne animal preter animal quod est homo non est homo. Similiter ex eisdem subcontrariis sequitur illa exceptiva primi ordinis omne animal preter animal quod non est homo est homo. Et ita dicendum est de illa universali omne animal est homo que est in parte vera et in parte falsa. Per exceptionem redditur vera isto modo omne animal preter animal non hominem est homo. Et ista universalis negativa omne animal non est homo si sit in parte vera et in parte falsa per exceptionem redditur isto modo vera omne animal preter animal quod est homo non est homo.

**42.** (Major *De Exponibilibus* 12v²)
Sed differentia videtur in exclusivis et exceptivis quia in exclusivis virtus signi non modo in subiectum cadit verum etiam in predicatum ut tantum animal est homo confundit confuse tantum subiectum et distribuit predicatum quare non est potior ratio quod sit pars subiecti quam predicati quare relinquitur quod non est pars unius illorum. Secus est de signo exceptivo quod solum natum est cadere in terminum immediatum si sit capax sui casus. Ergo videtur quod sit pars extremi cum illo ut hic omne animal preter hominem est irrationale ly preter cadit solum in ly hominem. Ergo debet esse pars extremi secum et in reduplicativis similiter.

**43.** (Major *De Exponibilibus* 12v²–13r¹)
Notandum est secundo quod ut patet ex doctrina nunc communi in speciali ponuntur octo genera exceptivarum. Primus modus est exceptiva in qua nulla ponitur negatio ut omnis homo preter Sortem currit. Secundus modus est contradictorius illi preponendo negationem negantem illi ut non omnis homo preter Sortem currit. Tertius modus quando sola negatio precedit copulam ut omnis homo preter Sortem non currit. Quartus modus est proponendo negationem negantem illi. Quintus est preponendo negationem immediate signo exceptivo ut omnis homo non preter Sortem currit. Sextus modus contradictorius illi. Septimus modus est preponendo negationem ante signum et aliam ante copulam ut omnis homo non preter Sortem non currit. Octavus est modus illi contradictorius. Et nunc ita dogmatisant omnes. Sed veteres dyalectici tantum quattuor modos posuerunt ut patet ex eorum monumentis. Sed michi videtur quod moderni male superaddunt illos quattuor modos et hic et in reduplicativis quod probo primo quia confundunt iuvenum ingenia in multiplicitate que est mater ignorantie quia facilius est ad pauca inspicere quam ad plura.

**44.** (Lokert *De Exponibilibus* 25v²–26v¹)
Inter signa reduplicativa magis in usu habetur ly inquantum. Sicut dicetur de illo proportionabiliter de aliis talibus signis est dicendum ly inquantum aliquando capitur specificative ut impedit appellationem rationis que fieret secluso tali signo ut in ista propositione Sortes cognoscit Platonem inquantum homo ubi ly cognoscit appellat ratio-

nem et conceptum illius termini homo qualiter non appellaret remoto signo specificativo. Isto modo non capitur in proposito sed reduplicative ut reddit propositionem exponibilem que communiter exponitur per quattuor exponentes. Et ponuntur quattuor ordines reduplicativarum sicut exclusivarum et exceptivarum in quibus propositionibus considerandi sunt signum reduplicativum terminus reduplicatus et est ille qui immediate sequitur signum reduplicativum et terminus precedens immediate signum reduplicativum qui ab aliquibus dicitur subiectum principale et aliud extremum ab illo in quo ponitur signum reduplicativum. Tunc pro expositione talium propositionum dicitur pro prima exponente accipienda est preiacens in forma que est residuum a signo reduplicativo et termino reduplicato. Secunda exponens in propositionibus primi et secundi ordinis debet esse affirmativa et negativa in propositionibus tertii et quarti in qua predicabitur terminus reduplicatus de termino precedente signum reduplicativum. Tertia exponens erit eiusdem qualitatis cum exponibili in qua predicabitur aliud extremum de termino reduplicato. Et quarta exponens erit conditionalis affirmativa in propositionibus primi et secundi ordinis et negativa in aliis cuius antecedens similiter erit affirmativum in quo predicabitur terminus reduplicatus de eius sinonimo vel transcendente et consequens eiusdem qualitatis cum exponibili in quo predicabitur aliud extremum de termino reduplicato vel relativo idemtitatis referente terminum reduplicatum in antecedente. Illud intelligendum est ut dicitur communiter exponendo tales propositiones concomitanter quia causaliter exponendo pro ultima exponente accipienda est propositio causalis proportionabiliter ut dictum est de conditionali. Istud declaratur. Talis propositio omnis homo inquantum rationalis est risibilis sic exponitur omnis homo est risibilis et omnis homo est rationalis et omne rationale est risibile et si rationale est rationale ipsum est risibile. Et ista secundi ordinis omnis homo inquantum rationalis non est asinus sic exponitur omnis homo non est asinus et omnis homo est rationalis et omne rationale non est asinus et si rationale est rationale ipsum non est asinus. Et opposito modo exponantur reduplicative tertii et quarti ordinis. Proportionabiliter pro ultima exponente accipienda est causalis causaliter exponendo tales propositiones.

Contra dicta arguitur primo superflue multiplicantur tot exponentes in propositionibus reduplicativis quod sic probatur. Talis propositio sufficienter poterit exponi per duas primas exponentes cum ultima conditionali. Et ita videtur quod sufficiunt exponentes date dempta prima. Ymo illarum trium primarum exponentium due inferunt aliam sillogistice. Igitur sufficienter exponitur propositio licet non expresse ponitur illa pro exponente que infertur ex aliis. . . .

Respondetur ad argumentum negando quod superflue ponantur tales exponentes propositionum reduplicativarum licet in propositionibus primi et secundi ordinis ubi non impeditur distributio termini reduplicati ut in pluribus prima exponens sillogistice inferatur ex secunda et tertia. In omnibus tamen illud non est verum ut patet consideranti. Nec etiam superflue ponitur tertia exponens ut patet in illa propositione omnis deus inquantum ens necessario est ens que redditur falsa pro tertia exponente precise.

**45.** ( Major *De Exponibilibus* 16r[1] )

Sed reduplicative possunt exponi longe facilius sufficienter per secundam et quartam exponentes sic Sortes inquantum rationalis est risibilis Sortes est rationalis et si aliquod est rationale ipsum est risibile quod patet quia tertia superfluit quia si illa conditionalis sit vera cum positione prioris exponentis oportet omne rationale esse risibile quod patet ex falsitate huius si aliquod est animal ipsum est risibile. Nec est opus dare primam exponentem cum illa implicetur in secunda et quarta.

**46.** ( Lokert *De Exponibilibus* 26v[2]–27v[2] )

Primo videndum est qualiter tales propositiones de ly immediate exponuntur pro quarum expositione presupponitur quattuor esse ordines talium propositionum proportionabiliter ut in precedentibus est dictum. Et propositiones primi vel secundi ordinis copulative exponuntur per duas exponentes et opposito modo disiunctive exponende sunt illarum contradictorie tertii vel quarti ordinis. Qualiter assignande sunt exponentes diverse sunt opiniones saltem de secunda exponente quia ab omnibus admittitur preiacens in forma prima exponens sicut dicitur de una proportionabiliter de omnibus dicatur. Communis modus dicendi exponeret istam propositionem immediate post hoc instans erit Sortes isto modo post hoc instans erit Sortes et nullum erit instans post hoc instans quin inter illud et hoc instans erit Sortes, et istam immediate post hoc instans non erit Sortes isto modo post hoc instans non erit Sortes et nullum erit instans post hoc instans quin inter illud et hoc instans non erit Sortes et opposito modo exponeret contradictorias illarum propositionum. Proportionabiliter diceretur de propositionibus in quibus ly immediate dicit immediationem spacii ut ista immediate post a punctum est b punctum si exponeretur post a punctum est b punctum et nullum est punctum post a punctum quin inter illud et a punctum est b punctum. Et ita alie propositiones conformiter exponerentur. Sed poterit improbari talis modus exponendi. . . .

Casu posito quod instans presens reproducatur post unum annum et erit Sortes per unam horam vel certam mensuram temporis circa medium anni cuius dictum instans est initiativum et similiter terminativum et non erit Sortes in alio tempore ista propositio esset falsa immediate post hoc instans erit Sortes ut constat et utraque exponens capta modo dicto esset vera. De prima non est dubium et secunda patet ex eo quod quocunque instanti signato post hoc instans inter illud et hoc instans erit Sortes.

Eodem modo improbari potest dicta expositio. Supposito quod instans initiativum hore future sit a et terminativum b et Sortes erit precise per mediam tertiam dicte hore sequeretur veritas huius propositionis immediate post a instans vel b instans erit Sortes et nullum erit instans post a instans vel b instans quin inter illud et a instans vel b instans erit Sortes. Illud tamen non esset concedendum nec immediate post a instans erit Sortes nec immediate post b instans erit Sortes. Et ita poterit improbari expositio dicta de illa propositione immediate post istam horam erit b instans et etiam de ista immediate post aliquod instans intrinsecum alicuius hore erit Sortes in dicto casu.

Propter aliquas istarum rationum taliter datur ab aliquibus secunda exponens propositionis de ly immediate taliter pro secunda exponente illius propositionis immediate post hoc instans erit Sortes capiendo istam propositionem nunquam post hoc instans erit ita quin sit vel fuerit Sortes. Et pro secunda exponente huius immediate ante hoc instans fuit Sortes dant istam nunquam ante hoc instans fuit ita quin sit vel erit Sortes. Sed notum est quod non valet talis modus exponendi. . . .

Casu posito quod Sortes fuisset in preteritum et non erit in futurum usque ad instans terminativum hore cuius instans presens est initiativum sequeretur veritas huius immediate post hoc instans erit Sortes ut demonstrando instans presens ut patet ex exponentibus datis. Falsitas tamen eius sufficienter patet ex casu. . . .

Alii dant secundam exponentem propositionis de ly immediate per propositionem de ly infinitum ut huius immediate post hoc instans erit Sortes dant istam secundam exponentem in infinitum propinque post hoc instans erit Sortes et proportionabiliter in aliis. Sed improbatur talis expositio querendo vel in illa secunda exponente ly infinitum capitur cathegoreumatice vel sincathegoreumatice. Non est dicendum primum taliter negarentur tales propositiones immediate post hoc instans erit instans immediate post hoc instans erit alique pars hore que tamen communiter conceduntur. Ly infinitum cathegoreumatice captum enim confudit terminos sequentes. Et quod non valeat expositio capiendo sincathegoreumatice patet quia taliter ista esset falsa immediate post istam horam erit hoc instans demonstrando horam

futuram et instans terminativum eius. Illud tamen est falsum postquam inter horam illam et datum instans nihil mediabit. Sequella
tamen patet ex falsitate secunde exponentis scilicet in infinitum propinque post istam horam erit hoc instans sive exponatur talis propositio isto modo aliqualiter propinque et non tam propinque quin propinquius etc sive isto modo aliqualiter propinque et in duplo propinquius et in triplo propinquius et sic consequenter.

**47.** (Lokert *De Exponibilibus* 28r¹)

Videtur probabilius quod secunda exponens propositionis de immediate danda sit per ly citius vel ly tardius ubi denotatur immediatio
durationis et per ly propinquius ubi denotatur immediatio situs vel
spacii taliter quod ista propositio immediate post hoc instans erit
Sortes sic exponatur post hoc instans erit Sortes et non citius post hoc
instans poterit esse aliquid quam erit Sortes post hoc instans. Et istius
immediate ante hoc instans fuit Sortes dabitur ista secunda exponens
non tardius poterat aliquid esse ante hoc instans quam fuit Sortes ante
hoc instans.

**48.** (Lokert *De Exponibilibus* 28r¹)

Presupponitur quod tempus nihil aliud est quam motus primi mobilis
licet cuiuscunque rei duratio vel cuiuscunque mobilis motus potest
dici tempus et inter quascunque partes temporis mediat unum in-
divisibile secundum durationem quod dicitur instans intelligendo de
partibus temporis secundum prius et posterius et non secundum
divisionem subiecti. Et ita in quocunque tempore quantumcunque
parvo sunt infinita instantia intrinseca mediantia inter partes ipsius
temporis sicut est unum instans initiativum et aliud terminativum
eiusdem. Et ex illo habetur quod in nullo tempore dantur aliqua duo
instantia immediata. Quibuscunque datis inter illa mediat tempus et
per consequens infinita instantia.

**49.** (Lokert *De Exponibilibus* 28v¹⁻²)

Ulterius est advertendum quod pro expositione propositionum de
incipit et desinit quattuor communiter attribuuntur instantia rebus
quoad inceptionem et desitionem scilicet primum instans esse et
ultimum instans non esse pro inceptione et primum instans non esse et
ultimum instans esse pro desitione.

**50.** (Lokert *De Exponibilibus* 28v²–29r¹)

Dupliciter aliqua res potest incipere esse. Ideo propositio affirmativa
exponibilis ratione illius verbi incipit disiunctive exponitur per duas
copulativas quarum una datur per affirmationem de presenti et negationem de preterito mediante illa determinatione immediate et hoc
pro inceptione per primum instans esse. Et alia copulativa danda est
per negationem de presenti et affirmationem de futuro mediante illa

determinatione immediate et hoc pro inceptione per ultimum non esse
taliter quod omnis res incipiens esse altero illorum modorum incipit
esse scilicet per primum esse vel per ultimum non esse. Et ita dupliciter res potest desinere esse. Et ideo propositio affirmativa de ly desinit
disiunctive similiter est exponenda per duas copulativas quarum una
datur per affirmationem de presenti et negationem de futuro mediante
ly immediate et hoc pro desitione per ultimum esse. Et alia copulativa
dabitur per negationem de presenti et affirmationem de preterito et
hoc pro primo instanti non esse taliter quod non stat aliquam rem
desinere esse quin desinat esse per ultimum esse vel per primum non
esse.
Ista declarantur exemplo. Talis propositio Sortes incipit esse homo sic
exponitur Sortes in instanti presenti est homo et Sortes non immediate
ante instans presens fuit homo vel Sortes in instanti presenti non est
homo et Sortes immediate post instans presens erit homo. Et ista
propositio Sortes desinit esse homo taliter est exponenda Sortes in
instanti presenti est homo et Sortes non immediate post instans presens erit homo vel Sortes in instanti presenti non est homo et Sortes
immediate ante instans presens fuit homo. In exponente negativa de
preterito vel futuro neganda est illa determinatio immediate. Et opposito modo copulative per duas disiunctas exponende sunt contradictorie illarum propositionum. In talibus propositionibus resolvendi
sunt sufficienter termini precedentes ly incipit vel ly desinit antequam
exponentur. Et propositiones modales vel de extrinsecis temporibus
reducende sunt ad inesse.

**51.** (Lokert *De Exponibilibus* 33v$^{1-2}$)
Comparativus aliquando capitur pro eius positivo ut in diffinitionibus
predicabilium capitur ly pluribus. Aliquando etiam improprie comparative capitur vel quando non denotatur positivus talis comparativi
convenire utrique comparatorum licet propositio sit affirmativa secundum quod conceduntur tales propositiones corpus est maius spiritu
homo est rationabilior asino. Proprie tamen capiendo comparativum
reddit propositionem exponibilem. Et si talis propositio sit affirmativa
exponenda est copulative et disiunctive si sit negativa per tres exponentes. In primis duabus que ponende sunt eiusdem qualitatis cum
exponibili debet predicari positivus comparativi de terminis import-
antibus res comparatas scilicet rem excedentem et excessam. Tertia
exponens erit opposite qualitatis ad exponibilem [et] ad alias exponentes in qua subiectum erit terminus importans rem excessam et predicatum complexum resultans ex altero comparatorum de illis terminis ita sicut cum positivo mediante inter illos. Et termini accipiendi
sunt eodem modo quoad suppositionem in exponentibus et exponibili

ut ista propositio Sortes est fortior asino sic exponitur Sortes est fortis et quilibet asinus est fortis et nullus asinus est ita fortis sicut Sortes. De eius contradictoria disiunctive exponenda est per oppositas exponentes.

**52.** (Lokert *De Exponibilibus* 33v²)

Propositio de superlativo etiam est exponibilis per tres exponentes. In primis denotabitur positivus talis superlativi convenire utrique comparabilium si propositio sit affirmativa. Et tertia exponens secundum diversam acceptionem superlativi poterit dari affirmativa vel negativa ubi predicabitur unum comparatorum de alio mediante comparativo talis superlativi ut ista propositio Sortes est fortissimus hominum sic exponitur affirmative capiendo superlativum Sortes est fortis et quilibet homo alius a Sorte est fortis et Sortes quolibet alio homine ab ipsomet est fortior. Et negative capiendo superlativum servatis duabus primis exponentibus datur ista tertia nullus homo alius a Sorte est fortior Sorte. Ideo dicitur superlativus vel complexum cuius superlativus est pars principalior affirmative capto superlativo non potest simul pro pluribus verificari.

**53.** (Lokert *De Exponibilibus* 34r¹)

Concedendum est sicut exponendo propositionem de comparativo in una exponente ponuntur ly ita et ly sicut sic in aliqua exponentium propositionis de ly ita et sicut ponitur comparativus et taliter exponentes talium propositionum non essent notiores et clariores suis exponibilibus.

**54.** (Lokert *De Terminis* 3v–4r)

Consequenter declarandi sunt aliqui termini pertinentes ad argumentationem. Unde antecedens est oratio ex qua denotatur inferri consequens. Consequens vero est oratio que denotatur sequi ex antecedente. Et si antecedens habeat duas partes principales copulative ad invicem unitas prima dicitur maior et secunda minor. Nota illationis est coniungibile ratione cuius consequens denotatur inferri ex antecedente et tota consequentia resultat ex antecedente consequente et nota illationis. Istud declaratur. Ista tota oratio omnis homo currit et Sortes est homo ergo Sortes currit dicitur consequentia cuius antecedens est hoc totum omnis homo currit et Sortes est homo. Consequens vero est illa propositio Sortes currit maior illa omnis homo currit. Minor est illa Sortes est homo. Et nota illationis est ly ergo . . .

Consequentia aliqua dicitur bona et est illa consequentia que sic se habet quod non potest ita esse sicut significatur per eius antecedens quin ita sit sicut significatur per eius consequens secundum talem significationem. Consequentia mala opposito modo diffinitur quando scilicet potest ita esse sicut significatur per eius antecedens non existente ita sicut significatur per eius consequens.

**55.** ( Lokert *De Sillogismis* 4r²)

Aliquis est sillogismus hipoteticus quando scilicet aliqua premissarum est ypothetica. Communiter exemplificatur de argumento a tota disiunctiva cum destructione unius partis ad positionem alterius et de argumento a tota conditionali cum positione antecedentis ad positionem consequentis vel cum destructione consequentis ad destructionem antecedentis. Constat tales consequentias non esse proprie sillogismos licet in modo loquendi dicantur sillogismi hipotetici. Aliquis est sillogismus cathegoricus quando utraque premissarum est cathegorica.

**56.** ( Lokert *De Sillogismis* 2r²)

Confirmatur de propositione in qua ponuntur infinite negationes neganter tente non videtur ratio quare potius dicenda sit talis propositio affirmativa quam negativa postquam paritas negationum nata est reddere propositionem affirmativam et imparitas sicut unica negatio reddit propositionem negativam. Modo multitudo infinita nec est paritas nec imparitas.

**57.** ( Lokert *De Oppositionibus* 33v²–34r¹)

Determinandum est de oppositione subalternata cuius lex talis est quod una propositionum subalternarum sit illativa alterius formaliter et de forma acceptionis terminorum et non econtra. Illarum propositionum illa que est illativa alterius dicitur subalternans et alia subalternata. Conditiones requisite ad talem oppositionem sunt iste. Prima propositiones subalterne debent esse eiusdem qualitatis participantes utroque termino et eodem ordine. Intelligo de propositionibus cathegoricis sicut in precedentibus dictum est de aliis oppositionibus. Secunda conditio aliqua universalitas propositionis subalternantis debet mutari in particularitatem in propositione subalternata. Nec oportet in talibus propositionibus quod maneat eadem universalitas vel eadem particularitas . . . Nec etiam oportet in propositionibus taliter oppositis quod quelibet universalitas unius mutetur in particularitatem alterius vel contra. Patet de illis duabus cuiuslibet hominis quilibet asinus est asinus et alicuius hominis quilibet asinus est asinus.

**58.** ( Lokert *De Oppositionibus* 5r¹)

Universalitas plus facit ad falsitatem propositionis quam particularitas et ita particularitas facit ad veritatem plus quam universalitas ex eo quod ad veritatem propositionis in qua ponitur universalitas plura requiritur quam ad veritatem propositionis in qua ponitur particularitas loco talis universalitatis ceteris paribus.

**59.** (Lokert *De Sillogismis* 10r$^{1-2}$)

Ponit [philosophus] aliquas regulas conversionum quas dicit tenere in modalibus de necessario et contingenter sicut in propositionibus de inesse. Prima regula universalis negativa convertitur in universalem negativam. Et talis conversio dicitur simplex quia in conversa et in convertente est similis qualitas et etiam similis quantitas. Secunda regula universalis affirmativa convertitur in particularem affirmativam. Et talis dicitur conversio per accidens quia servata simili qualitate in conversa et convertente non observatur similis quantitas. Tertia regula particularis affirmativa convertitur in particularem affirmativam et etiam dicitur talis conversio simplex sicut conversio universalis negative. De particularibus negativis dicit philosophus quod non convertuntur. Ideo patet quod solum determinat de conversione simplici et conversione per accidens.

**60.** (Caubraith *Quadrupertitum* 57v$^{1-2}$)

Ista consequentia non valet homo non est animal ergo non animal non est non homo quia ante creationem mundi ita erat sicut nunc significatur per antecedens et oppositum consequentis. Similiter affirmative non sequitur omnis homo est ens ergo omne non ens est non homo . . . Sed ad inveniendum modum arguendi formalem in hac materia adverte quod licet non sola conversa inferat convertentem formaliter per contrapositionem conversa tamen cum debita constantia formaliter infert convertentem de terminis contradictoriis ad terminos converse. Sed non semper eodem modo ponenda est constantia. Unde particularis negativa cum debita constantia subiecti eiusdem formaliter infert particularem negativam cuius predicatum est terminus contradictorius ad subiectum ipsius converse et subiectum eiusdem opponitur contradictorie ad predicatum converse. Sed propositio universalis affirmativa posita constantia contradictorii predicati infert universalem affirmativam de terminis contradictoriis ad terminos ipsius converse. Exemplum primi formaliter sequitur homo non est animal et homo est ergo non animal non est non homo. Exemplum secundi bene sequitur omnis homo est animal et non animal est ergo omne non animal est non homo.

**61.** (Lokert *De Sillogismis* 4r$^2$–v$^2$)

Debita dispositio premissarum consistit in debita ordinatione trium terminorum quoad subiectionem et predicationem scilicet quod unus illorum terminorum subiiciatur in una premissarum et predicetur in alia secundum dispositionem prime figure vel quod unus predicetur in utraque secundum dispositionem secunde figure vel quod subiiciatur in utraque secundum dispositionem tertie figure. Consistit etiam debita dispositio premissarum in debita quantitate et debita qualitate

ipsarum premissarum. Debita qualitas premissarum est quando una
est affirmativa. Ideo solet poni regula talis ex ambabus premissis negativis non licet inferre conclusionem sillogismi. Debita quantitas premissarum est quod una sit universalis. Ideo ponitur alia regula talis ex
premissis particularibus non sequitur conclusio sillogismi. Et intelligenda est prima regula de propositionibus pure negativis quia ex
premissis negativis pregnantibus vel quarum una est negativa pregnans sequitur bene conclusio ut patet in exclusivis exceptivis et pro
positionibus de contingenti specialiter capto. Similiter [secunda]
regula intelligatur de premissis particularibus particularitate medii et
non solum de particularibus particularitate subiecti enunciationis
taliter quod non maneat eadem particularitas ex parte medii in ambabus premissis. Solent poni due regule.
Prima regula si aliqua premissarum sit negativa conclusio debet esse
negativa que proportionabiliter intelligatur ut dictum est de prima
regula precedente.
Secunda regula si aliqua premissarum sit particularis conclusio similiter debet esse particularis que sic debet intelligi. Si in premissis
ponatur aliqua particularitas ex parte alicuius extremitatum talis particularitas servari debet in conclusione.
Ulterius advertendum est quod observande sunt conditiones sillogistice arguendo. Prima ex parte medii quod sit completa distributio
medii in premissis taliter quod nec formaliter nec equivalenter ex
parte eius maneret eadem particularitas in ambabus premissis ratione
cuius tales premisse vel alie in simili acceptione terminorum poterunt
pro diversis omnino verificari. Ista conditio virtualiter est eadem cum
secunda regula prius posita.
Secunda conditio requiritur quod medium in aliqua premissarum
ponatur in recto et secundum aliquos quod sit tale extremum in aliqua
premissarum. Illud maxime est verum negative arguendo. . . .
Observandum est similiter quod non arguatur a non distributo ad
distributum.

**62.** ( Lokert *De Sillogismis* 28r²-v¹ )
Sillogismus secunde figure reducitur per impossibile ex maiore et
opposito conclusionis inferendo oppositum minoris. Nec solus sillogismus de Baroco reducitur per impossibile ad primam figuram sed
quilibet silllogismus inevidens in quacunque figura vel in quocunque
alio modo poterit reduci per impossibile. Sillogismus in Cesare per
impossibile reducitur ad sillogismum in Ferio et sillogismus in Camestres taliter reducitur in Celarent et ut dictum est sillogismus de
Baroco ad sillogismum in Barbara. Et ita non inconvenit eundem
sillogismum reduci ad modum evidentem affirmativum et etiam ad

modum evidentem negativum. Patet de Camestres. Reducitur per conversionem et transpositionem premissarum ad Celarent et per impossibile ad Darii.

**63.** (Lokert *De Sillogismis* 33r²)

Similiter Disamis ad Celarent Datisi ad Ferio et Ferison ad Darii reducuntur per impossibile ex contradictorio conclusionis cum minore inferendo contradictorium maioris. Darapti tamen reducitur ad Celarent et Felapton ad Barbara per impossibile ex contradictorio conclusionis et minore inferendo [contradictorium] maioris.

**64.** (Lokert *De Sillogismis* 34r¹⁻²)

Aliquod est bonum argumentum in Darapti ex cuius maiore et subalternata minoris non sequitur conclusio in Datisi. Similiter est aliquod argumentum in Darapti ex cuius maioris subalternata et minore non sequitur conclusio in Disamis. Et eodem modo dicendum est de Felapton in ordine ad Bocardo et Ferison.

**65.** (Lokert *De Sillogismis* 33v¹)

Istud argumentum est bonum in Darapti omnis homo est animal et omnis homo possibiliter est risibile ergo risibile possibiliter est animal. Tamen sub illa maiore subsumendo subalternatam minoris non sequitur talis conclusio in Datisi. Et ita valet istud argumentum in Darapti omnis homo possibiliter est animal et omnis homo est risibile ergo risibile possibiliter est animal. Tamen ex subalternata maioris et minore non sequitur talis conclusio in Disamis.

**66.** (Lokert *De Sillogismis* 42r¹⁻²)

Presupponitur primo quod sillogismus expositorius est sillogismus cuius medium singulariter tenetur et aliquis est affirmativus et aliquis negativus. Potest etiam secundum dispositionem cuiuscunque figure fieri sillogismus expositorius sed non oportet tales esse in aliquo modo. Presupponitur ulterius expositorie arguendo observandum est similes conditiones ex parte extremitatum et medii sicut sillogisando cum medio communi in modo et in figura dempta distributione medii pro qua expositorie arguendo ponenda est sufficiens singularisatio medii.

**67.** (Major *De Oppositione* 53r¹)

Contrarie sunt universalis affirmativa et universalis negativa eiusdem subiecti et eiusdem predicati ut omnis homo currit [et nullus homo currit]. Subcontrarie sunt particularis affirmativa et particularis negativa eiusdem subiecti et eiusdem predicati ut quidam homo currit [et] quidam homo non currit. Oppositio capitur duobus modis uno modo realiter ut convenit rebus ad extra quemadmodum dicimus calorem frigori et humiditatem siccitati opponi. Alio modo capitur ut convenit signis et hoc dupliciter. Uno modo capitur pro terminis non potent-

ibus verificari de eodem termino singulari singulariter et univoce tento
in eodem genere cause vel de eodem termino communi distributo vel
non distributo sumpto cum relativo idemptitatis in creaturis. Et ex
consequenti convenit propositionibus talium terminorum. Exemplum Sortes est albus, Sortes non est albus, omnis homo est calidus,
omnis homo est frigidus, homo est videns, idem homo est cecus . . .
Alio modo capitur oppositio et diffinitur sic oppositio est due propositiones utroque termino participantes secundum eundem ordinem in
forma vel in valore opposite qualitatis tantum vel quantitatis tantum
vel qualitatis et quantitatis similiter.

**68.** ( Major *De Oppositione* 56v[1] )

Notandum est secundo quod oppositio contradictoria apud antiquos
vocatur maior ceteris oppositionibus extensive et intensive quod sic
intelligo. Est maior extensive quia extenditur ad omnia genera propositionum ad ypotheticas ad cathegoricas. Cetere oppositiones cathegoricis competunt et adhuc paucis earum. Intensive quia hic est
repugnantia in veritate et in falsitate sic scilicet quod nunquam contradictorie possunt esse vere nec possunt esse false. Secus est in ceteris
oppositionibus.

**69.** ( Lokert *De Oppositionibus* 2r[2]–v[1] )

Contrariarum lex est talis si una contrariarum est vera alia est falsa et
non econtra taliter quod propositiones contrarie non possunt simul
esse vere sed bene possunt simul esse false . . . Lex contradictoriarum
est talis si una contradictoria est vera alia est falsa taliter quod non
possunt dari contradictorie simul vere nec simul false. Et lex subcontrariarum est talis quod si una subcontrariarum est falsa alia est vera et
non econtra. Propositiones subcontrarie non possunt simul falsificari.
Poterunt tamen simul verificari.

**70.** ( Lokert *De Oppositionibus* 5r[2] )

Terminus in una contradictoriarum distributus in ordine ad terminum stantem confuse tantum disiunctim in altera contradictoriarum
stare debet determinate respectu termini distributi qui in alia stat
confuse tantum disiunctim ut ista propositio homo non est albus
habebit contradictoriam in qua ly albus stabit confuse tantum disiunctim.

**71.** ( Lokert *De Oppositionibus* 5v[1] )

Terminus distributus in una contrariarum respectu termini stantis
determinate in altera contrariarum stare potest distributive vel determinate in ordine ad talem terminum et talis distributus in una contrariarum respectu termini stantis confuse tantum disiunctim in alia
poterit stare distributive vel etiam determinate respectu talis termini
dummodo maneat aliqua eadem universalitas in ambabus.

**72.** (Lokert *De Oppositionibus* 5v²)

Terminus distribuibilis in una subcontrariarum respectu termini stantis confuse disiunctim in altera subcontrariarum poterit stare confuse disiunctim in ordine ad alium terminum distributum qui stabat confuse disiunctim in alia.

**73.** (Lokert *De Oppositionibus* 5r²)

Terminus distributus in una contradictoriarum respectu alterius termini stantis determinate in altera stare debet confuse tantum disiunctim in ordine ad illum terminum qui stabat determinate in alia . . . ista propositio *a* homo non est albus habet contradictoriam cuius predicatum stat determinate.

**74.** (Lokert *De Oppositionibus* 5v²)

Terminus distributus in una subcontrariarum respectu termini stantis determinate in altera subcontrariarum poterit stare determinate nulla posita universalitate . . . illius omnis homo est *b* animal non poterit [dari] alia subcontraria ab ista homo animal non est vel eius equivalente.

**75.** (Lokert *De Oppositionibus* 15r²–v¹)

Datis duabus propositionibus in quibus observantur conditiones requisite ad contradictionem dempto illo quod terminus qui debet stare determinate in ordine ad aliquam distributionem stat confuse tantum disiunctim in ordine ad talem distributionem ille propositiones subcontrariantur saltem de lege.

**76.** (Lokert *De Oppositionibus* 15v¹)

Datis duabus propositionibus in quibus observantur omnia requisita ad contradictionem dempto illo quod terminus qui debet stare confuse tantum in ordine ad aliquam distributionem stet determinate in ordine ad talem distributionem ille propositiones contrariantur.

**77.** (Lokert *De Oppositionibus* 35r¹–v¹)

Disiunctiva affirmativa subalternata est copulative affirmative composite ex similibus partibus . . . Ratio huius propositionis est talis omne illud quod requiritur ad veritatem disiunctive requiritur ad veritatem copulative . . . et non econverso.

Propositiones copulative affirmative composite ex partibus contradictoriis vel contrariis opponuntur contrarie. Et disiunctive affirmative composite ex partibus contradictoriis vel subcontrariis opponuntur subcontrarie. Copulativa affirmativa et disiunctiva affirmativa composite ex partibus contradictoriis contradicunt. Sed copulativa et disiunctiva composite ex partibus contrariis contrariantur. Et ita si componantur ex partibus subcontrariis subcontrariantur.

# NOTES

## CHAPTER ONE

1   *Acta Facultatis Artium*, 16 February 1418.
2   *Acta Facultatis Artium*, 14 November 1438.
3   *Acta Facultatis Artium*, 26 November 1415.
4   Antonio Coronel *In Posteriora Aristotelis* Paris (O. Senant) 1510.
    See prefatory letter to Coronel's brother Francisco.
5   'New light on John Major' by J. H. Burns, *Innes Rev.* vol.5, p.83.
6   Preface to the *Quartus Sententiarum Johannis Maioris* (1516 ed.).
7   Léopold Delisle *Notice sur un registre des procès-verbaux de la Faculté
    de Théologie de Paris pendant les années 1505-33*, Paris 1899, p.366.
8   A. Renaudet *Préréforme et Humanisme à Paris*, Paris 1953, p.614 fn.
9   cf. *History*, p.41.
10  *History*, p.cxxxiii.
11  *Scotland in the Later Middle Ages*, p.586.
12  G. Lax *De Oppositionibus* Paris 1512. See dedication.
13  *Bipartitum*, 49v, 57r-58r.
14  See the dedicatory epistle of his *Introductorium in Aristotelis
    Dilecticen* (1527).
15  *Bipartitum* esp. fol. 57r et seq.
16  *History* pp.172-3.
17  *Commentary on Matthew* fol.80.
18  *Acta Facultatis Artium* pp.cxxxiii-iv.
19  *History of the Scottish Reformation* (ed. Dickinson) vol.1, p.15.
20  *History of the Scottish Reformation* vol.1, p.15.
21  *History* vol.1, p.17.
22  Pierre Duhem *Études sur Leonardo da Vinci* Series 3, p.582.
23  *St Andrews Early Records* p.217.
24  Watt *Fasti* p.350.
25  Watt *Fasti* p.350.
26  See D. E. Easson 'The Collegiate Churches of Scotland' Pts I and II,
    *Rec. of Sc. Ch. Hist. Soc.* vols 6 and 7; also G. Hay 'The Architecture
    of Scottish collegiate churches' in *The Scottish Tradition* ed. G. W. S.
    Barrow.
27  D. E. Easson 'The Collegiate Churches of Scotland Pt I' *R.S.C.H.
    Soc.* vol.6, pp.195-6.
28  J. Durkan 'Education in the century of the Reformation' *Innes Rev.*
    vol.10.
29  *Rec. Scot. Ch. Hist. Soc.* vol.7, p.31.
30  *Early Records of St Andrews University* J. M. Anderson, p.xvii.

31    W. A. McNeill 'Documents illustrative of the history of the Scots College, Paris' *Innes Rev*. vol.XV, 1964.

32    ibid., see Warrender Papers i, 275-6.

33    J. Durkan 'Scots College, Paris' *Innes Rev*. vol.II, pp.112-13.

34    Delisle *Notice sur un registre* . . . pp.375-6.

35    F. Higman *Censorship and the Sorbonne* p.15.

36    Delisle *Notice sur un registre* . . . p.399; Higman *Censorship* . . . p.16.

37    F. Higman *Censorship* . . . p.23.

38    Delisle *Notice* . . . p.378.

39    Delisle *Notice* . . . pp.381-2.

40    See Delisle *Notice* . . . p.382 for list of names, and J. Farge *Bibliographical Register of Paris Doctors of Theology, 1500-36* (Toronto 1980) for bibliographical details. 'Silvanus', who occurs in the list in Delisle but is not mentioned by Farge, may well be Antoine Silvestre, in which case he is a seventh Montaigu man, and a very distinguished one, on the commission.

41    Delisle *Notice* . . . p.382.

42    Delisle *Notice* . . . p.383.

43    Delisle *Notice* . . . p.392.

44    J. K. Farge *Bibliographical Register* p.284.

45    *Reg. of Supplications* 2123, fols 106v-107; 2125, fols 33v-34. N.B. The assumption made in Watt's *Fasti* p.178 that 'George Herher' is to be identified with George Lokert is therefore wrong.

46    *Reg. Supp*. 2123, fol.107v.

47    *Reg. Supp*. 2123, fols 106v-107.

48    *Reg. Supp*. 2125, fol.185r-v.

49    *Reg. Supp*. 2131, fol.167.

50    *Reg. Supp*. 2132, fols 69v-70.

51    Watt *Fasti* p.178.

52    Watt *Fasti* p.156.

53    That his library contained such unorthodox works as the *De Causa Boemica* as well as certain political tracts by William of Ockham, written when the author was an excommunicate, hardly argues against this. See J. Durkan and A. Ross 'Early Scottish Libraries' *Innes Rev*. vol.IX, pp.124-5.

## CHAPTER TWO

1    *Terminorum* Ir[1].

2    ibid., see Appendix no.1.

3    Following Major *Terminorum* Ir[2].

4    Medieval logicians referred to mental terms in many ways. Major writes: 'A mental term is a concept of the mind, or an impression naturally signifying, and it is sometimes called an act of the understanding, a notion of a thing, a lively apprehension, an imitation [immutatio = imitatio], an image, a similitude, a cognition' [*Terminorum* 2r[2]].

5    This position is discussed by Major also, who invokes the authority of St Augustine for it. Major writes: 'And thus St. Augustine (*De*

*Trin.* xv) said: "If anyone be fed alone for ten years without seeing a man, then when he is presented with a man he will form a concept of a man, and there is no greater reason why that concept should be of one language than of another. Therefore it is of none"' [*Terminorum* 2r²].

6      This, at any rate, was Major's account of how the imposition was effected. He writes: 'Socrates will point first to something present e.g. a loaf or a book, and will say "A" to Plato, while pointing to the said book. And he will take the book again, put it down, and will repeat "A". At length Plato will understand that the aforesaid book is called "A" . . . From this I infer that this cannot be the origin of syncategorematic terms. This is proved since we cannot point to things signified by syncategorematic terms, since syncategorematic terms have no such significates' [*Terminorum* 3v²].

7      See also *De Opp.* 16v¹⁻², 20v².

8      For reference to the problem of the concept of the triune God for formal logic see Major *Liber Consequentiarum* 93r².

9      The idea of a non-auditory and non-visual means of communication did not first arise with Lokert. Major attributes the idea to St Augustine who wrote [*Christian Doctrine* Bk.II]: 'Of the signs with which men communicate with each other some belong to the sense of sight and fewer to that of hearing, and fewest to the other senses' [*Terminorum* 3v¹].

10     cf. W. Kneale 'Modality *de dicto* and *de re*' pp.622-33 in *Logic, Methodology and the Philosophy of Science*, eds Nagel, Suppes and Tarski (Standford 1962), where precisely this suggestion is made; and S. Kripke *Naming and Necessity* (Oxford 1980), pp.68ff, where Kneale's position is criticised on the grounds, identical to Lokert's, that Socrates would have been Socrates even if his name had not been 'Socrates'.

11     It may be noted that Lokert's position here follows Major's closely. Major imagines that Socrates was born today at 4 o'clock and that the name 'Socrates' was imposed on him at 12 o'clock. And he argues that at 12 this is true: '*This* [pointing to Socrates] was Socrates at 8 o'clock'. For *this* is named 'Socrates', and this same person existed at 8 o'clock. On the other hand, asks Major, could he really have been Socrates at 8, given that the name had not yet been imposed on him? And he replies that if someone were to have a mental picture of seeing at 8 o'clock him whom we now (at 12) call 'Socrates', the imaginer could say to himself truly 'This is Socrates' [*Terminorum* 12r¹] (see appendix, no.29).

### CHAPTER THREE

1      Major's initial list is longer than Lokert's. He refers also to 'all (taken collectively)' (as in 'All the disciples are twelve') and 'as . . . as' (as in 'A is as tall as B').

2      Or several exponible terms. Major gives the example: 'Only every man not excepting Socrates, in so far as he is rational, is stronger

than Plato' [*De Ex.* 1r¹].

3    Lokert was not alone in characterising exponibles in terms of their obscurity. Major had written: 'An exponible proposition is one whose sense is obscure on account of a sign placed in it' [*De Ex.* 3v¹]. By 'sign' here Major means a term, for he immediately points to a problem associated with the special quantifier *a*. He says: 'This is not an exponible proposition "Of a man *a* ass is every brayer" which has a rather obscure sense, but this is on account of [the problem of identifying] its contradictory and not on account of an exponible sign'. See appendix, no.33.

4    It should be noted that some authors, though not Lokert, treated even quantifiers as exponibles. Thus, and most importantly, Major said that universal affirmatives were exponibles. He writes: 'A universal affirmative proposition is expounded through its prejacent form and through the universal negative corresponding to it. Thus "Every man runs" is expounded as "A man runs and nothing is a man but that it runs"' [*De Ex.* 4r¹]. See appendix, no.34.

5    For Latin text see appendix, no.35.

6    Major *De Ex.* 4v². For Latin text see appendix, no.36.

7    This case is less straightforward than it looks. Major [*De Ex.* 5r²] accepted 'Only no man is not an animal' as a first order exclusive on the ground that it was equivalent to 'Only every man is an animal'. More puzzlingly, he assigns, contrary to the authority of Lorenzo Valla, 'Only you do not know, neither in war nor in peace, how to live' to the first order. Valla [*Dialectice Libri Tres* III cap.27] had argued that the proposition was negative since it had three negation signs before the copula. Major responded that the subject was 'you' and that the copula 'are' (which is virtually present in 'do not know' = 'are not knowing') precedes all three negation signs. It seems however that Valla, while accepting most of Major's analysis, could have replied that in 'You are not knowing' it is indeed the copula which is negated and that in consequence the sentence at issue cannot after all, *pace* Major, be in the first order of exclusives.

8    One point regarding the foregoing two examples, noted by Major [*De Ex.* 5v¹], is that in each case the exponible is opposite to its second exponent in both quantity and quality.

9    *Opusculum Exponibilium* in *Introductiones Dialectice* Burgis 1529, fol.90.

10   Sometimes *preterque*; Major adds *nisi* (= unless). Major distinguishes between *preter* and *preterque* on the one hand and *nisi* on the other, on the ground that the first two can appear in affirmative or negative propositions whereas the last occurs only in negatives [*De Ex.* 12v¹⁻²]; e.g. 'No animal except (*nisi*) a cock is free', which Major describes as a conditional rather than a true exceptive, presumably on the ground that it is to be understood as 'If an animal is not a cock it is not free'.

11   Major gives the same example, though referring to it as a 'disjunctive' exceptive [*De Ex.* 12v²].

12    Regarding the term immediately following the exceptive sign, a
      certain distinction, drawn more clearly by Major than by Lokert,
      can be made. Major writes: 'There is a difference to be seen between
      exclusives and exceptives. For in exclusives the scope of the ex-
      ponible sign includes not only the subject but also the predicate, so
      that in "Only an animal is a man" the sign gives the subject merely
      confused supposition while distributing the predicate. For this
      reason there is no more ground for saying that the sign is part of the
      subject than part of the predicate. And hence it is not part of one of
      them. But the exceptive sign is fitted to operate only on the immedi-
      ately following term. Hence it seems that it is part of the same
      extreme as that term; e.g. in "Every animal except a man is ir-
      rational" the "except" operates only on "a man". Consequently
      it must be part of the extreme containing "man"' [De Ex. 12v²].
      See appendix, no.42.

13    Though this is his standard example, Lokert would not hold that the
      case where the exceptive phrase is on the subject side of the copula
      has priority over cases (e.g. Major's 'Socrates sees every man except
      Plato') where the exceptive phrase is on the side of the predicate.

14    Major compromised by giving 1b-4b but with complaint: 'The old
      dialecticians gave only four kinds [1a-4a] . . . But it seems to me that
      the moderns are wrong to add the other four [1b-4b] . . . since they
      confuse the minds of the young with multiplicity which is the
      mother of ignorance, for it is easier to inspect fewer cases than more'
      [De Ex. 13r¹]. See appendix, no.43.

15    Major adds the synonyms *secundum quod*, *ea ratione qua* and *prout*.

16    Major's corresponding example is 'God hates Socrates in so far as he
      is a sinner'. Major argues that it is invalid to argue: 'God hates
      Socrates in so far as he is bad. Therefore God hates Socrates' [De Ex.
      15v²].

17    For discussion of this position see Major De Ex. 16r¹. For text see
      appendix, no.45.

18    Other philosophers considered other relations as well as spatial and
      temporal ones. Major, for example, mentions immediate cause, an
      ordinal number immediately after another, and an immediate pro-
      position in logic (e.g. 'Everything is or is not') [De Ex. 16r²].

19    See e.g. Major De Ex. 16v².

20    The corresponding example in Major's discussion is 'God is better
      than the devil' [De Ex. 24v¹] which he criticises [25r¹] on the ground
      that God is neither better than, worse than, nor as good as the devil.

21    Other sorts of case are discussed by other logicians. Major mentions
      as a particularly bad misuse (*impropriissime et abusive*) of the com-
      parative, 'It is better to sin venially than mortally' [De Ex. 24v¹].
      The reason why this is so unsatisfactory is that all three exponents
      are false, since venial sin is not good, nor is mortal sin, and neither is
      it the case that no mortal sin is as good as venial sin.

CHAPTER FOUR

1      These two definitions form a circle. Lokert does not comment on this fact, but Major does: 'Since the antecedent and consequent are said to be mutually relative they are defined in relation to each other. In the case of terms relative to each other a circular definition is not prohibited' [*Liber Consequentiarum* 80r¹].

2      Major mentions five marks of inference: *si* (= if), *quia* (= since), *ergo* (= therefore), *ideo* (= for that reason), *igitur* (= therefore) [*Liber Consequentiarum* 80r¹].

3      Major [*Liber Cons*. 80r¹⁻²] raises the question whether 'consequence' univocally signifies both good and bad consequences.

4      An important point arises here. Lokert and his contemporaries had a good deal to say about expressions which were propositional complexes rather than plain propositions. Such complexes are, for syntactical reasons, incapable of taking a truth value yet they could form the antecedent and consequent of a conditional. Major [*Liber Cons*. 80v¹] gives the example: 'If an ass were to fly it would have feathers'. 'An ass were to fly' cannot take a truth value (neither can the consequent if taken in its Latin version *haberet pennas*). Of course, if the verbs in the example were transformed from the subjunctive to the indicative mood the antecedent and consequent could both have a truth value. But it should be added that good consequences formed from propositional complexes do not conflict with the above account of a good consequence, since that account says what must follow *if* the antecedent is true. 'If an ass were to fly it would have feathers' cannot be a consequence in which the antecedent is true and the consequent false. But clearly the account has to be extended in order to deal with the case where the main verb in an antecedent or consequent is subjunctive. Lokert does not pursue this matter. The obvious move is to map the subjunctive onto the indicative form and to say that if the indicative case (i.e. the one where both antecedent and consequent are propositions) is a good consequence then so also is the corresponding subjunctive case (where antecedent and/or consequent are propositional complexes).

5      The modal nature of a good consequence is clearly expressed by Major: 'A good consequence is one the contradiction of whose consequent is inconsistent with the antecedent' [*Liber Cons*. 81r¹]. To avoid confusion it should be added that a good consequence is not the same thing as a true conditional. As Major puts the point: 'For a true conditional it is sufficient that when the antecedent is true the consequent is true. For the truth of this: "If you will come to me I will give you a horse", it is sufficient that if you come to me I will give you a horse; but it is not required that it be impossible that you should come to me without me giving you a horse' [*Liber Cons*. 91r¹].

6      Intelligenda est prima regula de propositionibus pure negativis quia ex premissis negativis pregnantibus vel quarum una est negativa pregnans sequitur bene conclusio ut patet in exclusivis [et] exceptivis.

7        Datis duabus propositionibus contrariis contradictoria unius illa-
         rum contradictoriarum est subalternata respectu alterius et ita datis
         duabus subcontrariis unius illarum subcontrariarum contradictoria
         erit subalternans respectu alterius.

8        Propositio de copulato divisive sumpto est subalternans propos-
         itionis de disiuncto divisive sumpto ceteris paribus.

9        Si aliqua propositio est subalternans alterius eadem est subalternans
         cuiuscunque subalternate illius alterius.

10       Consequenter conceditur quod propositio de termino non distributo
         est subalternans respectu propositionis de eodem termino distributo
         ceteris paribus.

11       Si aliqua propositio aliquo modo convertitur contradictoria talis
         propositionis contradictorio modo hoc est per propositionem contra-
         dicentem convertenti alterius converti debet.

12       Omnis propositio que convertitur in universalem etiam converti
         potest in particularem postquam si aliqua propositio infert subalter-
         nantem oportet quod etiam sit illativa subalternate illius subalter-
         nantis.

13       Rules relating propositions the same in subject and in quantity, but
         the opposite in quality, and with the predicate in one infinitised in
         the other.

## CHAPTER FIVE

1        Lokert, unlike his master Major, omits all discussion of non-lin-
         guistic opposition, for example, the opposition of heat and cold,
         humidity and dryness. See Major *De Opp.* 53r[1]. For Major's opening
         statement on oppositions see appendix, no.67.

2        In virtue of the fact that contradictories can be neither true together
         nor false together it is sometimes said that contradiction is 'in-
         tensively' the greatest of the oppositional relations. See Major *De
         Opp.* 56v[1], and appendix, no.68.

3        Major quotes George of Brussel's example 'No being is contingently
         God' and 'No being is contingently not God', which is a case of
         contraries as regards the mode of expression and not contraries as
         regards the law. In the case of George of Brussels' example, and this
         is what distinguishes it from Lokert's, what prevents the two pro-
         positions being contraries as regards the law is that both are true. See
         Major *De Opp.* 53v[2] for a discussion of this example. Major also gives
         an example of propositions which are contraries as regards the law
         but not as regards the mode of expression. The propositions are 'Of
         every man an ass runs' and 'No ass of a (certain) man runs'
         (*Nullus hominis asinus currit*). See ibid.

4        A further example, this time furnished by Major, is 'Of B every A is
         C $\leftrightarrow$ Of *a* B every A is C' [*De Opp.* 61v[1-2]].

5        It follows that another contradictory of 'Every A is *b* B' is 30a 'Every
         B A is not'. For, as Major [*De Opp.* 56r[1]] points out, '*a* A is not B'
         and 'Every B A is not' are equivalent. The two propositions 30 and
         30a are of the same quality, and have the same terms suppositing in

the same way. In particular, in 'Every B A is not' the 'A' has merely confused supposition (as in 30) because it is indirectly governed by the 'every' and not by the 'not' since it precedes the negation sign.

6    The first square also calls in question the view, attributed by Major to the 'ancients', that contradiction is 'extensively' the greatest of the oppositional relations. Major took that doctrine to mean that contradiction extends to all kinds of proposition, hypotheticals as well as categoricals, whereas the other kinds extend only to categoricals [*De Opp.* 56v[1]] (see appendix, no.68). The first of the above squares shows that in so far as hypotheticals can be contradictory they can also be contrary or subcontrary.

7    This point is clearly formulated by Major: 'One proposition does not contradict several non-equivalent propositions' [*De Opp.* 54v[2]].

## CHAPTER SIX

1    *Summulae Logicales* ed. De Rijk, p.1. The passage runs in full: Dialetica est ars artium et scientia scientiarum ad omnium methodorum principia viam habens. Et ideo in acquisitione scientiarum dialetica debet esse prior.

# LOKERT'S PUBLISHED WORKS

[1]  1514  *Scriptum in materia noticiarum* (Paris)
reprinted 1518, 1520 (twice), 1524 (twice), *c.*1534

[2]  1516  *Quaestiones et decisiones physicales insignium virorum* (Paris)
(edited with W. Manderston and G. Waim)
reprinted 1518, 1534

[3]  1516  *Tractatus proportionum* (Paris), printed as appendix to [2]

[4] *c.*1520  *Liber posteriorum* (Paris)
reprinted *c.*1520 (twice)

[5] *c.*1522  *Tractatus exponibilium* (Paris)
reprinted *c.*1522 (twice)

[6] *c.*1522  *Sillogismi Georgii Lokert* (Paris)
reprinted 1524

[7]  1523  *De oppositionibus* (Paris)

[8] *c.*1523  *Termini magistri Georgii Lokert* (Paris)
reprinted 1525

[9] *c.*1524  *Questio subtillissima de futuro contingenti* (Paris)

[10]  1528  *Habes candide lector tractatum oppositionum G. Lokert* (Paris)
(J. Farge speculates that this is a second edition of [7])

# BIBLIOGRAPHY

Anderson, J. M. (ed.) *Early Records of the University of St. Andrews: The Graduation Roll 1413-1579 and the Matriculation Roll 1473-1579*, Edinburgh 1926.

Ashworth, E. J. 'Propositional logic in the sixteenth and early seventeenth centuries', *Notre Dame J. of Formal Logic*, 9 (1968) 179-92.

— 'The doctrine of supposition in the sixteenth and seventeenth centuries', *Archiv für Geschichte der Philosophie*, 51 (1969) 260-85.

— 'Some notes on syllogistic in the sixteenth and seventeenth centuries', *Notre Dame J. of Formal Logic*, 11 (1970) 17-33.

— 'The doctrine of exponibilia in the fifteenth and sixteenth centuries', *Vivarium*, 11 (1973) 137-67.

— 'Existential assumptions in late medieval logic', *American Phil. Q.*, 10 (1973) 141-7.

— 'The theory of consequence in the late fifteenth and early sixteenth centuries', *Notre Dame J. of Formal Logic*, 14 (1973) 289-307.

— *Language and Logic in the Post-Medieval Period*, Dordrecht 1974.

— 'Multiple quantification and the use of special quantifiers in early sixteenth century logic', *Notre Dame J. of Formal Logic*, 19 (1978) 599-613.

Boehner, Philotheus 'Ockham's theory of signification', *Franciscan Studies*, 6 (1946) 143-70.

— 'Ockham's theory of supposition and the notion of truth', *Franciscan Studies*, 6 (1946) 261-92.

Burns, J. H. 'The Scotland of John Major', *Innes Rev.*, 2 (1951) 65-76.

— 'New light on John Major', *Innes Review*, 5 (1954) 83-100.

— 'The political background of the Scottish Reformation', *Innes Rev.*, 10 (1959) 199-236.

Cant, R. G. *The College of St. Salvator*, Edinburgh 1950.

Cowan, Ian B. *Regional Aspects of the Scottish Reformation* (Hist. Assoc. General Series 92), London 1978.

Delisle, M. Léopold 'L'imprimeur parisien Josse Bade et le professeur écossais Jean Vaus', *Bibliothèque de l'École des Chartes*, 1896, vol.57, pp.1-2.

— *Notice sur un Registre des procès-verbaux de la Faculté de Théologie de Paris pendant les années 1505-1533*, Paris 1899.

Dunlop, Annie I. (ed.) *Acta Facultatis Artium Universitatis Sancti Andree 1413-1588*, London and Edinburgh 1964.

Durkan, John 'John Major: After 400 years', *Innes Rev.*, 1 (1950) 131-9.

— 'The school of John Major, Bibliography', *Innes Rev.*, 1 (1950) 140-57.

Durkan, John 'Scots College, Paris', *Innes Rev.*, 2 (1951) 112-13.
— 'Education in the century of the Reformation', *Innes Rev.*, 10 (1959) 67-90.
— 'The cultural background in sixteenth century Scotland', *Innes Rev.*, 10 (1959) 382-439.
— 'George Lockhart', *Innes Rev.*, 15 (1964) 191-2.
— 'Grisy burses at Scots College, Paris', *Innes Rev.*, 22 (1971) 50-2.
— and Ross, A. 'Early Scottish Libraries', *Innes Rev.*, 9 (1958) 5-167.
Easson, D. E. 'The collegiate churches of Scotland, Pt. I', *Records of Scot. Church Hist. Soc.*, 6 (1938) 193-215.
— 'The collegiate churches of Scotland, Pt. II', ibid., 7 (1939) 30-47.
Élie, Hubert 'Quelques maîtres de l'Université de Paris vers l'an 1500', *Archives d'histoire doctrinale et littéraire du moyen âge*, 25-6 (1950-1) 193-243.
Farge, James K. *Bibliographical Register of Paris Doctors of Theology, 1500-1536*, Toronto 1980.
Geach, Peter T. *Reference and Generality* (3rd ed.) London 1980.
Hay, George 'The architecture of Scottish collegiate churches' in *The Scottish Tradition: Essays in honour of Ronald Gordon Cant*, ed. G. W. S. Barrow, Edinburgh 1974.
Henry, D. P. *Medieval Logic and Metaphysics*, London 1972.
Higman, Francis M. *Censorship and the Sorbonne: A biographical study of books in French censured by the Faculty of Theology of the University of Paris, 1520-51*, Geneva 1979.
Jardine, Lisa 'Lorenzo Valla and the intellectual origin of humanist dialectic', *J. of Hist. of Phil.*, 15 (1977) 143-64.
Kneale, William and Martha *The Development of Logic*, Oxford 1962.
Knox, John *John Knox's History of the Reformation in Scotland*, ed. by W. C. Dickinson, vols I and II, London 1949.
Kretzmann, N. 'Medieval logicians on the meaning of the *propositio*', *J. Phil.*, 67 (1970) 767-87.
Lukasiewicz, Jan *Aristotle's Syllogistic from the Standpoint of Modern Formal Logic*, Oxford 1957.
Mackay, Aeneas J. G. 'Life of the author', printed as preface to Major's *History of Greater Britain* (Scot. Hist. Soc. edn.).
McNeill, W. A. 'Documents illustrative of the history of the Scots College, Paris', *Innes Rev.*, 15 (1964) 66-85.
Moody, Ernest A. *Truth and Consequence in Medieval Logic*, Westport, Connecticut 1976.
Nicholson, Ranald *Scotland: The Later Middle Ages*, Edinburgh 1978.
Nuchelmans, G. *Late-Scholastic and Humanist Theories of the Proposition*, Amsterdam 1980.
Pannier, J. A. 'Quelques écossais professeurs et étudiants à Paris, du 12e au 17e siècle', *Rec. of Scot. Ch. Hist. Soc.*, 4 (1932).
Prior, A. N. *Formal Logic* (2nd ed.), Oxford 1962.
Quicherat, J. *Histoire de Sainte-Barbe, Collège, Communauté, Institution*, Paris 1860.

Renaudet, Augustin, *Préréforme et Humanisme à Paris pendant les premières guerres d'Italie (1494-1517)*, Paris 1953.

Ridley, Jasper *John Knox*, Oxford 1962.

Ross, Anthony 'Some Scottish Catholic historians', *Innes Rev.*, 1 (1950) 5-21.

— 'Scots College, Paris', *Innes Rev.*, 1 (1950) 68.

Watt, D. E. R. *Fasti Ecclesiae Scoticanae Medii Aevi ad annum 1638* (second draft), Edinburgh 1969.

# INDEX

Aberdeen University, founded 1495, 2

abstract terms, 73-4

additive exceptive, 96

affirmatives, convertibility of particular, 134-8; convertibility of universal, 134-8

Agricola, Rudolph, 184

Albert of Saxony, physics writings edited by Lokert, 21

Aleandro, Jerome, introduced teaching of Greek into Paris, 6; teacher of Major and Cranston, 6

'all', collective sense of, 94-5

Anderson, J. M., 234n30

animals, cognitive faculty of, 41

'antecedent', definition of, 125

Aristotle, 54, 134, 137, 138, 145-6

Arth, William, accused of heresy, 19

ascent, 46ff

Ashworth, E. J., vii, viii, 190

Balliol College, Scots attracted to, 2

Beaton, Cardinal David, death of, 18

Beaton, James, dedicatee of Major's commentary on First Gospel, 13-14; translation from Glasgow to St Andrews, 12

Berquin, Louis de, 13; his condemnation by the Theology Faculty of Paris, 27-8

Beda, Noel, his criticism of Erasmus, 29; a heresy hunter, 16; principal of Montaigu, 5; syndic of Theology Faculty, 26-7

Beza, Theodore, on early career of Knox, 17

Bishopric of Murray, relation of Scots College to, 25

Bocardo, proof of, 154, 156-7; its relation to Baroco, 155-6

Buridan, John, his physics writings edited by Lokert, 8, 21

Burns, J. H., 234n5

Camestrop, proof of, 153-4

categorematic terms, definability of, 34; negation of, 77; priority of, 44; all singular and common terms are, 74

categorical proposition, 35-6; exponible proposition classified as, 83

Caubraith, Robert, on convertibility of contrapositives, 140; description of his Quadrupertitum, 8; professor at College of Coqueret, 8; his proof of conversion of second-order exclusives, 91-2

causal conditional, 61

cessation, propositions of, 113-19

Chaplain, Peter, 24

'chimera', common signification of, 74-5

Christ Church College, Oxford, Major offered teaching post at, 15-16

cognitive faculty, mental term a modification of, 37

Colloquia, Erasmus's, censored by Faculty of Theology, 28

comparatives, 119-24; exposition of, 120; strict and non-strict, 120-1

conciliarism, 15

concrete terms, 73-4

conditional proposition, description of, 36-7; non-truth functionality of, 60-1

conjunction, 36, 59; commutativity of, 134-5; modalised, 60

consequence, modality of good, 125-6, 239n5; syntactic definition of, 36, 125

'consequent', definition of, 125

Constantia, 127, 139-40, 167

contradictories, law of, 166

contradictories, syntactic relation between, 167-8

contraposition, convertibility by, 139-40

contraries, law of, 166; syntactic relation between, 169-70

conventional term, strict signification of, 70

conversion, accidental, 134; mutual, 136; restriction of rules of, 136-137; rules of, 134-43; rules of, for exclusives, 90-2; simple, 134

Copernicus, 21

copula, 35-6; complex, 137

Coronel, Antonio, 3, 7, 234n4

Crab, Gilbert, 10

Cranston, David, buried beside Standonck, 17; death of, 8; fictitious discussion with Gavin Douglas, 10; from Glasgow, 8; member of Major's circle, 3; taught by Aleandro, 6; teacher of Lokert at Montaigu, 8, 20

Crichton, Collegiate Church of, description of, 21-3

Crichton, Sir William, founder of Crichton Collegiate Church, 22

Crockaert, Pieter, 7-8

*Darapti*, its relation to *Disamis* and *Datisi*, 158-60

*Darii*, proof of, 153

David I of Scotland, Major's criticism of, 7

definition, near, 33-4; relation between near definition and ordinary, 34-5; relation between remote definition and ordinary, 34; remote, 34; three requirements for a good, 33-4

definitum, near, 34; remote, 34

Delisle, Leopold, 235ns34,36,38-43

descent, 46ff; importance of order of, 47-8, 49

*Dici de nullo*, 147, 153

*Dici de omni*, 147, 153

*Desinit, see* cessation

determinable, priority of determinator over, 49

*De Terminis*, date of Lokert's, 24-5

*Disamis*, proof of, 153

disjunction, 36, 59; modalised, 60

division, nature of satisfactory, 38-9

double negation, law of, 126

Douglas, Gavin, 1, 16; church appointments of, 10; diplomatic role of, 10

Duhem, Pierre, on role of Lokert's edition of Buridan's physics, 21, 234n22

Dunbar, Gavin, death of, 30

Dunbar, William, his *Lament for the Makaris*, 1

Dunlop, Major vicar of, 14

Duns Scotus, 1

Durkan, John, viii, 234n28, 235ns33,53

Easson, D. E., on Collegiate churches, 22-3

entity, conventional and natural signification of, 40

equipollence, 140-3

equivalence, two kinds of propositional, 83

equivocation, 39

Erasmus, Beda's criticisms of, 29; a colleague of Major at Montaigu, 5; his problems with the Faculty of Theology, 13, 27-9

exceptive propositions, 95-102; description of, 96; eight orders of, 97-8; relation between superlatives and, 123; relation between universals and, 100-1; square of opposition for, 98-100; subalternation relations between, 133

exclusive propositions, 84-95; implicit negativity of, 129; subalternation relations between, 133

exponent, 84

exponible propositions, Lokert's definition of, 81; multiply, 123-4

exponible terms, existence of, 82-3; Lokert's list of, 83; obscurity of, 122-3

exponibles, topic of Major's first book, 6

extremes of proposition, 35-6

Faculty of Theology at Paris, conservatism of, 5-6, 26; its criticism of Berquin, 27; its independence of royal patronage, 29;

Faculty of Theology at Paris—*contd*
    its role as censor, 27-9; heresy
    among its members, 5; Sorbonne
    its headquarters in Paris, 5
Farge, James, 235n40
*Ferio*, proof of, 153
first figure, reduction to the, 152-3
'formal', 'virtual' contrasted with,
    35-6, 82
formal significate, 72-3
fourth figure, 145-6
François I, 13, 27; his support for
    Berquin, 27-8
function, categorematic term with,
    64-5

genitival relation, suppositional
    analysis of, 49-50
George of Brussells, 240n3
German Nation in Paris, Lokert's role
    in, 20
Gerson, John (Doctor Christianis-
    simus), 5
Gibson, William, Glasgow philo-
    sopher, 11
Glasgow, deanery of, 30
Glasgow University, 2; Major
    principal of, 9, 11
Gleghornie, the birthplace of Major, 4
Godshouse, Major's college at Cam-
    bridge, 4, 15
Gomez, Juan, his assessment of
    Major, 7
Guild, David, heresy charged against,
    18; subsequent career, 18
gustatory terms, 63

Halkerston, Thomas, Lokert's pre-
    decessor at Crichton, 21
Hamilton, Patrick, death of, 13;
    heresy of, 13-14; matriculated
    at St Andrews with Major, 12;
    pupil of Manderston, 9
Hangest, Jerome, accused Manders-
    ton of plagiarism, 9; on obscurity
    of exponibilia, 122-3
Hay, G., 234n26
Henryson, Robert, 1
Hepburn, James, bishop of Murray,
    25
Hepburn, Bishop John, accused Arth
    of heresy, 19
Higman, F., 235ns35,37

*History of Greater Britain*, date of, 11;
    Major's motives for writing, 6;
    message of, 15
Houston, Peter, 10
humanism, Aleandro's link with
    Paris, 6
hypothetical propositions, 36-7;
    relation of exponibles to, 83;
    square of opposition for, 180-2

identity, relative pronoun of, 118,
    162-3
immediateness, four orders of propos-
    itions of, 108; propositions of,
    108-13
impetus, Buridan's theory of, 21
imposition, conditional sufficient,
    42-3; formal definition of, 38;
    insufficient, 43; kinds of virtual,
    38; origin of, 43-4, 236n6;
    sufficient, 42-3
inception, 113-19; convertibility of
    propositions of, 117-19; order of
    descent under propositions of,
    115-16
*incipit, see* inception
indefinite propositions, classification
    of, 128-9
*Index Librorum Prohibitorum*, 26
infinity, categorematic and syncate-
    gorematic, 112
inherence, propositions of, 55
*in sensu composito*, modality, 55-6
*in sensu diviso*, modality, 55-6
instants, four kinds of, 114;
    indivisibility of, 113
intention, first, 79-80; second,
    79-80
Intrant, his role in election of
    St Andrews' rectors, 3
is, *secundum adiacens*, 54; *tertium
    adiacens*, 54

James v, dedicatee of Major's *History*,
    6

Ker, Thomas, 30
Kneale, William, 236n10
Knox, John, content of his first public
    sermon, 18; educated at Had-
    dington, 4; pupil of Major, 17-18
Kretzmann, Norman, 190
Kripke, Saul, 236n10

La Marche, College of, Lokert at, 21
Lamb, John, 30
Latin, lingua franca of academic
    discourse, 2; scientific, 186
Lauder, John, 30
Laurence of Lindores, first rector of
    St Andrews University, 1; his
    organisation of rectorial elec-
    tions, 3; a proponent of the
    nominalism of Buridan, 1-2
law of opposites, 166
laws of thought, 185
Lax, Gaspar, 234n12
logic, classical conception of, 184;
    terminist conception of, 188
Lokert, George, variant spellings of
    name in contemporary sources,
    viii; leading member of Major's
    circle, 4; the printing of his
    books, 11; reported by Knox as
    present at Arth's sermon, 19;
    probable date of birth, 20; youth
    of, 20; taught at Reims College,
    20; elected to Sorbonne, 21; his
    return to Scotland in 1521, 21;
    appointed provost of Crichton
    Collegiate Church, 21-22; incor-
    porated in St Andrews, 23;
    elected rector of St Andrews,
    23-4; work at St Andrews, 23-4;
    head of Scots College in Paris,
    25-6; his role in censorship of
    Erasmus, 28; final return to
    Scotland, 29; his role as dean of
    Glasgow, 30; death of, 31;
    historical significance of, 189-90
Lokert, John, half brother of George,
    20; incorporated in St Andrews,
    23; took degree in Paris, 20
Loyola, Ignatius, member of
    Montaigu, 5

Mair, *see* Major, John
Major, John, preeminence of, in
    Paris, 3; leader of Scottish intel-
    lectual life in Paris, 3-4; born in
    Gleghornie, 4; date of birth, 4;
    spent year at Cambridge, 4; date
    of master's degree, 4-5; taught at
    Montaigu, 5; doctorate of theo-
    logy, 5; hostility to aspects of
    ecclesiastical morality, 6; a
    prolific writer, 6; his *History of*

*Greater Britain*, 6-7; testimony
    to his teaching, 7; publications of
    his students, 7-8; principal of
    Glasgow University, 9, 11; work
    in Glasgow, 11-12; incorporation
    in St Andrews, 12; influence on
    exam procedures in St Andrews,
    12; his attitude to Patrick Hamil-
    ton, 13-14; his teaching on ex-
    communication, 14; conciliarism
    of, 15; his reasons for leaving
    Paris in 1531, 16-17; appointed
    provost of St Salvator's, 17;
    present at Knox's first public
    sermon, 18; supported William
    Arth, 19; worked with Lokert at
    St Andrews, 24; taught at St
    Andrews, 24; death of, 20; on
    circular definitions, 239n1; on
    contradiction, 240n2, 241ns6,7;
    on existence of exponible terms
    in mental language, 83; on in-
    finity, 238n19; on kinds of im-
    mediateness, 238n18; his list
    of synonyms of 'mental term',
    235n4; on imposition, 236n6; on
    modality of consequence, 239n5;
    on non-linguistic opposition,
    240n1; on non-strict compara-
    tives, 238n21; on relations be-
    tween exclusives and exceptives,
    238n12; on senses of 'term', 32,
    33; on synonyms of *inquantum*,
    238n15
major premiss, 144-5
major term, 145
malpractices, Arth's criticism of
    church, 19; Major's criticism of
    church, 14
Manderston, William, member of
    Major's circle, 3-4; from St
    Andrews, 8; graduate of
    Glasgow, 8; professor of College
    of St Barbe, 8; rector of Paris, 8;
    publications of, 8-9; accusation
    of plagiarism, 9; on justification
    by faith alone, 9; attitude to
    Hamilton's death, 14; teaching
    on grace and free will, 14; elected
    rector of St Andrews, 17, 23
material significate, 72-3
material supposition, 45
McNeill, W. A., 235n31

mental proposition, 36, 37
mental term, definition of, 62; immediateness of, 37; spoken and written terms mediated by, 37
middle term, 143-44; distribution of, 148
minor premiss, 144
minor term, 145
modal propositions, truth conditions of, 56, 60
modal terms, Lokert's list of, 55
Montaigu, College of, 28, 235n40; ascetic conditions at, 5; its conditions disliked by Erasmus, 5; Major taught logic and philosophy at, 5; Major a theology student of Standonck at, 5

Navarre, College of, Major's connection with, 5
negation, confused distributive supposition generated by, 47; double, 42, 78; implicit, 129-30; infinitising, 93; singular terms operated on by, 77-8; two kinds of, 77, 129
negative names, 77-8
negative propositions, classification of, 129; convertibility of particular, 138-9; convertibility of universal, 134-5; truth conditions of, 58
Nicholson, Ranald, his assessment of Major's History, 7
nominalism, realism versus, 1, 73-4
non-ultimate mental term, 68-72
non-ultimate significate, 68
non-ultimate signification, 68-9
notion, 20-1
Nuchelmans, G., vii, 190

oblique case, categorematic terms in, 67-8; synonymy of terms in nominative and, 67-8
obscurity, 81, 122-3
obversion, 156, 240n13
Ockham, William of, 55, 235n53; on universality of singulars, 129
olfactory terms, 63
'only', 84-95; common terms before, 88-9
opposition, relations of, 165; syntactic nature of, 165-6

Oresme, Nicole d', 5
otherness, conversion rules for exclusives of, 90-2; exclusives of, 84-92; exposition of exclusives of, 85; four orders of exclusives of, 84-5; relation between universality and exclusives of, 87-8

Paris, ch.1 passim; Scottish rectors at University of, 2
Parlement de Paris, its role as censor, 27-9
particular affirmatives, truth conditions of, 55
particular propositions, indefinites classed as, 129; singulars classed as, 128-9, 136
particularity, determinate supposition generated by sign of, 47
past tense propositions, ambiguity of, 57; inception and, 116; truth conditions of, 56-8
personal supposition, 45
Peter of Spain, 184, 241n1
plurality, ambiguity in exclusives of, 93; convertibility of exclusives of, 94-5; exclusives of, 92-5
predicate, denial of, 141
prejacent, 84
printing, Paris centre of, 11
proposition, basic form of the, 35-6, 81; conjunctive, 59-60; disjunctive, 59-60; exponible equivalent to hypothetical, 82-3; non-ultimate mental, 71; truth conditions of singular, 55; ultimate mental, 70-1
propositional complex, 239n4

quantifiers, non-standard, 50-4, ch.5 passim

rational conditional, 61
realists, 1
reduction procedure, 152-3; per impossibile, 155-8
reduplicative propositions, 102-8; convertibility of, 107-8; elements in, 102; four orders of, 102-3; square of opposition for, 106-7
Renaudet, A., 234n8
Ross, A., 235n53

Scots College of Paris, 12; description of, 25-6

Shaw, Robert, bishop of Murray, 25

signification, categorematic term with, 64; loss of, 41-2; semantic nature of, 45; universality of natural, 40-1

'signify', definition of, 37; division of, 38; its division into 'natural' and 'conventional' criticised, 39-40

Silvestre, Antoine, 235n40; edited a treatise by Cranston, 8

simple supposition, 45

singular propositions, classification of, 128-9; their role in expository syllogisms, 163-4

Sorbonne, College of, brief description of, 5; Lokert at, 12, 20, 21; Lokert elected prior of, 21

Soto, Domingo de, his proof of the equivalence of 'Only A is B' and 'Every B is A', 87-8

spoken term, conventional signification of, 38; definition of, 62; distinction between written term and, 63-4; mediateness of, 37

square of opposition, ch.5 *passim*; exceptives in, 99-100; exclusives of otherness in, 86-7

Standonck, Jan, banished from Paris 1499, 5; taught Major theology at Montaigu, 5

St Andrews University, examinations at, 24; founded 1411-12, 1; Knox a student under Major at, 17; Laurence of Lindores its first rector, 1; modelled on University of Paris, 3; rectorship of, 23-4; religious disagreements in, 16-17; role of rector in, 3; teaching of Albertist realism banned at, 1

St Augustine, 235n5, 236n9

St Barbe, Major's first college in Paris, 4, 13

St Salvator's College, Major the provost of, 17, 22; site of Hamilton's execution, 13

subalternate moods, 160

subalternation, 130-4; conditions of, 130-1; criticisms of conditions of, 132; justification of law of, 131; law of, 130

subcontraries, law of, 166; syntactic relation between, 169-70; relation between exceptives and, 101

subtractive exceptive, 96

superlatives, 119-24; affirmative, 121; descent to singulars under, 123; exposition of, 121; negative, 121

supposition, 44ff; confused distributive, 46-7; determinate, 46; merely confused, 46; merely confused conjunctive, 94-5; non-standard quantifier conferring determinate, 51, 53-4; non-standard quantifier conferring merely confused, 50-1; quantifiers *c* and *d* conferring mixed, 51-3; syncategorematic terms lack, 45-6; syntactic nature of, 45

syllogism, categorical, 143ff; direct *versus* indirect, 145; expository, 162-4; hypothetical, 143; middle term of, 143-4; need for distributed middle term in, 148; number of figures of, 144-5; number of valid moods of, 152; rules of valid, 147

syncategorematic terms, difficulty of imposing, 44; indefinability of, 34-5; non-ultimate, 71-2; no singular or common terms are, 74; parallel between categorematic and, 65; role of, 35; signification of, 65; ultimate, 71-2

syndic, role of, at Sorbonne, 26-7

Tempete, Pierre, principal of Montaigu, 20

term, absolute, 72-4; abstract, 73-4; categorematic, 64-8; common, 74-8; concrete, 73-4; connotative, 72-4; contradictory, 78; kinds of exponible, 83-4; Lokert's sense of, 33; Major on senses of, 32-3; mental, 37, 62; negative, 77-8; non-ultimate, 68-72; singular, 74-8; spoken, 37, 62; superior, 96; syncategorematic, 64-8; transcendental, 78; ultimate, 68-72; written, 37, 62-4

terminists, advances made by, 187
Teviotdale, archdeaconry of, 29-30
Trinity, quantifying into the, 53-4
truth, partial, 100-1
truth conditions, 55-9

ultimate mental term, 68-72
ultimate significate, 68
ultimate signification, 68-9
universal affirmatives, relation be-
    tween exceptives and, 100-1;
    truth conditions of, 55
universality, confused distributive
    supposition generated by, 46-7
univocity, 75

Valla, Lorenzo, 184, 237n7
virtual presence, 35-6
Vitoria, Francisco de, 87

Walterston, Robert, a fellow regent of
    Major at Montaigu, 5; provost of
    collegiate church, 23
Watt, D. E. R., 234ns24,25,
    235ns45,51,52
Weddall, John, Lokert's successor at
    St Andrews, 25
Wishart, George, death of, 18
Wolsey, Cardinal, relation between
    Major and, 15-16
written term, conventional sig-
    nification of, 38; definition of, 62